Garibaldi And The Making Of Italy

GARIBALDI AND THE MAKING OF ITALY

BY THE SAME AUTHOR
Uniform with this Edition

GARIBALDI'S DEFENCE OF THE
ROMAN REPUBLIC
GARIBALDI AND THE THOUSAND

GARIBALDI

AND THE

MAKING OF ITALY

JUNE–NOVEMBER, 1860

BY

GEORGE MACAULAY TREVELYAN

THOMAS NELSON AND SONS, Ltd.
LONDON, EDINBURGH, AND NEW YORK
1921

*The Library Edition, with Notes, Appendices, and Illustrations,
is published by Messrs. Longmans, Green, and Co.*

To

C. P. T. AND M. K. T.

First published 1911

PREFACE

FOURTEEN years ago, when I began to study the life of
Garibaldi, and nine years ago, when I published the last of
the three volumes of this series, I certainly did not expect
that I was going to serve for more than three years with the
Italian army, becoming intimate in the field with the sons
and grandsons of men recorded in these pages, in the final
war of the *Risorgimento*, waged, during its first year, against
that very Kaiser Franz Josef whose soldiers hunted Anita
and Garibaldi in 1849.

Before the war history seemed to most men a· thing
outside the main current of life ; the past was like a turbu-
lent but distant ocean, on which we looked out ·through
magic casements from the agreeable bow-window of the
present. To-day that flood has broken banks.; we· are
ourselves tossed on the living stream ·of history. We
have been at war with Metternich and Bismarck. We
have fought for the principles of 1688 and 1789. We·have.
settled the undecided issue of 1848. Cavour and Garibaldi
gave us Italy for an ally, while Washington and Lincoln
gave us America. " The tombs were uncovered ; the dead
came to war." Each nation proved to be that which its
forefathers had made it. Because of the strange, romantic
history recorded in these volumes, Italy in our day fought
on the side of freedom. But for that history she would
still have been a province of germanised Austria.

The paradox of Italy is this : her civilisation is the oldest in modern Europe, while she herself is the youngest of the great States. In the thirteenth century of our era Italians were already supreme in art, in literature, and commerce, and in the appliances and amenities of civic and civilised life ; but the Italian State and the Italian nation sprang into being only sixty years ago. The events of the Risorgimento, a large portion of which are recorded in this Garibaldian trilogy, are therefore to the Italian of to-day more than any single epoch of English history can be to us. They are to him all that the story of Washington and Lincoln together are to the American. To be friends with Italy, we must begin by understanding and sympathising with the movement that gave her birth.

In this edition I have omitted not only the illustrations, but the elaborate system of references to authorities for statements made, which in Messrs. Longmans' Library Edition occupy so many pages of bibliography, appendix, and footnotes. For several years these books have run the gauntlet of historical criticism, clad in the armour of those references—on the whole with a singular immunity. I would, therefore, venture to refer the student to Messrs. Longmans' edition. The present reprint has been arranged in order to place the volumes within the reach of a larger class of reader.

CONTENTS

7

LIST OF MAPS

GARIBALDI AND THE MAKING
OF ITALY

————•————

INTRODUCTION

THE choice of this title for a volume of which the principal theme is Garibaldi's part in the events of June to November 1860 requires, not apology, but comment. It is true that the 'making of Italy' had begun two generations before, when General Buonaparte crossed the Alps with his hungry French Republicans, and was completed in 1870 when Victor Emmanuel entered Rome after the news of Sedan: but 1860 was the decisive year in that long process, the year when Italy was made. After considering whether I should call the book *Garibaldi and the Fall of the Neapolitan Kingdom,* I have rejected any such title, not only because it would fail to cover some of the most important events described—the battle of Castelfidardo and the liberation of the greater part of the Papal provinces—but also because the motive that inspired Garibaldi from the first to the last moment of his great campaign in the South was less the desire to destroy the Kingdom of Naples than the desire to make the Kingdom of Italy. The reader's mind should not be diverted from the national and constructive character of the Italian revolution by the interesting but subsidiary fact that the Bourbon system of government in South Italy collapsed in 1860 for the fourth and last time. The revolution of that year differs from those of the Napoleonic epoch and from those of 1820 and 1848, in that it created a free State stretching from the Alps to Sicily, which has since maintained its place in the family of nations as securely as France, Germany, or Spain. Although at the end of 1860 the Austrian was still in possession of his Venetian territories and the Pope of the small province that contained the city of Rome, the union effected between the other parts of Italy rendered the absorption of Rome and Venice merely a question of time.

This volume, starting from the accomplished fact of the capture of Palermo by Garibaldi and the Thousand described in a previous volume, narrates the events of the following half-year which brought this new State into being. The story has variety and scope enough. It is a complicated tale of war, regular and irregular, of diplomacy open and secret, of politics high and low. It carries us into palaces and peasants' huts from one end of Italy to the other and into half the capitals of Europe. And it has all the interest of long protracted suspense. For even after the taking of Palermo in June, it was by no means certain that, when the winter snows descended again on Aspromonte, four-fifths of Italy would be united and free. The turn of complicated events brought this result about, but in June it was no more a foregone conclusion than the break-up of Austria-Hungary or the reconstruction of Poland, events which were confidently expected in Garibaldi's camp, and of which at least the former entered as a probable contingency into the schemes of Cavour.

In the following pages the reader will see by how

narrow a margin Italy in her great year escaped another
disaster like that of 1848; with what skill and fortune
she avoided foreign interference while she achieved her
union against the will of all the great European Powers
except England; what gross political and military mistakes stultified the powerful resistance which the Pope
and the King of Naples might have set up; how Garibaldi's luck and genius and the psychological atmosphere
of a triumphant revolution again and again produced
military results contradictory to the known science of
war; how the bullet that might, in any one of a hundred
scuffles, have reversed in a moment the fortunes of the
campaign, never passed nearer than through his poncho
or his felt hat; how the first check to his career northwards, when Capua held out against him in September,
occurred at the very moment when the wiser friends of
Italy were beginning to pray that he might get no nearer
to the walls of Rome; how in the contest waged for six
months between Cavour from his chamber at Turin and
Garibaldi from his shifting bivouacs on the Southern Apen-
nines, the divergent views of the two patriots as to the
utmost pace at which the redemption could be pushed
on were finally compromised exactly at the right point,
so as to secure the essential union of Italy without the
immediate attack on Rome and Venice which must have
imperilled all.

The mass of the nation supported both Cavour and
Garibaldi, and it was this that saved the situation. But
many of the principal actors were naturally forced to
group themselves behind one or other of the two chiefs.
If either party had completely got the upper hand, if
Cavour had succeeded in annexing Sicily in June, and if
he had been relieved from the competition of the revolutionary bands, the great Powers would not have per-

mitted him to attack either Naples or the Papal territory. If on the other hand the Garibaldini had succeeded in attacking Rome, Napoleon III. would have been forced to undo all that they had accomplished for Italy. The principle of audacity and the principle of guidance, both essential for successful revolutions, had each in 1860 an almost perfect representative. But the death of Cavour in 1861, and the subsequent deterioration of Garibaldi, deprived both parties of the splendid leadership of the great year, so that the last stages of the Italian *risorgimento* were shorn of their meed of glory. Venice and Rome were ultimately acquired, but in a back-handed manner. Between 1861 and 1870 the ship of Italy's fortunes drifted and whirled amid shallow eddies, but was swept at last safe into port, because in 1860, when bold and skilful hands were still on board, the great flood tide had lifted her over the breakers at the bar.

CHAPTER I

THE CONSEQUENCES OF THE CAPTURE OF PALERMO IN NAPLES, PARIS, TURIN, AND LONDON

> 'You've seen the telegram?
> *Palermo's taken, we believe.*'
> MRS. BROWNING. *Garibaldi.*

IN the first days of June 1860, the news spread throughout Europe that the capital of Sicily, guarded by 20,000 regular troops, by forts and artillery, and by the Neapolitan fleet in the harbour, had been taken after three days' fighting by Garibaldi and a thousand North-Italian volunteers in plain clothes, aided by a mob of half-armed Sicilians. How soon, men asked, and how far would the revolution advance?

When last Palermo had expelled its garrison in January 1848, half Europe had followed suit. To the excited hopes of patriots and exiles, to the indignant fears of kings and their chancellors, Palermo seemed but the first point fired in a train of gunpowder laid through Messina and Reggio to Naples, through Naples and Rome to Venice, through Venice and Pesth to Vienna, through Vienna perhaps to Warsaw and back to the Tuileries. It was in the interest of every monarch who was not, like Victor Emmanuel, out for revolution, to check by force or by diplomacy the progress of the red-shirted portent. The 'filibuster,' having failed to be shot in the authorised manner,* seemed an incar—

* '*Le Flibustive* [sic] movement at Naples is very shameful. . . . Col. Walker [the Nicaraguan filibuster] has been shot, and Garibaldi, who comes

nation of the improbable, and for a while aroused hopes and fears, of which some were wildly extravagant.

> ' A Cæsar he, ere long, to Gaul,
> To Italy an Hannibal,
> And to all States not free
> Shall climacteric be.'

It was a case for a Holy Alliance of sovereigns to restore order in Sicily, or, if that were no longer possible, at least for a Concert of Europe to prevent the further spread of mischief. The first person to invoke the protection of the Powers by an appeal to the common interest of all established governments, was the unfortunate King Francis II. of Naples, whose house was already on fire at one end, and was packed from roof to floor with combustible matter.*

The Neapolitan appeal for protection might take one of two forms. Either it might be addressed primarily to the powers of reaction, Russia and Austria, and would in that case be accompanied by vigorous conduct of the war in Sicily and by continued repression on the mainland ; or else, as actually occurred, it might be addressed primarily to the more Liberal powers, to England and France, in which case efforts must be made to patch up a truce with Garibaldi, and a constitution must be granted on the mainland. As the latter course was the actual path by which King Francis descended so rapidly to his

out of that self-same school, is divinised.' *The King of the Belgians to Queen Victoria.* Nov. 2, 1860, *Queen's Letters,* Vol. III.

* On June 7 Odo Russell, the British Representative at Rome, wrote to his uncle, Lord John : ' The other day the young King of Naples was seized with such a panic that he telegraphed five times in twenty-four hours for the Pope's blessing. Cardinal Antonelli, through whom the application had to be made, telegraphed the three last blessings without reference to his Holiness, saying that he was duly authorised to do so. The Convents are awfully scandalised at this proceeding.'

doom, it is easy to say now that the bolder policy would
have had a better chance of success.   But the House of
Bourbon had twice before weathered the revolutionary
storms of the Bay of Naples by granting a charter, to be
set aside when the danger had passed by ; and no one in
the Neapolitan Camarilla had the nerve of a Strafford or
a Bismarck openly to continue in the reactionary course
with Garibaldi in Palermo.   The only man among all
Francis II's. counsellors was his Bavarian Queen, Maria
Sophia, and she, though ready, as she afterwards proved,
to fight for her crown behind the cannon of Gaeta, honestly
desired a constitution and a complete change of system.*

   Besides this, Russia and Austria, though more willing,
were less able to afford protection than either France or
England.   Russia, who had dominated the European
situation in 1849, when she had invaded rebellious
Hungary on behalf of Austria, had since then had a fall
on the ramparts of Sebastopol.   In whatever light the
Crimean war may be viewed from the standpoint of British
or near-Eastern interests, there is no doubt that from
the point of view of Continental Liberalism and the freedom of action of independent States, it had done much
to secure the 'liberties of Europe,' the phrase inscribed
at Macaulay's suggestion on the monument to our
soldiers at Scutari. The great power of darkness had
been disabled and discredited in pan-European affairs,
and the new Czar had even begun the work of liberation
at home. Austria, too, who had the most immediate
reason to support the old governments in Italy, and to
check Garibaldi's advance, was in like manner recovering

* For Maria Sophia see *Garibaldi and the Thousand*, chap. vii. The
queen in Daudet's *Rois en exil* is admittedly based on Maria Sophia, but while
Daudet's queen was an ultra-royalist, Maria Sophia had Liberal inclina-
tions, at least while on the throne. Also the king in the *Rois en exil* has
positive vices which were wanting to the real Francis II.

from her Crimea, the Lombard war of 1859. She dreaded
that if she again moved to interfere in Italy the Hungarian rebels would rise behind her, this time without
fear of the Russian armies, for the ingratitude shown by
Austria to Russia during the Crimean War had dissolved
the political friendship of the two Powers. Napoleon III.
and Cavour were both in constant communication with
Kossuth, and Cavour had a Hungarian rising ready primed
to fire in case of an Austrian war.

Partly for these reasons, and partly because the Sicilian
and Neapolitan situation was more easily commanded
from the sea, it was necessary for Francis II. to appeal
not so much to the Eastern as to the Western and naval
powers. In spite of the constant bickering between France
and England, the deepest line of diplomatic division lay
between East and West. The idea of an alliance with
the principles of Russian despotism, even for the purpose
of scoring a point against a near neighbour, was abhorrent
to Napoleon III. on one side of the Channel, and to Palmerston and Lord John Russell on the other. In fact
when Russia early in July proposed to join with France
in policing the Mediterranean against Garibaldi's transports, the offer coming from that quarter was promptly
rejected. If Napoleon interfered on behalf of Naples,
it would be in concert with Great Britain, and, if possible,
with Piedmont, and only on behalf of a reformed constitutional Kingdom.

The decision of the young King of Naples to adopt a
Liberal policy, to abandon the friendship with Austria
and Russia so long traditional in his family, to appeal to
Napoleon III. for help, and to conciliate France, England,
and his own subjects by the grant of a constitution, was
taken in principle at Councils held on May 30 and June 1,

1860. They were the first-fruits of Garibaldi's success. On June 1 the King also sanctioned General Lanza's proposal to retreat with 20,000 royal troops from the Palace to the suburbs of Palermo, and on June 4 he sanctioned his further proposal to capitulate with Garibaldi and to ship the whole royal army back from Palermo to Naples.*

The chief promoter in the Council of these important decisions was General Filangieri, the veteran Prince of Satriano, who had served with equal fidelity the Napoleonic Kings of Naples, and the restored House of Bourbon, who had reconquered Sicily for the Crown in 1849, and ruled it with wise moderation until recalled by his reactionary enemies at Court. He had often and in vain advised *Bomba* and his son after him to break with Austria and the reaction, and to come to an understanding with France abroad and with the Constitutionalists at home. His advice, rejected year after year so long as it would have saved the throne, was now adopted a month too late, and was with his own full concurrence coupled with the fatal policy of military surrender at Palermo, at a moment when a renewed attack on Garibaldi and the rebel town, headed by General Nunziante or by the King in person, would not improbably have turned the tide of war.

It might have been expected that Filangieri, having at length completely overborne his reactionary enemies at the Council-board, would have helped to carry out the hard task, which he had himself set to his royal master, of changing horses in the bed of a roaring torrent which had already swept them all off their feet. But he preferred to retire to his country-house near Sorrento, whence at his ease he could watch the troubled city of Naples across the full breadth of the Bay. When the King sent

* Readers of *Garibaldi and the Thousand* will observe that the last pages of that book and the first pages of this one overlap chronologically.

General Nunziante to beg him to return to the head of affairs and to revive the body politic by a constitutional regimen, he replied with brutal frankness : ' Would you have me repeat the miracle of Lazarus ? I am not Christ, but a miserable mortal.' His interlocutor, Nunziante, hitherto a staunch reactionary, who had been loaded with honours and emoluments by the late King, and was esteemed and trusted by Francis II. as the ablest man in the Neapolitan service after Filangieri himself, had recently consented to take up the command against Garibaldi, and had drawn up plans for the reconquest of Palermo, but he was so deeply impressed by these words of Filangieri that he at once determined not to go to Sicily, and then and there began to calculate how best to desert the falling house of Bourbon, and to carry over the army intact to the service of the House of Piedmont and United Italy.

Before the end of June the King himself crossed the Bay of Naples to try his own powers of persuasion on the recluse of Sorrento. When the royal yacht was unexpectedly seen approaching the landing-place below the villa, Filangieri fled to his bedroom and jumped into bed. Not having time to take off his clothes, he drew the blankets over him up to his chin, and received his royal visitor so. Was ever monarch before or since received in such fashion by the first subject in his kingdom ?

Francis II. held an hour's private conversation by the bedside of the malingerer, and then returned to Naples. Filangieri, perhaps a little ashamed of himself, never disclosed even to his nearest and dearest what had passed in that strange interview, but no one doubted that he had again been pressed to form a constitutional Ministry, and that, pleading his feigned illness, he had again refused.

Early in August, Filangieri went into voluntary exile at Marseilles. After the revolution was accomplished he returned to Italy, and till his death in 1867 resided as a loyal subject of Victor Emmanuel, refusing office and honours from the new Government, but never regretting the old. The ideal of his life had been an independent South Italy, with a progressive and civilised Government of its own, such as that which in his youth he had helped Murat to conduct. After Waterloo the restored Bourbons and their subjects had left that path, and had since failed in numerous attempts to return to it again, in spite of the efforts of men like Poerio and Filangieri. Poerio, convinced after 1848 that South Italy was by itself incapable of maintaining a tolerable Government, had quickly come to believe in the Union of all Italy as a positive good; and even Filangieri was at last forced to admit, after the event, that Union was the least bad of all practicable solutions.

Discouraged but not deterred by Filangieri's refusal to lend a hand in carrying out his own policy, Francis II. continued in the prescribed course. In the first days of June he had frankly thrown himself on the protection of France. De Martino had been sent as the bearer of an autograph letter of the King of Naples to the Emperor. Accompanied by Antonini, the regular Neapolitan Minister at Paris, he went out to Fontainebleau on June 12 to interview Napoleon. The envoys met with a chilling reception from the French courtiers. Even Thouvenel, the Foreign Minister, though no friend to Italian aspirations, was brutally rude to the representatives of the falling cause, and before the conference began was overheard by them saying in a loud voice in the antechamber, 'Now I must go and hear what lies the two Neapolitan orators will tell the Emperor.' Napoleon himself, though courteous and humane, held out no hope that he would actively interfere. He explained the difference between the claims of the King of Naples on his protection and those of the Pope. 'The French flag,' he said, 'is actually waving on the Pope's territory, and then there is the question of religion. The Italians understand that if they attacked Rome I should have to act.' But in the case of Naples he declared that as the victor of Solferino and the liberator of Lombardy, he was bound not to stultify his own past by using his troops on behalf of an opposite principle in South Italy. '*Les Italiens sont fins,*' he said; 'the Italians are shrewd; they clearly perceive that since I have shed the blood of my people for the cause of nationality, I can never fire a cannon against it. And this conviction, the key to the recent revolution, when Tuscany was annexed against my wishes and interests, will have the same effect in your case.' The King of Naples' concessions, the offer of the constitution, failed to impress him. 'It is too late,' he said. 'A month ago these concessions might have prevented everything. To-day they are too late.'

It was now June 12. On April 15 Victor Emmanuel had written to his 'dear cousin' of Naples, suggesting a mutual alliance on the principle of Italian nationality and freedom, and ending with the words: 'If you allow some months to pass without attending to my friendly suggestion, your Majesty will perhaps experience the bitterness of the terrible words—*too late.*' Eight weeks had sufficed to fulfil the prophecy, and the 'terrible words' were now on the lips of Napoleon himself.

But there was still, said the Emperor to the Neapolitan envoys, one chance for their master. Let him humbly ask for the Piedmontese alliance, which he had himself rejected earlier in the year when Victor Emmanuel had made the advances. 'Piedmont alone,' said Napoleon.

'can stop the course of the revolution. You must apply not to me but to Victor Emmanuel.' 'We French do not wish,' he added, 'for the annexation of South Italy to the Kingdom of Piedmont, because we think it contrary to our interests, and it is for this reason that we advise you to adopt the only expedient which can prevent or at least retard that annexation.' For the rest, he would be delighted if the Neapolitan Royalists proved able to defeat Garibaldi and the revolution with the force of their own arms, but he could not help them himself, partly for the reasons which he had already given, and partly because he was determined to do nothing contrary to the wishes of England.

His advice therefore to the Neapolitan envoys at Fontainebleau was nothing more than a reasoned repetition of the programme which his representative Brenier had several days before urged upon the Court at Naples, namely :—

First, a scheme of Sicilian Home Rule under a Prince of the Royal House of Naples.
Secondly, a Constitution for the mainland.
Thirdly, an alliance with Piedmont.

This triple programme was perforce adopted by the Neapolitan Court, but the first item depended for its fulfilment on Garibaldi and the Sicilians, and the third on Cavour and the Piedmontese. The Constitution, indeed, could be published by the King without the consent of any other party, but whether it would at this twelfth hour conciliate the population of the Neapolitan provinces still remained to be seen.

The question was soon put to the proof. A Council of Ministers sat on June 21, and after Antonini's report of the interview at Fontainebleau had been read to them, decided by eleven votes to three to adopt the triple programme laid down by the French Emperor. A short while back the same men would have voted by an equally large majority against any concession, but in these weeks life-long opinions were changing with a rapidity peculiar to the crisis of a great revolution. Since the taking of Palermo most of the reactionary party, headed by the King's uncle, the Count of Aquila, had become ardent Constitutionalists; while the Constitutional party of former years, headed by the Duke of Syracuse, another uncle of the King (the Philippe Egalité of the Neapolitan revolution), had turned against the dynasty, and were working to bring in Victor Emmanuel. 'A year ago,' wrote Elliot, the British Minister, ' there was hardly an annexationist to be found in this part of Italy, and now pretty nearly the whole country is so for the moment.'

But even after the Council of June 21 the feeble King still hesitated. Although he would not go to Sicily and lead on his troops against Garibaldi, he was almost equally unwilling to publish the Constitution and to declare for the Piedmontese alliance. All the pieties and instincts of his dumb nature were averse to the change, and he was upheld in his passive resistance by the clamours of his stepmother Maria Theresa, ' the Austrian woman,' whom he had been accustomed since boyhood to obey. But on the other side was his wife, Maria Sophia, whose influence upon him was constantly growing throughout his brief reign, corresponding to a perceptible increase of manliness on his part. For some days after the Council of June 21 a final struggle was waged between the two Marias, ending in the victory of the younger. Her demand for constitutional reform was urgently supported by the King's uncle, the Count of Aquila, and by the French Minister, Brenier, who were now in close partnership. De Martino, meanwhile, had been sent to Rome to obtain the Pope's leave for the change of policy, which was grudgingly given on condition that any alliance with Piedmont was not to be made at the expense of the Papal territories or the privileges of the Church. The Pope's consent turned the scale in the King's mind, and on June 25 the Sovereign Act was published recalling to vigour the Constitution of 1848, granting Home Rule to Sicily under a Prince of the Royal House, and announcing that an alliance would be made with Piedmont—the complete triple programme advised by Napoleon. The tricolour flag, symbolic of Italian nationality, was hauled up on all the public buildings and on the ships of the fleet ; * the political prisoners were let loose throughout the Kingdom ; the exiles returned amid processions and rejoicings; pending the elections to Parliament, a Ministry of Moderate Liberals took over the authority of the State. As far as the Government was concerned, everything was done in the most approved manner according to the pattern of one of those joyous Constitution-givings of the spring of 1848, when monarchs and peoples had wept in each other's arms. But on this occasion it was only the monarch who opened his arms and embraced the empty air. When on June 26 the King and Queen drove out in an open carriage to receive the ovations of liberated Naples, hats were respectfully raised, but hardly a cheer was heard in the whole length of the Toledo.

The Constitution was still-born. In some upland villages, especially in the district between Naples and

* Victor Emmanuel's flag, used by Garibaldi, was the tricolour with the cross of Savoy upon it ; that is now the flag of all Italy. There was no cross on the tricolour of the short-lived 'Constitutional' Kingdom of Francis II. of Naples.

the Roman border, it was regarded as a Jacobinical betrayal
of religion ; while the great mass of the King's subjects
in the capital and in the provinces south of the capital
regarded it merely as a first step in the direction of Italian
unity, a means of freeing themselves from the police and
the censorship, so as to be better able to welcome ' him '
when he came.   ' He ' was at Palermo, he would soon
be at the Straits, and it was in that direction and not to
the Palace of Naples that all men's thoughts were turned.
The newly granted liberties were used to destroy the
Government that had conceded them.   Newspapers sprang
up by the score ; books, pamphlets, and proclamations
appeared everywhere, and nearly the whole output of the
liberated press was anti-dynastic.   Its only disputes turned
on the rival merits of Cavour and Mazzini, of Federation
and Annexation, and whether or not to await Garibaldi's
coming before beginning the revolution.

The new Ministry formed by Spinelli, with De Martino
in charge of Foreign affairs, consisted chiefly of mediocre
but honest men, desirous of working the Constitution
and saving the dynasty.   But with one exception they
had neither influence nor popularity, at a time when the
mere possession of office lent but little authority to the
opinions of its holder.   Yet even the Ministers, without
intending to do so, further undermined the stability of
the throne.   For they busied themselves, as indeed it
was their duty to do if the Constitution was to be a reality,
in turning out reactionaries and putting in old constitutionalists as prefects, magistrates, and police, regardless
of the fact that the old constitutionalists were now for
Garibaldi almost to a man.   The expulsion of genuine
royalists from the public service alienated the enthusiasm
of the King's friends, without reconciling his enemies,
to whom it gave the civil power in every Province from

Calabria to Abruzzi. The bishops, more reactionary than their clergy, were the only persons in authority who could not be summarily dismissed, but they were watched by spies who reported their sayings and movements to the Minister of the Interior : some of the prelates fled from their dioceses in real or affected fear for their personal safety. In every town the new authorities formed and armed the National Guard, chosen out of the middle class, which became in effect a military force prepared to support the coming revolution.

The army alone was loyal to the King, but as it still consisted of about 100,000 well-armed and well-drilled men, it might still defeat Garibaldi, and if it could once drive the red-shirts in rout, no one doubted that the Constitution, the National Guard, the Ministry, the press, and the tricolour flags would all be huddled away in twenty-four hours. After all, there had been a Constitutional Ministry in 1848, and shortly afterwards the principal Ministers were serving their time in irons. It was this supreme consideration which made real loyalty impossible for any man, however much he cared for the dynasty, if he also cared for the Constitution. No one except the reactionaries really wished to hear of a victory over the man who was in name the national enemy, and in reality the national deliverer. It was for this reason that the new Ministers were so unwilling to take the offensive against him in Sicily. For no Cabinet can be expected to conduct a war with vigour, when a decisive victory would mean twenty years' penal servitude for each of its members. General Pianell, the new War Minister, was a faithful and honest man, but he erred in accepting a post of which he could not, by the nature of the case, heartily fulfil the duties.

Don Liborio Romano, the new Prefect of Police, was

the sole exception to the rule that the Ministers had neither popularity nor influence ; and he was also the exception to the rule that they were passively loyal to the King. '. Don Liborio,' as he was called in these days, was a native of lower Apulia, skilled in the insinuating manners and arts of political intrigue which the inhabitants of the region between Taranto and Brindisi are said to have inherited from their Greek ancestors.   He had been an active Liberal as early as 1820, and had often suffered as such at the hands of the police.   But he belonged essentially to the world of Levantine intrigue, rather than to the world of European revolution.   For this reason he was able from June to September, 1860, to preserve the confidence of the inhabitants of the capital by a kind of masonic mutual understanding or sympathy of character, which a more straightforward man would have failed to establish with the Neapolitans.   After his retirement he always asserted that he had taken office, not in order to save the dynasty, which he believed to be already lost, but in order to preserve his fellow-countrymen from anarchy and civil war.   This account of his motives, if a considerable allowance be also made for his vanity and ambition, is accepted by the most competent and unbiassed authorities who knew the Naples of that day well, and they are also of opinion that at the moment of entering office he did actually achieve his purpose and save the city and perhaps the whole Kingdom from a terrible disaster.

The circumstances were as follows.   On June 27, two days after the proclamation of the Sovereign Act, when all the authorities of the old *régime* had lost their power, but before the new Ministry was well in the saddle, and before the National Guard or the new police had been formed, disorders broke out in Naples.   The police of the old Government were hunted down, and their archives burnt. Unless the mob was checked, anarchy would soon prevail in its most hideous form. But there was at the moment no armed force deriving its authority from the Constitution, and if the regular army, aflame with reactionary passions, had been called out to shoot the mob, civil war would have begun at once. In the circumstances Liborio Romano was entreated to become Prefect of Police, on the ground that no one else could save Naples. He accepted the post on June 27, and on the next day the Prefecture of Police, till then execrated by every one, became the resort of the leading Liberals. But the Liberals alone could not control the vicious and non-political criminal class of Naples. The *camorra*, hitherto in tacit league with the old Royal Government, had now turned against all government. Don Liborio, to avoid the imminent social catastrophe, struck a bargain with this secret association of criminals, in the name of the new Government, or at any rate of its Prefect of Police. The chiefs of the *camorra* were given places in the new police force, along with other more respectable members of society. The consequence was that there were no more disturbances in Naples during the next three months of turmoil, panic, and revolution, except on occasions when the reactionary soldiers broke loose from their barracks. In this ignominious manner Naples was saved. The price paid by the Italian Government in later years was high, but possibly not too high for the escape of society from promiscuous bloodshed and rapine.

Having thus tided over the immediate danger, Don Liborio formed the National Guard from among his own adherents in the respectable middle class. The National Guard, the police, and the *camorra* were now at his disposal, not only in Naples but throughout the provinces. He was master of the situation, and held the stakes until

either the King or Garibaldi had conquered. Throughout July and August he was the real ruler of the country
for all domestic purposes except the command of the army.
Francis II. hated and distrusted Don Liborio, but dared
not dismiss him.

While the House of Bourbon was thus engaged at
home in clothing its enemies with authority and its friends
with confusion, the Piedmontese alliance, to obtain which
all these sacrifices were being made, was eagerly solicited
at Turin. Twice during the last twelve months Piedmont
had asked for an alliance and been rebuffed by the counsellors of Francis II.; it was now their turn to sue for the
settlement which they had so recently refused. The House
of Bourbon was on its knees, clad in the Constitution and
the Tricolour for a garb of penitence. But the record of
its perjuries prevented all confidence, and the record of its
cruelties all forgiveness. The 'Neapolitan prisoners,' *
whose woes Mr. Gladstone had made famous, the victims
of *Bomba's* dungeons, were now many of them residing in
Turin, several as Deputies in the North Italian Parliament,
which was then in full session. Others, like Braico, had
gone to Sicily with the Thousand. When the news of the
fall of Palermo arrived, the Neapolitan exiles in Turin met
at the house of Mancini, one of their number, and at the
instance of Carlo Poerio declared for the deposition of the
Bourbons. When, some three weeks later, there arose
the question of the alliance of Piedmont with Naples, the
uncompromising attitude of these men strengthened Cavour's
hands to resist the proposal. Poerio, the Conservative
Minister of the late King during the Parliamentary *régime*
of 1848, had been rewarded for his undisputed loyalty to
Crown and Constitution by a sentence of twenty-four years
in irons obtained by notoriously false witness, at the in-

* See *Garibaldi and the Thousand*, chap. iii.

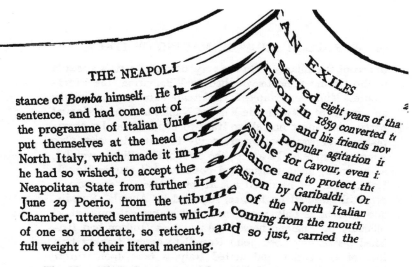

stance of *Bomba* himself. He h[ad] sentence, and had come out of [prison in 1859 converted to] the programme of Italian Uni[ty. He and his friends now] put themselves at the head o[f popular agitation in] North Italy, which made it im[possible for Cavour, even if] he had so wished, to accept the [alliance and to protect the] Neapolitan State from further in[vasion by Garibaldi. On] June 29 Poerio, from the tribu[ne] of the North Italian Chamber, uttered sentiments which, coming from the mouth of one so moderate, so reticent, and so just, carried the full weight of their literal meaning.

The Neapolitan Government,' he said, has the tradition of perjury, handed down from father to son. That is why it now offers to swear to the Constitution, because it is clear that in order to be perjured it is necessary first to swear. I trust that the Ministers of Victor Emmanuel will not stretch out their hands to a Government which certainly is the most declared of the enemies of Italian independence.'

The roar of applause that followed him as he returned to his seat showed that the North Italian Deputies had already made up their minds about the proposed alliance.

The Neapolitan exiles, while they held this language in public, expressed themselves with no less vigour and decision in their private correspondence. Writing to Panizzi, the Librarian of the British Museum, and one of the chief unofficial agents of the Italian cause in our country, Poerio and his fellow-martyr Settembrini urged that the hour had struck to weld Italy into one State, and that if a truce were now patched up, when the trumpets should be sounding the final charge, 'enthusiasm would cool with time,' and the principle of 'dualism with all its terrible consequences' would for ever divide the Italian Peninsula.

Cavour was from the first aware that it was impossible

to accept the alliance. On the very day of Poerio's speech in the Chamber, he telegraphed to Villamarina, the Piedmontese Minister at Naples : ' Take care to render impossible an agreement between the King of Naples and the national party. We must not allow Italy to believe that by complaisance or weakness we are ready to fraternise with the King of Naples.' To accept the Neapolitan alliance would, as he knew, mean schism and possibly civil war in North Italy. And yet he dared not at once close the door on a proposal initiated by France, regarded by Austria, Russia, and Prussia as only too liberal, and at present supported officially by England herself. As soon as Hudson had finished persuading Lord John Russell to accept frankly the idea of annexation and united Italy, a task upon which he was busily engaged in a private and unofficial correspondence,* Cavour might take a bolder course. But ' even if we were helped by England,' he wrote to Ricasoli on July 8, ' we could not fight both on the Mincio and on the Alps,' against both Austria and France. So he could not ' reject scornfully a proposed settlement presented under French auspices and by French advice.' He determined, therefore, to entertain the Neapolitan envoys, Manna and Winspeare, and to treat about the alliance on such terms as were certain to be refused by King Francis, making demands tantamount to the cession of Sicily and the further partition of the Pope's territory for the benefit of Piedmont.

But the fear that the Italian people would suppose even these negotiations to be serious constantly haunted him. ' If we consent to the alliance, we are lost. If we reject it, what will Europe say ? In my life I was never more embarrassed.' To retain the confidence of the patriotic party Cavour more and more openly hastened the equipment and

* See Appendix. at end of book.

departure of the expeditions of volunteers to join Garibaldi, and that portion of the press which he inspired was observed to be scornfully hostile to the Neapolitan alliance. At the same time he tried to cut the knot of his difficulties by engineering an immediate revolution in Naples. The Piedmontese diplomatic representative, Villamarina, was the centre of this movement and the Piedmontese Legation its house of call. Even in April, under the old *régime* of repression, Villamarina's house, with its immunities against police search, had been used for the meetings of conspirators, and the forwarding of their letters to North Italy. And now in July he was instructed to act with Piedmontese agents of high character like Emilio Visconti-Venosta, and with the best of the Neapolitan exiles like Spaventa and Nisco, who openly came into Naples, some as naturalised Piedmontese subjects, others trusting to the civil rights enjoyed under the new Constitution. Some came with money supplied by Cavour and Farini to start newspapers ; all came to talk to their old friends in the army and elsewhere, and to stir up an annexationist movement. Within a few days of his arrival in Naples, Venosta wrote home to report that the army was Bourbonist in sympathy, and that the people only understood the idea of revolution as connected with Garibaldi, for whom they were waiting as for a second St. Januarius. But it was not until the end of August that Cavour could be persuaded by his agents that a revolution without Garibaldi was impossible.

It was indeed neither a dignified nor an honest policy to pretend to treat for alliance with the Government of a country while arming bands of volunteers to invade its provinces, and sending emissaries to excite a revolution in its capital. But that was the system pursued by Cavour during July and August, because he believed the alternative to be the Austrian bayonets in Milan and the French

in Turin. Danton once thundered out for all the world to
hear, *Que mon nom soit flétri, que la France soit libre.* Cavour's
intellectually aristocratic temper had no such unsafe con-
fidences for the people at large, but he said quietly to his
friends one day : ' If we had done for ourselves the things
which we are doing for Italy, we should be great rascals.'
The magnificent integrity of Cavour's private character and
the entire disinterestedness of his public conduct, lends
peculiar force to this saying. It must indeed be confessed
that he bequeathed to the statesmanship of the new Italy
the old traditions of duplicity, which have sometimes become low cunning in the hands of successors with neither
his virtues, his abilities, nor his dire necessities for their
excuse. But before we condemn Cavour we must decide
whether without a large degree of duplicity he could, supported by England alone, have made Italy against the will
of a hostile Europe—against the destroyers of Poland, ' the
man of December,' the Pope, and the perjured dynasty of
Naples. This question I am unable to answer, and I believe that no answer, however confidently given, can be
anything better than a reasoned guess.

There were not wanting at the time well-informed observers who believed that Cavour could have avoided all
this chicanery, that even in June he could have carried out
the bold and straightforward policy on which he finally
embarked in September. ' I wish,' wrote Elliot to Lord
John Russell on June 25, ' Victor Emmanuel would throw
off the mask like a man and go to war. It would certainly
be a very easy matter for him to roll down this rickety
dynasty, and he would be received with enthusiasm by the
nation.' It was natural for the British Minister at Naples
to write in this confident manner, for what Elliot had close
under his own eyes was the rottenness of the Government
to which he was accredited. But it was not any fear of

resistance at Naples that with[out fear]
of counter-attack from Vien[na were]
many riddles in the complic[ated problem he]
had to solve, but the chief one [was]
of the chameleon of the Tuile[ries]: it was the fear
the Pope, the friendly foe of Italian unity. There were
loose the nation straining at the problem which Cavour
war on Naples and invaded the Papal had to guess the true colour
would Napoleon merely protest, the Liberal protector of
fere? Or if Austria attacked Piedmont Italian unity. If Cavour let
engaged in liberating the South, leash, if he made legal
would Napoleon lend his protection? Papal Marches and Umbria,
or would he actively inter-
Piedmont when she was
on what terms, if any,

On this, the supreme problem of that summer, Cavour
obtained a decided opinion from the Emperor's cousin,
Jerome. This prince, a whole-hearted friend of Italian
unity, deserves more credit than he has got for his successful efforts in 1859–60 on behalf of that policy, which
for ever cut him off from all hope of an Italian kingdom
in Tuscany or elsewhere. On June 30 he wrote to Cavour
that the time had come when he could attack South Italy
without fear of the Emperor's veto. The letter is one of
the most important in the history of Italy, for it foreshadows
the course which Cavour adopted two months later.

Italy,' wrote Prince Jerome, ' is in a supreme crisis. She
must emerge from it united under the sceptre of my father-
in-law [Victor Emmanuel] with Rome as her capital, or else
she will slide back under the oppression of priests and
Austrians, at Turin as well as at Naples and everywhere else.
The die is cast. . . . Daring alone can save you to-day. Be
strong. Don't trust to yourself, no illusions, no vanity; you
have need of France and you can get her by means of the
Emperor. (*Il vous faut la France par l'Empereur*.) Be then
completely open with him. No more *finesse*; that served your
turn for Tuscany; it will not serve your turn with Sicily.

Naples, and Rome. Explain to him your views of the future, not only your end but your means and your conduct.'

Cavour did not at once adopt the course here prescribed for him by the Prince, but he did so before two months were out, when he opened his innermost counsels to Napoleon, and mobilised the Italian army to invade the territories of the Pope and of the King of Naples. The question is whether he could safely have ventured upon this policy in the first days of July, on receipt of the Prince's letter, or whether in fact it was necessary, as he judged, to wait until the unofficial revolution under Garibaldi had spread from Palermo to the gates of Naples. Perhaps Prince Jerome ante-dated the readiness of his Imperial cousin to condone the making of Italy. It is true that Napoleon at the end of August accepted it as the only alternative to anarchy, but it was by no means the only alternative prior to Garibaldi's victory at Milazzo and march through Calabria. Would Napoleon at the beginning of July have consented to throw over, at Cavour's request, all the proposals which he himself had just made for a reformed Neapolitan kingdom allied to Piedmont? It may be doubted—although the Emperor's gloomy words to the Neapolitan envoys at Fontainebleau perhaps imply a weakening of his resistance to Cavour. But on July 6 Brenier, the French Minister at Naples, declared strongly against annexation. And at Turin the French Minister, M. de Talleyrand, was pressing Cavour hard to grant the Neapolitan alliance, claiming first and foremost that Victor Emmanuel should at once write to Garibaldi to bid him make a truce. Talleyrand found that Cavour ' sheltered himself behind England,' and put off his demands with fair words and excuses to gain time. Victor Emmanuel was conveniently away hunting in his beloved Alps,' and his return must be awaited.

Meanwhile, in the bette[r] woods and beneath the mora[l] generations of hunting ruler[s] to his companions of the cha[se] talk gruffly and freely, to eas[e] weight of simple emotions. 'He wrote one of these after their retur[n] said he envied Garibaldi, and would about him, like the Nizzard general. really loves Garibaldi.'

world up there, in the pine ...es, the descendant of twenty of Savoy unbosomed himself the men to whom he could his rugged nature of its talked much about Sicily.' return to the plains. 'He would like to be able to lay general. Victor Emmanuel

The affection for Garibaldi which the Italian King could only express to his confidants in the depths of the Alpine forest, was being proclaimed aloud in the streets by all classes in Great Britain. In the uncertain diplomatic situation, England's decided attitude became the governing factor. If at the beginning of July, when France asked for her support in forcing a truce on Garibaldi in Palermo, England had supported the other Powers in such a programme of interference, it is difficult to see how Sicily could have been annexed to Piedmont. But England refused, and without her concurrence Napoleon, who at this time highly valued her friendship, was unwilling to proceed to definite action.* And again at the end of July, as will be told in a later chapter, she refused to participate in Napoleon's scheme to prevent Garibaldi from crossing the straits, and thereby enabled the red-shirts to invade the mainland. This policy of Lord John's was not that of

* 'As to Southern Italy I am free from engagements and I ask nothing better than to concert matters with England on this point as on others ' (e.g. Syria). ' Since the peace of Villafranca my only thought has been to inaugurate a new era of peace and to live on a good understanding with all my neighbours, particularly with England.' Napoleon III. to Persigny, July 27, 1860.

intervention in Italian affairs, but of non-intervention with an implied veto on the intervention of others.

The action of Great Britain in this summer, without which Italy could not have been made, was due partly to the steady pressure of public opinion, press, and Parliament on the Cabinet, and partly to the personal attachment of the Minister for Foreign Affairs to the cause of Italian freedom. Lord John Russell had been brought up in boyhood and youth among the friends of Fox, that small group of Liberal aristocrats who, no fair-weather friends of freedom, had sacrificed their popularity and their chance of influence and power for forty years, on behalf of the principles of civil and religious liberty. Russell had inherited their traditions, had in early manhood led the great attack that re-established freedom in Great Britain in 1832, and now in old age was prepared to do all that in him lay to overturn on Italian soil worse tyrannies than had ever been known in England. In this task Lord John was opposed by the Court, but he was supported by the public, by the press, by the petitions of great municipalities, and by his two chief colleagues, Palmerston and Gladstone, both converts, at different dates and for different reasons, from those authoritarian principles in Church and State to which he himself had sworn eternal hatred while he was still a boy.

The British Minister for Foreign Affairs was therefore ready to take any step consonant with British interests that would assist Italian freedom, and fortunately he had for his advisers, at Naples and at Turin respectively, two men of marked ability who sympathised with these aims. Elliot and Hudson conducted a private correspondence with Lord John behind their official despatches, and so enabled the British Minister to keep abreast of the rapid development of the Italian situation in 1859–60. It was

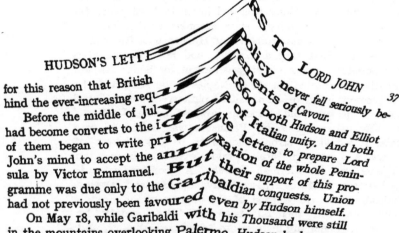

for this reason that British policy never fell seriously behind the ever-increasing requirements of Cavour.

Before the middle of July 1860 both Hudson and Elliot
had become converts to the idea of Italian unity. And both
of them began to write private letters to prepare Lord
John's mind to accept the annexation of the whole Peninsula by Victor Emmanuel. But their support of this programme was due only to the Garibaldian conquests. Union
had not previously been favoured even by Hudson himself.

On May 18, while Garibaldi with his Thousand were still
in the mountains overlooking Palermo, Hudson had argued
in a long private letter to Russell that the fusion of North and
South Italy in one State was difficult because of the intervening of Papal territories, and not desirable because of
the moral corruption of the South. He had recommended
as a compromise the possession of the throne of Naples and
Sicily by a cadet of the Royal House of Piedmont.* But the
fall of Palermo at the end of May converted him to the idea
of complete Italian unity.

Meanwhile Lord John had not taken up with any warmth
his suggestion of placing a cadet of the House of Piedmont
on the throne of Naples, and ' the tidal wave of unity which
the victory of Palermo set in motion carried that idea to
the frozen sea of diplomatic nostrums,' as its author cheer-
fully acknowledged. Therefore on July 16 Hudson wrote
to Lord John again, declaring himself thin ⸻
and entirely ' in ⸻

of her own on that throne.' On July 27 he again wrote in favour of annexation ' as less prejudicial to British interests (of which you remind me) than the anarchy of Sicily and Naples, and the discontent of North Italy.' Finally on July 31 he wrote a long reasoned letter to Lord John to prove that Italian unity was in accordance with British interests. In this important letter Hudson uses two main arguments. First that annexation had now become the only possible form of stable government for South Italy : ' are the respectable classes of Naples to be subjected to the inconvenience of being shot, plundered, burnt, and violated because the Foreign Powers dislike Unity ? ' Secondly, when the whole Peninsula was united in one State, it would be strong enough to be independent of France, and would naturally gravitate to friendship with England and the German Powers. A good understanding between Austria, Prussia, Italy, and England, argued Hudson, would rid Europe of the nightmare of French domination which then oppressed her. ' It is my duty,' he concluded, ' under my instructions to support Duality, and I have done so. But I should greatly fail in my duty if I did not point out to your Lordship the difficulties (I may say the impossibility) which prevent its accomplishment.'

These arguments, in which, as will be seen, the fear of French predominance was the chief, sufficed to persuade the British statesmen of 1860 that their earnest desire to help Italian freedom was compatible with the material interests of Great Britain, and that it was not only their pleasure but their duty to bring about the union of the whole Peninsula under Victor Emmanuel. Side by side with the love of Italy, the fear of France then dominated Englishmen, and not least among them Lord John Russell. He was in constant anxiety at this period lest Cavour should purchase from Napoleon the right to annex the rest of Italy by ceding the island of Sardinia and the Genoese Riviera to France. The rumour was in fact baseless. But although Cavour and Farini hastened to deny it with the utmost solemnity, Russell could not feel easy, remembering the protestations of innocence that had preceded the barter of Nice and Savoy. Hudson endeavoured to relieve his chief's fears, pointing out that Genoa was a vital part of Italy, whereas Nice had been a mere outpost. At the same time, with admirable skill, he turned Lord John's remaining fears on this head into an argument that England herself should support the Italian claims unconditionally, and so outbid the French by doing the work for nothing. 'I perceive,' he wrote on May 31, replying to Lord John's fears about the alleged cession of Genoa, 'that the more you hang back the more easy do you make the propagation of French notions in Italy.' It is difficult to see where Lord John had been guilty of 'hanging back.' In any case he was never seriously open to the charge again, but made himself thenceforth a willing auxiliary to the plans of Hudson and Cavour.

CHAPTER II

> 'Oh giornate del nostro riscatto !
> Oh dolente per sempre colui
> Che da lunge, dal labbro d' altrui
> Come un uomo straniero, le udrà !
> Che a' suoi figli narrandole un giorno,
> Dovrà dir sospirando : io non c'era ;
> Che la santa vittrice bandiera
> Salutata quel dì non avrà.'
>
> ALESSANDRO MANZONI.

'Oh days of our country's ransoming ! Unhappy for ever shall he be who shall like a stranger hear of it from afar, from the lips of others ; who when he tells the tale to his children on a time, must say sighing, " I was not there ; " who shall not have hailed on that day of days our holy, conquering banner.'

A NEW nation cannot be made solely by the skill of a great statesman playing on the mutual jealousies of Foreign Powers. The making of nations requires the self-sacrifice of thousands of obscure men and women who care more for the idea of their country than for their own comfort or interest, their own lives or the lives of those whom they love. Cavour, with the help of England's attitude of ' non-intervention,' could, at best, only keep the ring while the revolutionaries struck down the Neapolitan Kingdom. It remained to be seen whether volunteers would go out in sufficient numbers to enable Garibaldi to defeat the 100,000 Bourbon troops who, even after the fall of Palermo, refused to embrace the national cause [...] had produced martyrs by the [...] produce effective soldiers by the hundred; could it now produce them by the thousand? The active patriots came from among all [...] classes of the town population, and from the leaders of rural districts, but the common peasantry of the North, though most of them had now been converted to the national cause, did not cross the sea to join Garibaldi. A severe strain was therefore put on the cities of North Italy, not at that date as wealthy as they have since become, to supply at a few weeks' notice, out of the civil population, a complete army of volunteers. The strain was the more severe because so large a portion of the patriotic youth of the Peninsula had already enlisted in the regular army of Piedmont, which, so long as Garibaldi was on the warpath, was urgently required for home defence against a possible attack from Austria. Yet within three months of the capture of Palermo more than 20,000 volunteers were shipped off south from Genoa and Leghorn.

The great majority of these Northerners proved in the battle of the Volturno that they could fight bravely. And it is reasonable to suppose that nine-tenths of them went to the war mainly from patriotic motives, for there was no compulsion to enlist except public opinion, no reward except mental satisfaction. The pay offered was insufficient to supply their daily needs on a campaign where the plunder even of food was punished by death, and where the improvised commissariat was always insufficient, and often non-existent. When Garibaldi at Palermo heard complaints of the irregularity of the paone franc or less. The Intendant General calculated two francs per man as the average for pay and maintenance combined, including both officers and privates in the estimate.

Neither was there any prospect that at the end of the war the spoils would be divided among the actual victors. For the South was to be liberated, not conquered ; and furthermore the Garibaldini well knew that they were fighting to win a kingdom for a Royal Government suspicious of them if not of their leader, and fully equipped with place-hunters of its own. Financially, far more was given up than was gained by the Garibaldino—though exceptions could be named. Physically, the campaign was no holiday ; in the mountains of Sicily and Calabria these town-bred youths of an unathletic community were exposed to the utmost hardships of hunger and thirst, heat, cold, and rain, and to the thousand petty miseries of campaigning in a half-barbarous country, all of which, as privileges of a patriot's life, the old South-American guerilla expected his followers to enjoy as much as he did himself.   All this they endured, and the tortures of wounds treated in ill-provided field hospitals, with an uncomplaining courage which aroused the wonder of their British companions in arms.

The difficulty of raising at a moment's notice a purely volunteer army, and of leading it to victory over regular troops, is one on which modern military authorities lay ever-increasing stress. In the light of these doctrines it will be seen that the improvised campaign narrated in this volume, even when full allowance has been made for the inferior quality of the Bourbon troops, remains a remarkable feat.   It proves that fine elements of character were widely spread in the cities and market-towns of North Italy, and were brought out and fused together by the

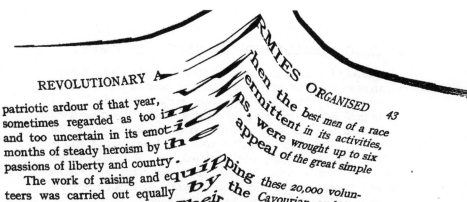

patriotic ardour of that year, ...hen the best men of a race
sometimes regarded as too i... ...rmittent in its activities,
and too uncertain in its emot... ...ns, were wrought up to six
months of steady heroism by th... ...appeal of the great simple
passions of liberty and country.

The work of raising and equipping these 20,000 volunteers was carried out equally by the Cavourian and by
the more advanced parties. Their rivalry for the affections of the people, and their quarrel for the right to
direct the revolution, had the effect of stirring each side to
greater activity on Garibaldi's behalf. Since the friends
of Mazzini and of Cavour could not have sat side by side
in one office, there were three or more separate organisations engaged in the work. First, there was Bertani's
Central Committee in Aid of Garibaldi, seated at Genoa,
conducted in the interest of the advanced groups; secondly,
the more moderate *National Society*, seated at Turin, of
which Cavour's agent La Farina was now President, in
place of Garibaldi resigned; thirdly, the *Million Rifles
Fund*, with its armoury at Milan, founded by Garibaldi
but conducted from first to last under the control of the
Government. The Million Rifles Fund did not, like Bertani's
Committee and the National Society, actually enlist and
equip men, but it supplied the National Society with a
great part of its arms and money, and was itself secretly
supplied, to this end, with large sums from the Royal
treasury, which in this roundabout manner helped to
finance Garibaldi's operations in June and July.

One or both of the rival organisations, Cavour's National
Society and Bertani's Committee, had local branches and
agents collecting money and enlisting men in every chief
town of free Italy, from Turin to Rimini, from Brescia
to Leghorn.

In the enslaved provinces there was more secrecy but

scarcely less activity; the conspirators of the Papal States were in constant correspondence with Mazzini and Bertani, who urged them not to send their young men to Sicily but to hold them in readiness for a rising which Bertani pledged himself to assist with an invasion of volunteers from the North. But from Austrian Venetia, the liberation of which was not immediately contemplated, several thousands of young men escaped over the Lombard frontier by help of a committee that sat for the purpose at Milan and sent them on by way of Genoa to join Garibaldi.

An English engineer named Denton, who was travelling on business through North Italy that summer, described the excitement he found in every town and village; the patriotic newspapers read aloud at the street corner to satisfy a 'rapacity' for news 'astonishing to an Englishman'; Garibaldi's name overheard every moment; Garibaldi's photograph seen in every size and shape, from the shirt-stud to the 'big poster on the town's walls'; the volunteers openly departing by the light of day in their red shirts and képis. When Mr. Denton crossed into Austrian Venetia he found the flame burning not the less intensely for being forced to smoulder. He was able to see below the surface, because every patriot thought it safe to open his heart to him, when no stranger was by, on no other security than the fact that he was an Englishman. One Venetian merchant, leaving his home because the Austrian spies and police had at length rendered his life unbearable, said to him: 'That is my nephew, and he is going to join the ranks of the future liberator of Venetia. He will make the fifth nephew I shall have serving Garibaldi, and out of sixteen young men I had in my counting-house ten have left me' for Sicily. 'So it will be,' he said, 'throughout Venetia: there will not be a young man of spirit left at home.'

No class and no party an[d] was behindhand in the offering[s] ... no district in North Italy ... lives or of money. Rich and poor sent their private ... ferings from all over the country, in sums which to ou[r] ... English standards are not immense, but which represente[d] ... the widow's mite in many straitened Italian households. ... The Cavourian munici-pal bodies of great towns like Milan voted large sums out of rates to the Million Rifles Fund. Cremona alone, a town well below thirty thousand inhabitants, sent nearly a thousand volunteers and gave over 130,000 lire, partly by subscription, partly by a loan which the municipality raised in order to aid Garibaldi's expedition.

But Bergamo, Brescia, and Pavia were the chief Garibaldian cities, next to Genoa herself. In Pavia the Cairoli exercised a supreme influence, based upon nothing more material than the respect of their fellow-citizens for their integrity and their leadership in patriotic endeavour. The father, Carlo Cairoli, Professor of Surgery, had been made Podestà of his native city in 1848, and had died soon after its re-occupation by the Austrians, leaving his five boys to the influence of his widow Adelaide. 'The mother of the Cairoli' had first lost Ernesto at Garibaldi's battle of Varese in 1859. In 1860 Benedetto and Enrico had gone with the Thousand and were both lying wounded in Palermo, when Luigi, aged twenty-two, threw up his commission in the regular army and followed them to Sicily. In September he died of typhus, the result of the hardships of the march through Calabria. During the days when he was contracting his fatal illness, he wrote a long and cheerful letter to his mother and to his betrothed, from the remote Calabrian village of Spezzano Albanese. 'Mama,' so the letter ended, 'I must tell you one thing, which I have tried to be silent about so as not to alarm your modesty, but which I can no longer leave untold.

Yesterday evening my hosts asked me my name. You should have seen the effect which it had on them to hear that I was a Cairoli, or rather a son of the Cairoli mother, of Pavia. And this is not the first time that it has happened to me. Garibaldi's proclamation to the women of Sicily,' [in which Adelaide's patriotic sacrifices were held up for their imitation,] ' was greedily read in all Sicily and the Neapolitan continent, and so your name is already venerated by every good Italian of the South. . . . Good-bye, Mama, good-bye, Adriana.' Luigi died a fortnight after writing this letter, but Benedetto and Enrico recovered of their wounds. Seven years later Enrico, and Giovanni the youngest of the five, received their death-wounds from the Papal troops at Villa Glori, while attempting at the head of a small band of men to force their way into Rome. Benedetto, the eldest, and the mother Adelaide alone survived the wars of liberation. The story of the Cairoli, all bound together by ties of the strongest affection, all devoted wholly to their country's cause, all free from any taint of self-interest, of bombast, or of violence, was revered by Garibaldi and his contemporaries, and has become traditional with posterity as the most perfect example of that family life which fostered the purest qualities of the Italian *risorgimento*.

The papers of Bertani's Central Committee in Aid of Garibaldi have been preserved. The historian can turn over voluminous masses of accounts, bills, purchases of steamers, lists of arms, uniforms, and stores acquired and despatched, besides many documents more poignantly human. There are hundreds of letters for May, June, and July offering service, or rather imploring to be allowed to serve under Garibaldi. In many cases the writer offers to throw up for life some well-paid civil or military post under Government, the Italian idea of bliss, in order to be able to serve Garibaldi for six months. Frequently the aspirant states his age to be seventeen, apparently as the ideal age for a soldier. Sometimes the letter speaks for a group of persons preparing to come. Sometimes it serves to introduce a would-be volunteer who brings it by hand. We can imagine Bertani, his emaciated body propped up on the pillows of his sick-bed, working night and day with the light of fever, almost of madness, in his eyes; his hand shakes as he tears open one after another of these letters, and dashes off a line of answer to each—an almost indecipherable scrawl. Racked by an incessant cough, unable to speak articulately, unable to swallow food, he had not in the middle of June the strength to leave or return to bed except by his friends' help; when they told him he would die if he continued to work, he replied, 'What does it matter?' To their surprise he recovered as the summer drew on.

The misery of some who met with Bertani's positive blank refusal to accept them as volunteers is depicted. Meanwhile their piteous second appeals, refusing to be denied.[*] while Genoa was crammed full of volunteers who had been duly forwarded by their local committees or who had paid for their own journey thither on the chance of getting a passage to Sicily; all these complained bitterly if they were not shipped south by the very next steamer.

One important group of letters proves that Bertani faithfully carried out Garibaldi's instructions that officers of the regular army should be restrained from sending

[*] A girl of the Genoese working class writes to him confidentially on July 4: 'Genoa and the world weary me, so far from the heroes of Italy... My parents may perhaps be adverse to my decision to go to Sicily, but you who are, like Garibaldi, the incarnation of the Italian mind and heart.

in their papers, and men from deserting the ranks in order
to join him. Garibaldi, when he sailed for Sicily, had
left behind him a proclamation exhorting Italian soldiers
to remain at their posts, and Bertani, as we find, had a
formula réady drawn out to the same effect, copies of which
were stacked in his office. When, as often happened,
he received an application from some officer in the royal
army, desirous of joining Garibaldi, it was his custom to
sign a copy of this formula and send it off to stop him.
He made some exceptions, but this was his usual policy.
In spite of it many royal officers, sergeants, and corporals
appeared in Sicily, not a few having been sent out by the
Cavourian agencies. Some had the tacit consent of Victor
Emmanuel or of the military authorities, who knew that
Garibaldi stood in need of drill masters ; but others risked
and in many cases lost their careers. Without such a
stiffening of regulars, it is doubtful whether the volunteers
could have conquered. But if Garibaldi and Bertani
had not done their best to keep the movement within
limits, the discipline and numbers of the royal army might
have been dangerously weakened.

Meanwhile Mazzini was lying hidden in Genoa, secretly
exerting through Bertani and others an important influence on events.

The great exile, who in the 'thirties and 'forties had
raised the Italian movement into a religion by which thousands lived and died, had since 1848 remained behind in
his old position, while the national cause to which he had
given the first vital impulse rallied under other leaders
and moved forward to final victory. He was out of touch
with the new age. Even this year 1860, which saw Italy
united in fulfilment of his dream dreamt thirty years ago,
seemed to him merely another chapter of national shame

and weakness. Since the sacrifice of personal happiness is
was the soul of Mazzini's teaching and character, there his
artistic fitness in his life-long disappointment; and have
old age, though sad, is far above our pity. He would have
been wiser as a statesman, but less great as a prophet,
if he had reconciled himself to the monarchy and settle
down to die content in the country which he had
nation. But, as he wrote to Bertani at this time,
I have helped to make Italy one under the King,
go back to London and write to tell the Italians t
are idiots.' He clung to his Republicanism, to h
for Cavour's methods and for royal officialdom.
ally he erred, but spiritually he thus found a
telling himself the truth that the Italians of the
archy were not the regenerated mankind whose i
advent he had prophesied with Shelley-like ardo
great days of his youth. 'I shall have no mo
Italy,' he wrote, 'I shall have none, even if t
the Unity were to be proclaimed from Rome. The
with its contempt for all ideals, has killed the sou
me.' If he deceived himself, it was never to gai
ease. If it was delusion in him to believe that by
their State a Republic his countrymen could ma
increase their own chance of being great and good
there was Spartan courage in his acknowledgment of
fact that the Third Italy was not the Kingdom of
which he had set out to establish on earth. He saw
Kingdom of Italy established instead, and it pleased
not. But if the reformation of human nature had
the making of Italy was a sufficiently remarkable fea
Carlyle was driven to confess for all his scorn of Mazzini's
doctrines. It showed that the pre-scientific idealists
of whom Mazzini and Garibaldi were the survivors from
an earlier age, had a power over the springs of human

action which the politics of materialism may despise or explain, but can never imitate.

At the beginning of May, Mazzini had left London for Genoa. He came out intending to sail with Garibaldi and the Thousand, but finding that they had left Genoa two or three days before his arrival, he determined not to follow. ' I am tired,' he wrote, ' of being misunderstood. If I was to go to Sicily now, every one would say that I had gone to undermine Garibaldi, or God knows what. Besides, as far as Sicily is concerned, it would be too late. And for what we intend to try on the mainland, I cannot hope to change Garibaldi, who loves me not.'

Mazzini's presence in his native city was a secret kept by a few friends. He had to escape detection by the police, for Cavour would have been glad to deport or imprison him during the crisis. He strolled about, often by night and sometimes even by day, through the deep, narrow alleys of old Genoa, the scenes of his childhood and of his brooding student youth. He had no disguise beyond a shaven chin and a low felt hat pulled well over his tell-tale forehead and eyes. Thus attired he amused himself by stopping Cavour's spies and asking them to lend him a light for his cigar, or to tell him the way up some familiar street. By day he wrote notes to Bertani ; by night he came to visit his sick-bed. It was a delicate situation : for Bertani, being now Garibaldi's agent, wondered how far he ought, in that capacity, to connect himself again with his old master. His evident hesitation grieved Mazzini, who was already suffering from a political difference with Aurelio Saffi, his fellow-exile in England, once his fellow-triumvir of the Roman Republic : Saffi, dearly as he loved Mazzini, did not feel justified in entrusting to him the expenditure of the money raised in Great Britain for Garibaldi's expedition.

Bertani, however, in spite of occasional misgivings, fell once more under the spell of *l'amico*—' the friend' as Mazzini was called by the whole subterranean world of Italian conspiracy. Indeed, from ' the friend's' first arrival in Genoa early in May, Bertani entered with him into the great plan for invading the Papal States.

It was the intention of Bertani's Committee in of Garibaldi to send the volunteers whom they for his service, not to join him at once in Sicily, meet him at Naples, going by the land route, and li Umbria and the Marches from the Pope on their wa The city and district of Rome, being garrisoned b troops, was to be avoided for the present, but it w that when Garibaldi from the south and Medici north had met in triumph at Naples, the enthu unity would overcome all obstacles, and they woul before the year was out to proclaim Victor E King of Italy from the Capitol. This plan had entirely foreign to Garibaldi's own intentions sailed for Sicily with the Thousand. He had then to Medici the task of leading the next expedition, ins him to send reinforcements both to Sicily and also Papal Marches and Umbria, where a rising was, sai baldi, about to take place. Whether Medici in was to go with the reinforcements to Sicily or with invaders of the Pope's territories, was left undecid Garibaldi's letter.*

* Garibaldi's letter reads as follows :— ' GENOA, May 5, 1860.

' DEAR MEDICI,—It is better that you should remain behind, and you can be more useful so. Bertani, La Farina, the Directors [of the Million Rifles Fund] at Milan will furnish you, on the presentation of this letter, with all the means you will require. You must not only make every effort to send reinforcements of men and arms into Sicily, but to do the same for the Marches and Umbria, where there will soon be a rising and where soon it will be necessary to support it to the utmost. Tell the Italians to follow

Such were the vague instructions which he left behind, obviously requiring a good deal of interpretation. Bertani, under the influence of Mazzini, decided to divert practically the whole of the reinforcements to the Papal States. Neither of them military men, they were both under the delusion that Garibaldi could overrun Sicily and cross the Straits with his Thousand alone, aided by the islanders. ' Sicily is safe,' said Mazzini, ' let us think of the rest. . . . You do not know the genius of Garibaldi and the indomitable determination of the Sicilians to be rid of Bourbon rule. Henceforth we must help Sicily from Central Italy by way of the Abruzzi. Garibaldi has with him a body of good officers,' who would suffice to drill and lead the Sicilians. ' To the Centre every one : Umbria and the Marches liberated, we will reach Garibaldi across the Abruzzi.' *

The supposition that Garibaldi could have advanced from Palermo without strong reinforcements from North Italy was perhaps the crudest of the mistakes involved in this scheme, and was, moreover; the only point where the scheme deviated from Garibaldi's own instructions. But it may further be doubted whether a few thousand volunteers, under a chief other than Garibaldi himself, would have sufficed to liberate Umbria and the Marches. Mazzini told Bertani that all would go well because the Papal troops would join the liberators in the hour of battle. But the Pope's fighting regiments, his newly levied Austrian, Irish, and French crusaders, were about as likely to join the red-shirts as the red-shirts were to join them. These

you in entire confidence, and that the time has come to make the Italy that we all yearn for.'

* See also a letter of his to Bertani prior to the landing of Garibaldi : ' Collect money, but don't send it to Sicily. If Garibaldi does not get there it is not needed ; if he gets there, it is equally not needed. His presence there will suffice.'

SICILY OR THE CENTRE?

Papal troops put up a gallant though hopeless fight against in the superior force of the Piedmontese regular army would September, and there is no reason to think that they Medici's not have opposed a very serious resistance to the field scanty volunteers in June. Even if victorious in the how could an army of irregulars without siege guns taken Ancona? But if the plan to liberate the M... and join Garibaldi at Naples was to succeed at all, i... succeed completely and at once.

For not only the Papal army but the Foreign had to be considered. Austria, who until 1859 h... self garrisoned the Marches for the Pope, had si... beginning of 1860 been pouring into the port of thousands of Austrian subjects to be enlisted in th... army. Would Austria, then, have watched unmo... capture of these districts by Revolutionary bands as to France, even if Medici had left Rome un... would Napoleon have allowed the red-shirts to Umbria in June what he allowed Cavour to do ... September?

On May 7, the day after Garibaldi's departure, still regarded the invasion of the Papal States as hi... probable destiny;* but when all these grave considera... —the weakness of Garibaldi's military position on Si... the strength of the new Papal army and the old P... fortresses, and the probable action of Austria and Fra... were laid before his cool judgment by Cavour's agents Farina, Amari, and Melenchini, he was not long in ... ciding for Sicily. As early as May 12, even before the of Garibaldi's landing at Marsala had arrived, Medici had been won round to Cavour and common sense, and had

* 'I have remained behind to support the bold enterprise by a second expedition, or better still by a powerful diversion elsewhere.'—Medici's letter to Panizzi, May 7.

declared that he would take his expedition by sea to join
Garibaldi.

The quarrel that divided Mazzini and Bertani's Committee on the one side, from Cavour, Medici, and the
National Society on the other, arose on this question of
the destination of the volunteers, not on the question of
Republic or Monarchy.   On the latter point even Mazzini
had, for the time being, surrendered.*   But on the former
the quarrel was in full vigour even before the fall of Palermo.
It first arose on the question whether Medici should go
to Sicily or to the Papal States, and it was revived in the
same form over the departure of every large consignment of
volunteers that left Genoa in June, July, and August.

If Bertani's plan of invading the Papal States had
been carried out, Garibaldi would have been left locked
up at Palermo for want of men, and Italy would probably
have met with a great disaster in the centre.   And yet
Bertani's policy, though it would have been fatal if put
into practice, proved invaluable as a stimulus to Cavour.
The constant threat of the advanced party to send their own
men into the Papal States, coupled with Garibaldi's success
in the South, finally drove Cavour to invade the Papal
States himself when the time was ripe.   Mazzini and
Bertani, wrong in detail, were right in their two general
principles—first, that the Pope and the King of Naples ought
to be attacked this year while the revolutionary enthusiasm
created by Garibaldi's success was at its height ;   and
secondly, that they ought to be attacked from both north
and south at once.

At present Cavour was content to help Garibaldi.
Having won over Medici to abandon the Papal States and

* In one of his almost daily notes to Bertani, written in June, he says :—
' I have no republican intentions.   I strive for nothing but the Unity.
The cry *Viva la Repubblica* would seem to me a real mistake at this moment.'

D'AZEGLIO'S SCRUPLES

to go direct to Sicily in Bertani's despite, the Government was bound to fit him out and send him with all possible speed. Medici's expedition, and the expedition of Cosenz a few weeks later, were armed, clothed, and shipped at the expense of the Cavourian National Society and the Million Rifles Fund. Since these organisations had no offices in Genoa, the port of departure, it was necessary for Me and Cosenz to set up there a *Military Office* of the as they did not wish to be dependent on Bertani' mittee. Dr. Bertani did, however, fit out the am for their expeditions, and both of them, when spectively sailed, parted from him on speaking term

The Bertani Committee also supplied the Office of Medici and Cosenz with a good many of recruits, in addition to the men whom the Ca raised for themselves in Milan and elsewhere. steamers, the arms, and the money for the exped June and July came almost entirely from the C agencies. It was only in August that Bertani friends sent out the great expeditions which the selves had paid for and equipped. In June an hundreds of thousands of *lire* were secretly supp the King's Government to purchase the steamer equip the men for Medici and Cosenz. Over 6000 fire were obtained for them by Cavour from the armoury the Million Rifles Fund at Milan, which had been close Garibaldi himself a month before by the inconv scruples of Massimo D'Azeglio, the Governor of the Cavour now eased D'Azeglio's conscience by purchasing weapons with the alleged intention of arming the Nat Guard,—and then sent them to Medici at Genoa.

In the course of the summer D'Azeglio gradually dis covered that he was being fooled. When in obedience to the ostensible orders of Government he tried to put diff.

culties in the way of recruiting volunteers in Milan, he found
that all the neighbouring Governors gave him the cold
shoulder.   Finally a private letter from a highly-placed
official to one of D'Azeglio's subordinates served to open the
Governor's eyes : ' It seems,' said the letter, ' that at Milan
you are not much in touch with the real intentions of the
Government.'   Finally D'Azeglio retired, alleging the ground
of ill-health.   To the end of his life he would never allow
that Cavour's underhand methods had been right.

CHAPTER III

GARIBALDI AT PALERMO—THE RECONSTRUCTION OF ь
ARMY—THE ADVANCE THROUGH THE ISLAND

'Addio, mia bell' addio
L'armata se ne va ;
Se non partissi anch' io
Sarebbe una viltà.' *

'Farewell, farewell, my true love,
The army's on the move ;
And if I stayed with you, love,
A coward I should prove.'

THE three steamers which were to carry Medici a
men to Sicily had been purchased from a French con
nominally on behalf of De Rohan, a Yankee devot
the Italian cause. They had been hastily rechris
the *Washington*, *Oregon*, and *Franklin*, and the U
States Consul at Genoa, accompanied by Gariba
Englishman,' Peard, who was starting with the expediti
went on board the *Washington* and hauled up on it t
stars and stripes. A little before dawn on June 10 Med
sailed with the *Washington* and *Oregon* from a spot a
miles west of Genoa, where a midnight embarkation h
taken place, and on the same day the *Franklin* sailed f
the shore between Pisa and Leghorn, where she had tak
on board the Tuscan volunteers. These two parts of Medici's

* There is always some popular song that is being sung, whistled, and
hummed *ad nauseam*. In the Italian armies of 1860 it was 'Addio, mia
bell' addio.'

expedition met safely at Cagliari, the port in Southern Sardinia which became henceforth an important place of call for successive shiploads of Garibaldini. But two other vessels, the small *Utile* and the American clipper *Charles and Jane*, which were also expected at Cagliari with another thousand men, were captured on the way by Neapolitan cruisers, and taken into the harbour of Gaeta. Medici, after awaiting them for some time in vain, left Cagliari with the *Washington, Oregon,* and *Franklin,* containing 2500 men, 6000 or 8000 rifles and muskets, and an immense store of ammunition. This was the first aid despatched to Garibaldi from the mainland, with the exception of sixty men and a stock of arms and powder which the *Utile,* since captured by the Neapolitans, had run through to Palermo by way of Marsala on an earlier and more fortunate voyage.

Medici's three vessels left Cagliari early on the afternoon of June 16. Shortly before nightfall of the following day, when they were nearing the Sicilian coast and entering the zone of greatest danger from the Neapolitan cruisers, they saw a Piedmontese war-vessel steering towards them. When she came alongside she turned out to be the *Gulnara,* whose commander came aboard the *Washington* to speak with Medici. He had orders from his admiral, Persano, to conduct the expedition safely to Castellamare, the landing-place agreed on between Persano and Garibaldi. The commander of the *Gulnara* also made in Persano's name a strange request for the instant surrender of Mazzini. Medici was able to assure him that, although the Republican Alberto Mario and his English wife, Jessie White Mario, were on board, Mazzini himself had not accompanied the expedition. A few hours later they reached Castellamare and began to disembark before midnight. Garibaldi came to meet them, and they marched in high spirits to

CAVOUR MAKES A MISTAKE

Palermo, arriving there on the 19th and the two following days, just as the last of the Neapolitan garrison took their departure under the terms of the capitulation.* The new era in Garibaldi's enterprise had now fairly begun.

The demand made by the commander of the Guiscarda for the surrender of Mazzini out at sea was the end of a curious story. Cavour, who after the fall of Palermo had adopted the policy of aiding Garibaldi—upon te —instructed Admiral Persano to lend him what co help he could, but at the same time sent out a confide agent of his own to represent to the Dictator of Sicil wishes of the Government of Turin. Cavour's choi this purpose had fallen on the Sicilian, La Farina, Pre of the National Society, who, like Bertani, had done to bring Cavour and Garibaldi together in old day: like Bertani seemed now to aim at undoing his own He was already an object of dislike in Garibaldian when Cavour unwisely chose him for this delicate Those of Cavour's friends who knew Garibaldi fo inevitable disaster. La Farina arrived in Palermo d the first week of June, and began almost at once to qu with the new masters of the city. He turned his repor Cavour into a series of bitter attacks on the Dictator and administration, some just and some unjust, but all culated to alienate the two men on whose alliance t welfare of Italy depended.

On June 12 Cavour, misinformed by his spies at Gen as to Mazzini's movements, sent the following message Admiral Persano :—

‘ We are assured that that Mazzini and Miss White [Jessie Mario] have embarked on board the *Washington* that is taking volunteers to Palermo. Send La Farina to Garibaldi to invite

---

* These events are narrated in the last pages of *Garibaldi and the Thousand.*

him in the King's name to arrest Mazzini, and to give him into your hands. He must tell him that Mazzini's presence in Sicily would necessitate the recall of the squadron and ruin the national cause in Europe. You will send Mazzini to Genoa on board the *Carlo Alberto*. . . . Should Garibaldi refuse to have Mazzini arrested you will immediately prepare to depart with the fleet and will send the *Authion* to Cagliari to receive instructions.'

This letter proves that there were limits to Cavour's understanding of Garibaldi, though it was large compared with Garibaldi's understanding of Cavour. It was an error to expect Garibaldi to hand over to prison his former master and honoured rival, now in the decline of years and prosperity, and a folly to enforce the demand by a threat to the liberator of Palermo in his hour of triumph. Cavour had never had the chance of studying Garibaldi and his friends at close quarters ; otherwise he would have known that Garibaldi himself was above all things a gentleman, and that Mazzini was regarded by the whole world of exiles and advanced patriots, even when they most differed from him, with a reverence which to Cavour was foolishness.

La Farina flatly refused to carry out the mission, saying that he had no influence with the Dictator, and compelled the Admiral to take the message himself. Persano, who was at this time popular with all parties, was not ordered out of the room as La Farina would probably have been, but Garibaldi replied that he would not arrest Mazzini unless he began to intrigue against the monarchy of Victor Emmanuel. Persano, fully realising Cavour's mistake in tactics, determined, instead of making preparations to leave Palermo, to effect the arrest of Mazzini before he landed in Sicily. That was why he commissioned the commander of the *Gulnara*, when he went to meet Medici, to make the arrest out at sea. But since Mazzini was all the while in Genoa the incident ended in fiasco.

The main object of La Farina's mission to Sicily was to secure the immediate annexation of the island to Piedmont. Cavour was unwilling to allow Garibaldi, by prolonging his Dictatorship, to acquire a civil and military establishment of his own, independent of the Royal Government. It was necessary to send out arms and men to Garibaldi, but it was impossible not to dread some of the uses to which he might turn those arms and his own immense popularity. Surrounded as he was in great measure by friends of Mazzini and Bertani, by the Marios, by Nicotera, it was probable that, while continuing as ever to the monarchy, he might grow less and less amenable to the advice of the King's Ministers. Cavour, struggling to keep his feet in a flood of diplomatic troubles which Garibaldi thought it unpatriotic even to consider, and yet the Dictator's independent actions were the ignored factor in the diplomatic situation of which he ignored the very existence. There were also grave political dangers of an internal character in a prolonged Dictatorship: Cavour was endeavouring to build up the unity of Italy on the only possible basis, that of a constitutional monarchy, and if the advanced parties were to get all the credit of the revolution in South Italy and enjoy an indefinite tenure of power in the Provinces which they liberated, it would be a bad beginning for the principle of authority in the new State as represented by the King's Parliamentary Cabinet at Turin. Therefore Cavour desired as soon as possible to dominate the revolution, and like the falconer to lure his hawk back after it had struck the prey.

These motives and these principles of action were sound in themselves, but there remains always the question of particular application. If indeed the enemies of Italy

had already been struck down by Garibaldi, or if Cavour
had been prepared to strike them down himself in open war,
then no date would have been too early for the annexation
of Sicily.   But the House of Bourbon still reigned on the
mainland, and could be overturned by Garibaldi alone.
When Cavour attempted to obtain the annexation of Sicily
in June and early July, he was acting on the mistaken belief
that an annexationist revolution could be engineered by his
own agents in Naples.*   He imagined that the rank and
file of the Neapolitan army was prepared to come over to
the Italian cause, and that a civil and military *pronuncia-
mento* would speedily bring the Bourbon dynasty to an end
by the act of the Neapolitans themselves.   If such a revolution had been possible, it would no doubt have been safer
to dispense with Garibaldi's further service as an independent chieftain, and to bring him back to the place which
he had occupied in the war of 1859, as the leader of volunteers fighting in front of the royal armies of Italy, whenever
they should next be led against Pope or Austrian.   But
Cavour had yet to learn by experience that the Neapolitans
would effect no revolution for themselves, and that as he
was not himself prepared to declare war on Francis II.,
Garibaldi must be allowed to cross the Straits of Messina if
Italy was to be free.

If in June the Dictator had yielded to the cry for immediate annexation which La Farina stirred up among the
Sicilians, the island would have passed officially into the
hands of Piedmont, and before Garibaldi had marched
onward from Palermo, Victor Emmanuel would have found

---

* On July 14 Cavour wrote to Admiral Persano :—
  ' On the one hand, we must at all costs prevent Garibaldi from passing
on to the continent, and on the other, we must provoke a revolution in
Naples.   If this succeeds, the government of Victor Emmanuel would be
proclaimed without delay.'

himself completely responsible to the Powers for every act of every red-shirt in Sicily. In that case Garibaldi, who even as it was came very near to being stopped at the Straits of Messina by the Powers, would most certainly have been prevented from crossing to the mainland, since Cavour could no longer have pleaded inability to control his action. Then, when the Neapolitan revolution had missed fire the great statesman would have discovered too late the flaw in his plans, and the Pope and the King of Naples would have continued to govern Central and Southern Italy.

All this was clearly foreseen at the time by not a few Cavourians, including Michele Amari, the wise and learned historian of the Sicilian Vespers, who was just returned from exile to his own Palermo to work there for Italian unity. Amari was certain that the Dictator did right to refuse annexation in June, because annexation would almost certainly have confined him to the island; but he was equally certain that he was wrong to refuse annexation when once he had crossed the Straits.*

For nearly a month La Farina laid siege to Garibaldi. At his instigation, petitions were sent up by Sicilian ministers and municipalities, and demonstrations were held in the streets of Palermo, which showed a genuine popular desire for immediate annexation. The attitude of the islanders was neither that of Cavour nor that of Garibaldi. They desired annexation at the earliest possible moment, because they saw in it the best security against reconquest by the Neapolitans and the quickest way to a settled government. They cried Italia Una with no feigned zeal.

---

* Emilio Visconti Venosta, an out-and-out Cavourian, sent by Cavour to Naples in 1860 to stir up the revolution there, told me in 1910 that in his opinion Cavour made a mistake in desiring the annexation of Sicily before Garibaldi had crossed the Straits. Cadolini himself, politically the wisest and the most Cavourian of the red-shirts of 1860, expressed to me the same opinion.

when they saw their protectors, the red ~~~irts, and hoped
for the Bersaglieri to follow, as averted ~~~~ Bourbon reconquest; but they cared little whether the ~~~~ated Neapolitans were or were not brought into the Union ~~~~and only the
more enlightened individuals among them ~~~~ongly supported Garibaldi's project of crossing the ~~~~its. But
while, from these selfish motives, they favour~~~ Cavour's
plan of immediate annexation, on the other ha~~~, their
devotion to *Garibardi*, who had come to their res~~~ like a
Paladin of old, was so powerful a compound of su~~~ition
with pure human gratitude and love that no di~~~ of
political opinion could wear it away. As late as the ~~~dle
of September, when Garibaldi was clearly wrong in de~~~ to show
the annexation any longer, he had only to come to show
himself in Palermo, and although he was standing in the
way of the popular desire, all opposition was silenced in
heartfelt shouts of welcome and applause. When, therefore, in June, La Farina represented the island to Cavour
as being already on the point of ‘a terrible explosion’ of
popular wrath against the Dictatorship, he was writing
nonsense such as only an angry man can write. Garibaldi
said in effect to the people of Palermo and to his Sicilian
ministers: ‘I know you desire to vote the annexation at
once, but I desire to free the rest of Italy first. I have
freed you, and in return I ask you to wait while I free your
brothers. Fight first and vote afterwards.’ They consented to wait, less for the sake of their brothers than for
the sake of the man who asked of them this slight return
for all that he and his Thousand had done.

La Farina, in his letters to Cavour, not only represented
the Sicilians as more hostile to Garibaldi than they eally
were, but he also represented the island as falling into a
state of anarchy, whereas in fact the disturbance was
merely such as war and revolution must necessarily bring

their train among a population unaccustomed to self government. Bitter personal animosity to Crispi, Garibaldi's factotum in the island, goaded on La Farina to ... exaggerations. The two Sicilians were deadly rivals ... the affections of their countrymen. La Farina was ... far right that Garibaldi was utterly unfitted to cope ... any purely political or administrative situation, or to ... order out of the chaos of revolution; but the chaos ... not of the kind which destroys society. La Farina was ... in saying that annexation was desirable at the earliest ... possible in the interests of administration in Sicily, ... as Amari pointed out, the gendarmerie of North Italy ... the only force capable of restoring complete order in ... land. Yet Sicily continued under the Garibaldian ... nearly six months without any positive catastrophe. Nor, ... stration, did the Cavourians find it an easy task. ... years the island was in a continual state of unrest.

The 'hermit of Caprera' was the last man likely to succeed as administrator or politician. Beyond the life of the sailor, the poet, the farmer, and the soldier in active service, he understood nothing of the ways of men. His friend and biographer has justly said :—

'Finance, police, taxation, law courts, bureaucratic machinery were to him artificial and oppressive additions to the life of nature, invented by the wickedness or craft of man; if he could, he would have swept them all away. As he could not, he resigned himself to submit to them, but in his heart despised and abhorred them. Now for one holding these ideas, it is not easy to govern States well, or even to choose the best men to govern them, and so it was with Garibaldi. . . . One thing he saw with unerring vision during his Dictatorship, from his landing at Marsala till his arrival in Naples, and that was that he must put off the annexation of the Kingdom to

3

the Monarchy of Victor Emmanuel until the revolu
was to lay the foundations of Italian Unity, had
accomplished fact.'

Garibaldi endured La Farina for a month, and then
his patience gave way. He had always held high ideas of
the Dictatorial Power in times of crisis, when the freedom
of the country was at stake. He was determined to advance on Naples and make Italy, and if Cavour's agent strove
to lock him up in Sicily by arousing there a movement for
premature annexation, the man must take the consequences.
He decided to send him back to his master.

On July 7 La Farina's house was surrounded by the
police ; he was made prisoner, taken on board the Piedmontese flagship and handed over to Admiral Persano,
from whom La Farina's captors had the impudence to
demand ' a receipt ' for his person. Nor was this all. A
notice of his expulsion from the island was inserted in the
official paper of Sicily in terms of malignant insult. La
Farina was spoken of as expelled with two other men,
Griscelli and Totti. ' The three men thus deported,' said
the official journal, ' were in Palermo conspiring against
the existing order of things.' Now Griscelli and Totti were
two of the meanest of mankind, who had narrowly escaped
execution on a charge of plotting to assassinate the Dictator, and La Farina had no more to do with them than he
had with the beggars on the steps of the Cathedral.

For the decision to deport La Farina there was much
to be said. It restored political peace at Palermo, and
cut short a controversy which could not safely be conducted
in the face of the enemy, who had still 20,000 troops in
the island. But the manner of his deportation was most
offensive, and leaves a stain on the chivalrous character of
Garibaldi. It is not known whether the details were
planned by him or by some ill-natured follower, but it is

certain that he never punished or reproved the gross insult offered to the emissary of the Royal Government.

The expulsion of La Farina from Sicily, and still more the manner of the expulsion, embittered the quarrel of Cavourian and Garibaldian throughout the Italian world. But the nation as a whole, with a political instinct inspired by the supreme nature of the crisis, continued to regard Cavour and Garibaldi as partners in the great work. The Dictator had now cut the knot of Sicilian politics and was free to advance and cross the Straits if he had the military strength. Indirectly he had done Cavour a service, of which the latter was quick to take advantage. The incident could be used as a proof to diplomatic Europe that the Royal Government had no control over the Dictator's actions. 'Cavour,' wrote Hudson to Lord John Russell, 'says that the Government have no influence with Garibaldi, who has ordered La Farina to quit Sicily.'

In spite of La Farina and the vexed question of immediate annexation, June and July were full of happy days for Garibaldi, for the Sicilians, and for the volunteers who came pouring in by every steamer from the North. All classes of the population of Palermo, with priests and monks conspicuous among them, trooped down to the harbour to work at dismantling the Castellamare, the fortress whence the Bourbons had so long held Palermo in awe. The Church in Sicily lost none of its enthusiasm for Garibaldi on nearer view. The Archbishop was friendly, and even consented to bless the troops. In the nunneries of Palermo, where almost every noble family had a daughter shut up for life, the enthusiasm for 'Giuseppe' and his young followers, who had in several cases during the street fighting saved them and their churches from the brutality of the Neapolitan soldiers, was shown in many pretty and pathetic ways. Garibaldi, writing to Ruggiero, the veteran statesman of Sicily's former revolutions, described the feelings which he shared so fully with the people. ' This brave people is free. Joy is written on every face, the country echoes with the glad cries of the liberated.'

Garibaldi had good reason to be happy. He was fulfilling, by his own methods and with his own followers, the dream of his life which had seemed foolishness to the wise. The vision of all that he might some day do for Italy had first risen before his mind's eye more than twenty years before, as he rode over the Pampas leading a few dozen partisans to nameless skirmishes in long-forgotten wars. The vision had drawn near, only to vanish again like a mirage on the walls of Rome. Dim with fears of failure, it had yet given him strength to endure in the marshes of Ravenna and in the trading vessel on the faraway Pacific. It had cheered his farm life at Caprera with a steadier glow of hope. And now all Europe was watching this poet's daydream enact itself in the world of living men.

Bixio and many other volunteers, officers, and privates wounded and whole, lodged in the Trinacria, the famous hotel looking out upon the esplanade. Its host, Ragusa, a worthy Piedmontese, announced that for thirty days he would dine any of the Thousand for nothing, but next year he told an English guest that there had not been a man of them but had insisted upon paying his bill.

The Dictator and his aides-de-camp lived at the other end of the town, in the so-called ' Observatory ' of the Palace over the Porta Nuova. It had two balconies, one looking eastward down the mile-long Toledo to the sea, the other westward across the Conca d'oro to the mountains above Monreale. Its interior consisted of a modest hall of audience with the beds of the four officers on duty concealed behind screens in the four corners, and two little bedrooms beyond for Garibaldi and his secretary. The manners and way of life of the Dictator in the Palace at Palermo, as afterwards in Naples and Caserta, were in no way different from those on his Caprera farm. Formality there was none. Important visitors were sent to him to have audience whatever he was doing. Not infrequently they found him combing out his hair, to which he still gave long and careful attention, although the thick, flowing locks which had adorned the defender of Rome no longer fell over his shoulders. On another occasion, with more despatch, he evacuated his red shirt and grey flannels and retired into bed, still discussing the business in hand with his astonished visitor.

The terrace roof, connecting the Observatory, where the General lived, with the main part of the Palace, was a *rendezvous*, in the summer evenings, for the principal Garibaldini. for the ladies of Palermo, and for the officers of the Piedmontese and British navies. Eager questionings and endless stories about the battles and adventures which had led them thither so far, were mingled with confident prophecies of the coming campaign. All were agreed that they would enter both Rome and Venice before the winter. The perfumes rising from the gardens of the plain, the sun setting behind the distant mountains where the Thousand had suffered and fought, ' the place, the time, the events produced a sort of delicious ecstasy which annihilated distances and transfigured facts. Nor was this a mere effect of the southern temperature, for English officers shared those emotions, those illusions, those errors of enthusiasm.'

Among this happy crowd on the terrace appeared one evening, like death at the feast, a group of young men, prematurely aged and bent, looking about them with eyes that seemed to gaze without seeing. They

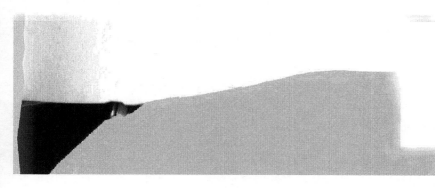

were the eight remaining followers of Pisa* who had started with him three years before from enza on his rash attempt to overthrow the Bourbon power. Since their defeat and the death of their leader and companions, they had lain in the dungeons of the island of Favignana, whence, only six weeks ago, they had seen through the prison bars the *Piemonte* and *Lombardo* sail past with the Thousand to Marsala. The revolution had now reached Favignana and set them free, and they had come straight to Palermo to demand places in the forefront of Garibaldi's battles. The first person whom they met on the terrace was the long-bearded Antonio Mosto, leader of the Genoese Carabineers. As soon as he had recognised his friends beneath the changes that misery had wrought in them, he granted them the privilege, sought by many in vain, of enlisting as privates in his little company that fought in the van of the army and bore the highest proportion of the losses. They were then taken into the Observatory to see the General. He was deeply moved. ' This,' he said, ' is a type of human life. We, whom fortune favoured with victory, lodge in royal palaces. These brave fellows, because conquered, are buried in the vaults of Favignana. Yet the cause, the undertaking, the audacity was the same. . . . The first honours are due to Pisacane. He led the way and these brave fellows were our pioneers.' Their leader, Nicotera, who had been Pisacane's lieutenant, was sent to organise the new expedition of volunteers preparing in Tuscany, where his incorrigible Republicanism soon caused trouble. The others marched with Garibaldi, and a few weeks later five out of the seven fell dead or wounded on the field of Milazzo.

But the terrace and Observatory were sometimes besieged by less disinterested visitors. Even before the

* The Sapri expedition. See *Garibaldi and the Thousand*, chap. iv.

capture of Palermo was complete, even before the Bourbon troops had signed the capitulation, no less than 3000 petitions for employment had been sent in, each petitioner setting forth his own claims on the State in terms of fulsome panegyric. If Garibaldi had placed Northerners in the governorships and magistracies, these duties might have been more effectively fulfilled, but in so disposing of patronage he would have alienated the Sicilians. This must be remembered by those who criticise the undoubted maladministration under the Dictatorship. Many of the better sort of Sicilians, especially the returning exiles, retired into private life, disdaining to advance their real claims on the State, but the worst class of petitioners set upon him like yelping hounds. He was utterly unfitted to choose among the pack: 'The Dictator says *yes* to every one and leaves me to disentangle matters,' complained Nievo the poet of the Thousand, now Vice-intendant of the National forces in Sicily. 'Every one makes court to me,' he wrote in disgust, 'Princes and Princesses, Dukes and Duchesses by shovelfuls, coveting salaries of twenty ducats a month.' On the civil side Crispi made selection among his fellow-islanders, for better, for worse. Garibaldi's only way of dealing with this foul Levantine disease of State-sycophancy was to apply the ineffectual remedy of his own example. The Dictator took ten francs a day for his civil list, and did not add to it by any indirect means. Once when he burnt a hole in his clothes he was hard put to it for a change. To Alexandre Dumas, who had come over in his yacht to see historical romance in the living reality, Garibaldi said one day: 'If I were rich I would do like you, I would have a yacht.' Dumas was much moved, for he had just seen him sign a cheque for half a million francs of public money.

It was fortunate for Garibaldi that North Italy was

so generous with the purse, and that by one of
pieces of luck he had captured from the Neapolitan government an immense sum of ready money which had been
called in for re-coinage and lay in the mint at Palermo.
For by the middle of July the Sicilians had subscribed
voluntarily no more than £5000 : the British Consul, who
had seen them win and lose their freedom in 1848–1849,
observed the same characteristics once more, passion
wreaked on the statues of the Bourbons and the stones
of the Castellamare, flags, shoutings, bombastic processions,
but no foresight, no fruitful fear of reconquest, no general
and public self-sacrifice. Since on this occasion they had
North Italy to protect them, their sense of security was less
ill founded. But Garibaldi's edict of conscription remained
a dead letter, and he was soon induced by deputations from
the upland communes to suspend it ' until the agricultural
work of the year was over,' that is, until the Greek Calends.
Most of the *squadre*, or irregular bands of peasants, went
back to their homes before or after the capitulation of
Palermo. But several thousands of Sicilians volunteering
for more regular service were formed into regiments and
drilled by native, by North Italian, and by English officers.
They proved far more efficient than the *squadre*, and
although the degrees of courage which they displayed
in the coming campaign varied from time to time, on
the whole they did credit, both in their own island and
on the mainland, to the officers who had in a few weeks
knocked them into soldiers.

Some of the upper class of the island behaved poorly,
refusing to serve unless they were at once given commissions, although scores of the noble and wealthy families of
North Italy had sons doing the meanest duties of the
camp, and thinking a red shirt better wear than epaulettes.
There were indeed many of the Sicilian upper class who did

their duty well, but the island regiments consisted of the lower orders of the population to a greater degree than did the regiments from the North.

Dunne's 'English regiment,'* in particular, was largely recruited from the corner-boys of Palermo, who under discipline and good influences behaved with marked courage in Milazzo fight. Many of these lads had passed a fortnight or three weeks in the 'Garibaldi Foundling Hospital,' established and conducted on excellent military lines by Alberto Mario. Happy as they were in this institution, they deserted from it fast to join Dunne's regiment, because they were told that under '*milordo*' they would go sooner to the wars with *Garibardi*. *Milordo* himself was one of the most romantic figures in the Garibaldian camp. Dunne had a share of the mysterious power of Nicholson or Gordon to inspire confidence, discipline, and courage into untrained races. He had commanded Turkish levies for the British Government in the Crimea. Shortly before the capture of Palermo he accepted, at Hudson's suggestion, a dangerous mission from Cavour and La Farina to carry a political message through to Garibaldi and to smuggle into Sicily the Cavourian agent Scelzi, disguised as his servant. Scelzi and Dunne had landed in North Sicily, raised several hundred *squadre* on their own account, skirmished with the Bourbon troops, and entered Palermo at the head of their men a few days before the capitulation was signed. Dunne then discarded his *squadre* and set to work to make a real regiment out of apparently unpromising material. Aided by Wyndham, an Englishman, formerly of the Austrian army, by a dozen civilians just come from Great Britain and Ireland for love

* Though it was so-called, only a part of the officers were English and the men were Sicilian. It must not be confused with the British Legion that only appeared at Naples in October.

3 a

of Garibaldi, and some ex-sergeants of the P
army, he soon manufactured a force of 600 your
whom the Dictator could have ill spared in th
battle.

Whatever his political errors, Garibaldi had a firm
hold of the military situation, and did not waste a day.
On June 20, twenty-four hours after the departure of the
last Neapolitan troops, and while Medici's men were still
arriving in Palermo, a column under Türr started for the
centre of the island with orders to march by way of
Caltanisetta to Catania on the eastern sea. The force,
when it left the capital, numbered little more than 500
men, consisting chiefly of members of the original Thousand, together with a small company of foreign deserters
from the Bourbon army, and a dozen Sicilian gentlemen.
This 'brigade,' as it was called, was the more formidable
in report because of two obsolete cannon retrieved from
the ignominious position of posts in the streets of Palermo,
remounted and dragged across the island as 'artillery.'
The foreign company had good Enfield rifles, but the
majority of the force, the remnant of the Thousand, still
had their old bad muskets. Ammunition was procured
on the way in the sulphur district of Caltanisetta.

Being the first column to leave Palermo for the front,
Türr's 'brigade' created great interest. It was accompanied by some of the best war-correspondents in Europe,
and by Alexandre Dumas with a female midshipman in
tow. The vain, good-natured, luxurious giant, liked by
some, disliked by others, and laughed at by all of his
companions on the march, left them half-way and returned to headquarters at Palermo. The expedition,
though romantic and picturesque, was uneventful. At
Misilmeri the population, which had shown fierce en-

thusiasm and sent its *squadre* for the attack on Palermo when Garibaldi passed that way three weeks before, was found to be sullenly hostile because of the edict of conscription. When they learnt that it was to be inoperative, they recovered their cheerfulness, and enjoyed the eloquence of Garibaldi's friar, Father Pantaleo,—which produced two volunteer recruits. Here Türr fell dangerously ill and was forced to return to the continent for a few weeks to recover his health. The command of the column devolved on his fellow-Hungarian Eber, who did not on that account give over his functions as *Times* correspondent. Eber was a reserved and quiet gentleman, known and respected in the English Lake district, where he had passed many years of exile, and in the best London society. He had neither Türr's military experience and vigour nor his popularity with the troops, but he had an easy part to play and fell into no capital errors. Passing through the heart of the island by Enna and the rock citadel of Castrogiovanni, which commands the finest view in Sicily, Eber and his men skirted Ætna on the South and entered Catania unopposed on July 15. After Misilmeri they had been well received, in most places with real enthusiasm, and they had put down some incipient brigandage; but they did not pick up many recruits in the course of their march from sea to sea.*

On June 25, less than a week after the departure of Türr's and Eber's column, Bixio left the capital with another 'brigade' of about 1200 men, consisting partly of Sicilians and partly of Northerners under Caldesi, who had come out in Medici's expedition. Passing through Piana dei Greci, where he enlisted sixty of the warlike Albanians, through Corleone and by the temples of Girgenti, Bixio reached the southern coast, sailed along it from Licata to Terranova, and marched thence straight

* See Map VI., at end of book, for routes of Eber's and Bixio's columns.

across country to Catania, where he joined Eber
in the latter half of July.

Meanwhile, as will be recounted in the next chapter,
Medici with a far better organised, better armed, and
better disciplined force was moving along the north coast
towards Milazzo. This Northern detachment could be
most quickly supported by Garibaldi himself with the
reserves which he was busily forming in Palermo. The
columns of Eber in the centre and of Bixio in the South
were to a large extent stage armies, not therefore the less
effective in paralyzing the Bourbon generals at Messina.
Garibaldi justly relied on the inactivity of those veteran
warriors, or else he would not have sent two weak columns
to roam at large through the island, and finally to unite
at Catania, not far from Messina, where lay fifteen to twenty
thousand Bourbon troops. Judged by the rules of ordinary
war, the division of the Dictator's slender forces into three
appears an absurd error. But under the actual conditions
he was justified in making the division, because, while
the force with which he intended to strike home on the
north coast was immensely the strongest and proved sufficient for its purpose, the other two flying columns served
to alarm the Bourbon generals and to render them less
willing to advance from Messina and attack his real force
in front of Milazzo with the requisite vigour. But the
chief purpose of the columns of Eber and Bixio was not
military but political. They established the authority of
the Dictator in three-quarters of the island, they nipped
in the bud the beginning of anarchy and brigandage, they
obtained several thousand recruits, mostly after their
arrival on the east coast, and they set up before Europe
the claim of Garibaldi to the real possession of the island.'

But that claim had still to be made good in the battle
of Milazzo.

CHAPTER IV

THE BATTLE OF MILAZZO

'Who is the happy warrior ?   Who is he
Whom every man in arms should wish to be ?
—It is the generous spirit, who, when brought
Among the tasks of real life, hath wrought
Upon the plan that pleased his childish thought :
Whose high endeavours are an inward light
    That makes the path before him always bright.

. . . .

Whose powers shed round him in the common strife
Or mild concerns of ordinary life
A constant influence, a peculiar grace ;
But who, if he be call'd upon to face
Some awful moment to which heaven has join'd
Great issues, good or bad for human kind,
Is happy as a lover ;   and attired
With sudden brightness, like a man inspired ;
And through the heat of conflict, keeps the law.
In calmness made, and sees what he foresaw.'
                                                    WORDSWORTH.

By June 19 Palermo and most of the other garrison towns in Sicily had been completely evacuated, but there still remained 18,000 effective Bourbon troops in Messina, 2000 in Syracuse, over 1000 in Milazzo, and 500 in Augusta.* On the mainland were some 80,000 more, of whom large numbers could be shipped to the island from Naples in a few hours.   In these circumstances two rational courses were open to the Royalists.   Either

* Of the 18,000 in Messina, 3000 or more were sent under Bosco to Milazzo on July 14.

a vigorous counter-attack might be made, first on the columns which Garibaldi was sending out from Palermo, and then upon that city itself, before the three thousand North-Italian volunteers had grown to ten, fifteen, and twenty thousand. Or else the opposite course might be chosen—a course less ambitious indeed but more consistent with the grant of the Constitution and the new diplomatic attitude adopted towards France, England, and Piedmont : Sicily might be written off as lost, and the troops in it confined to garrison work within the sea-fortresses of Messina, Syracuse, Milazzo, and Augusta. These places, if supplied and assisted by the fleet, could not be taken by the means at Garibaldi's disposal. Further fighting would thus be avoided in the island, and a claim would thereby be established on the good offices of England and France. The sea powers, pleased at such moderation in the Court of Naples, might not improbably use their fleet to stop Garibaldi at the Straits of Messina. With or without such aid, the military defence of the new constitutional kingdom could be reorganised on the Calab-

Straits. The Ministers had goo[
[far]ther hostilities, for while a vict[
overthrow the dynasty, a defeat o[
throw the Constitution, and their
on the maintenance of dynasty and

While the Ministers remained i[
ways of peace, neither the King at
at Messina had the nerve to wa[
war in their despite. But the rea[
entirely without influence on eve[
It had sufficient power in Court an[
between the Ministers and the Cr[
Sicily a feeble and partial offen[
Colonel Bosco, of which Garibaldi t[
the danger of an armistice, to win
and thereby to create the panic am[
on the Straits which enabled him to
to Naples. Such, in brief, is the sig[
narrated in this chapter.

Augusta.
et, could
disposal.
sland, and
ood offices
d at such
nprobably
Messina.
f the new
he Calab-
sina as a

the de-
nce they
be made
between

It had sufficient power in Court and camp to sow distrust between the Ministers and the Crown, and to initiate in Sicily a feeble and partial offensive movement under Colonel Bosco, of which Garibaldi took advantage to escape the danger of an armistice, to win the battle of Milazzo, and thereby to create the panic among the Bourbon troops on the Straits which enabled him to march almost unresisted to Naples. Such, in brief, is the significance of the events narrated in this chapter.

General Clary had distinguished himself on May 31 in suppressing an attempt of some local *squadre* to occupy Catania. When, immediately after this little victory, he was ordered to abandon Catania and retire to headquarters at Messina, he obeyed under protest. As one of the very few Generals who had shown any spirit during the operations in May, Cl.

their hopes, proved after all to be of much the same calibre as the other Generals. For as soon as he was ordered to advance, the tone of Clary's reports changed wonderfully ; he began to write of the unfitness and unwillingness of his troops, of the necessity of remaining on the defensive, of the probability that if he left Messina with a part of his force, Garibaldi would slip in behind his back, as he had slipped into Palermo behind the back of Von Mechel. But again, as soon as the Ministry countermanded the advance and bade him remain on the defensive, Clary recovered his courage and complained bitterly that such orders damped the spirits of his men.

Meanwhile King Francis was consulting his Generals and Ministers at Naples on a proposal to send strong reinforcements from the mainland to reconquer Sicily.   In a council held on July 13 the Ministers opposed it, giving their voices in favour of armistice and diplomatic action, and their arguments were supported by Generals Nunziante and Pianell, the two best soldiers in the service since Filangieri's retirement.   The plan was therefore

and Constitution, and bid them : white flag of the Bourbons, with s was afterwards done with som months too late.   No troops c the Constitution and at the same the man who was the cause of the

But whatever Pianell's plan a fair trial, for on July 14 Marsha with 3000 picked troops along the with orders to occupy the open and Barcellona.   This half-hearte the knowledge of Pianell, had all t merits of the defensive plan decre of the offensive desired by the Kir

Bosco was the fighting man o that he had been sent into the (his own was regarded by every o quest of Sicily.   Yet the actual the Colonel on the day before h divided counsels of the Royalist and Constitution, and bid them march forward under the white flag of the Bourbons, with the King in their midst, as was afterwards done with some success at Capua a few months too late. No troops could feel enthusiasm for the Constitution and at the same time fight loyally against the man who was the cause of the Constitution's existence.

But whatever Pianell's plan was worth, it never had a fair trial, for on July 14 Marshal Clary sent Colonel Bosco with 3000 picked troops along the north coast from Messina, with orders to occupy the open country between Milazzo and Barcellona. This half-hearted measure, taken without the knowledge of Pianell, had all the faults and none of the merits of the defensive plan decreed by the Ministers, and of the offensive desired by the King.

Bosco was the fighting man of the army, and the news that he had been sent into the open field with a force of his own was regarded by every one as a bid for the reconquest of Sicily. Yet the actual orders given by Clary to the Colonel on the day before he left Messina reflect the divided counsels of the Royalist camp. In this document Bosco is reminded that the Ministry has forbidden any fresh attack to be made; he must therefore leave it to the enemy to begin the fighting, but when attacked himself he has the right to make a counter-attack and dislodge the Garibaldini from their positions; the object of the expedition is defined as being to guard the threatened garrison of Milazzo from a blockade—though in fact this end could have been far more simply effected by the use of the fleet; for this purpose Clary advises Bosco to occupy Archi and certain other places some miles outside Milazzo; he is not to proceed farther westward than Barcellona, even if victorious, but is to await orders there. These instructions, which might be interpreted in many different ways, when thus placed in the hands of a spirited officer, left Messina, Medici, in command of 2000 Garibaldini, had already for a week made Barcellona his headquarters, and had been scouting with his friends on the mountains that tower above the plain of Milazzo.

Giacomo Medici, who had held the Vascello for four weeks against the French army on the Janiculum, was the friendly rival of Bixio for the first place among Garibaldi's lieutenants. To him the General had entrusted the leadership of the most important of the three columns now advancing through the island on Messina, that one which was to keep the north coast and be supported in case of need by Garibaldi himself and the reserves from Palermo. Medici left the capital with 1800 of the well-armed volunteers whom he had brought from North Italy, Simonetta's Lombards and Malenchini's Tuscans.* The General's orders were that he should occupy Castroreale (*see Map II., at end of book*), a strong position in the mountains above Barcellona, and there await orders. But when he found the coast towns enthusiastic in the national cause, when he was joined by several hundred local volunteers and bands from eastern Sicily, he felt unwilling to retire into the mountains on Bosco's approach, leaving his kind hosts at Barcellona to the Bourbon vengeance. Such a retreat would inflict a wound on the growing prestige of the Garibaldian armies, which stood to them in the place of cavalry, artillery, and big battalions. In order, therefore, to protect Barcellona, Medici moved his headquarters to Meri, and there awaited the enemy's attack, drawn up behind the broad *fiumara*, or torrent bed of white stones, that passes in front of the village on its way from the

* The remaining 700 of those whom Medici had brought to Sicily—namely, Caldesi's battalion—had gone south in Bixio's column.

neighbouring mountain gorge to the sea. (*See henceforth Map I., p. 89 below.*)

On July 15 Bosco and his three thousand approached by the high road from Messina to within a short distance of the *fiumara*, where Medici's men lay eagerly awaiting them ; the Royalists, however, wheeled off sharply to the right, and marched across the plain to Milazzo. It is possible that Bosco declined battle on account of his instructions from Clary not to initiate hostilities. On his arrival in the town, beneath the precipice on which the mediæval fortress is perched, the inhabitants fled for refuge into the thick olive groves that cover the hills of the peninsula beyond, where they remained hidden during the events of the following week. Bosco and his army occupied the deserted town and put themselves into communication with the garrison on the castled rock overhead.

Medici, encouraged by Bosco's refusal of battle, sent out detachments across the *fiumara* of Meri to occupy Coriolo and Archi, hamlets sheltered among the olives of the last foot-hills that overlook the plain of Milazzo. Now one part of Bosco's instructions had been to occupy Archi, and therefore, in spite of that other part of his orders which forbade him to be the first to attack, he felt justified in recapturing Archi, now that a Garibaldian outpost had occupied it and thereby cut off his connection with Messina. He had passed through the village on the 15th on his way to Milazzo, but had neglected to leave any guard behind. And so, early in the morning of July 17, he sent back across the plain four companies,* with cavalry and artillery, under Major Maringh, with orders to retake Archi. The hamlet and surrounding hills were defended by 300 Lombards under Simonetta and about seventy Sicilians. Maringh

* A company in the Neapolitan army was supposed to be 160 men ; a battalion was about 1000 men, and Bosco had three battalions of infantry.

ing Malenchini's Tuscans, and fierce fighting took place in the street of Coriolo and along the *fiumara* above which it stands. The street was taken by the Bourbon troops and retaken at the point of the bayonet. Marra's men tried to turn Medici's flank by penetrating up into the mountains towards Sta. Lucia, but they were headed off near S. Filippo. At the end of an arduous day Coriolo remained in Medici's hands, and Archi in those of the Royalists. But at midnight Bosco, who had come out when the fighting was over to review the situation, ordered a retreat to the town. He had been presuaded that Medici had 7000 men, whereas in reality he had scarcely more than 2000 all told.

Although Bosco's deserved reputation for courage saved him from wholly losing the confidence of his men, his conduct on this day had been neither spirited nor wise. He should have come earlier to direct the action himself, and he should not have sent out such small detachments if he seriously intended to occupy the slopes of the mountains, and so debar the further advance of the Garibaldini along the north coast. He had allowed Medici to out-manœuvre him, to drive him down off the hills, to get between him and Messina, and to lock him into the plain of Milazzo with his back to the sea. The Garibaldini were elated at their success, and rejoiced over an intercepted letter of Bosco's to Clary, written in the

line of complaint against his subord
fresh men and fresh officers, although
cacciatori the best regiments of the
the 15,000 officers and men left idle
they ought at once to be led to the
Bosco, who was far more popular
Marshal, who had already quarrelled
at Messina as well as with Bosco him
reinforcements which he demanded, b
to make excuses and to explain that
horses, carts, or ships to carry an a
to Milazzo. Clary's inactivity was
telegrams which he received from
ordering him to remain on the defe
Bosco in the strongest language
hostilities.

But although Medici had drawn a
it was a very thin line, and if Bos
was being contained not by 7000
might attack once more. In the
the Dictator his success of July
reinforcements. Nor had he long
were already on the way. On th
into Meri Dunne's regiment of 6

I am left to do everything, everything, everything (*tutto, tutto, tutto*). The officers are so many nullities.' But if he were reinforced from Messina either by sea or by land, he boasted that he would enter Palermo ' on Medici's horse.' Those of his despatches which reached Messina, being signalled by semaphore, were conceived in the same tone of complaint against his subordinates, and demanded fresh men and fresh officers, although in fact he had in the *cacciatori* the best regiments of the army. The feeling of the 15,000 officers and men left idle in Messina was that they ought at once to be led to the rescue of the gallant Bosco, who was far more popular than Clary. But the Marshal, who had already quarrelled with his subordinates at Messina as well as with Bosco himself, sent him, not the reinforcements which he demanded, but a Captain Fonsecca to make excuses and to explain that there were not enough horses, carts, or ships to carry an army by sea or by land to Milazzo. Clary's inactivity was in part due to the telegrams which he received from the Minister of War, ordering him to remain on the defensive, and denouncing Bosco in the strongest language for having resumed hostilities.

But although Medici had drawn a cordon round Milazzo, it was a very thin line, and if Bosco discovered that he was being contained not by 7000 but by 2000 men, he might attack once more. In the telegram reporting to the Dictator his success of July 17, Medici begged for reinforcements. Nor had he long to wait. Some troops were already on the way. On the 18th there marched into Meri Dunne's regiment of 600 Sicilians with its English officers, and Cosenz with a first detachment of the excellent troops whom he had just brought to Palermo from Genoa.

The Dictator, on receiving Medici's telegram in the small hours of the morning of the 18th, made one of those

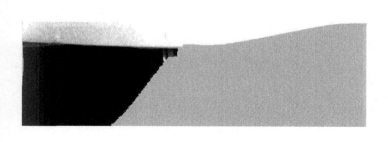

: as the flash of a sword, that with
he end of a long period of suspense.
i his engagements in Palermo, and
his departure, he went on board an
:amer called the *City of Aberdeen* that
eers from Genoa a few days before
:o be in the harbour. At four in the
arrangements for her use with her
aptain, who were passionately devoted
person. He instantly put on board
the Thousand, and those of his *aides-*
could muster at a moment's notice.
about to weigh anchor, there happened
the steamer *Amazon* from Genoa, bear-
volunteers, captured a month before in
Jane, and now released from their cap-
)y the Constitutional Ministers of King
if the policy of friendship with Piedmont.
sent back to Genoa, but had instantly
;icily in another ship ; on account of this
were henceforth known as the ' Gaeta
.baldi ordered them not to land, but to
. the *City of Aberdeen*. The transfer of
ammunition was effected in half an hour,
it in the morning the cattle-steamer left
the whole expedition on board. She was
)y the Piedmontese war-vessel *Carlo Al-*
orders from Persano to see them safely
disembarked at Patti before dawn on July
his men to march after him, the General
lop towards Barcellona and Meri.
lona the principal church was employed as a
[edici's wounded. As Garibaldi passed through
: noise of his reception in the street penetrated

into the quiet of that gloomy hall, where a gigantic crucifix looked down upon the sufferers. In an instant they were struggling off their couches and crawling to the door on hands and knees. As they lay crowded on the steps of the church, he waved his gentle salutations and thanks to them, and passed on towards Meri. One young Lombard who had been shot through the lungs crawled to his bed again, fell back on it, and died.

When Palermo discovered that the Dictator had gone, the streets were filled with angry and inquiring crowds. His departure was a complete surprise. The Palermitans felt only half safe in his absence, and many of his old followers and friends were aggrieved because he had left them behind in the hurry of his departure. Such was the eagerness to follow him that in a few hours nearly all the North Italians in the Sicilian capital had thrown up the civil or military posts which kept them from the front. In many of these cases substitutes were found among the wounded, who were unwilling to remain in hospital at such a time. Those who could, set out post-haste for Milazzo, and quiet was restored.

There was little doing at Meri on July 19. Medici and Cosenz were away scouting, and their men were eating their dinners in the filthy houses of the village, or beside the white stones of the *fiumara*, glowing in the midday heat, when an open carriage was noticed coming along the highroad from Barcellona. As it drew near they saw whom it contained. In an instant all the camp was in an uproar. The uneaten dinners were left smoking, and the volunteers rushed to seize him as he stepped from the carriage. It was his official birthday, being celebrated at that hour in Palermo with flags and speeches,* but he had come to spend it among friends in the field. Confidence and joy were in

* His real birthday was July 7, but they celebrated it on the 19th.

pressed round him. They now knew that on the morrow they would fight and conquer. He did not linger in **Meri,** but took horse to find his old companions in arms, **Medici** and Cosenz, and to spend the rest of the day riding **with** them over the mountains of Sta. Lucia, surveying through his spy-glass the plain below, where Bosco was in the act of taking up a new and formidable position to cover the approaches to Milazzo.

The plain of Milazzo is enclosed to north and west by the two sea-beaches that converge on the town and castle at the neck of the peninsula. To the south and east the plain is bounded by the white *fiumare* of Meri and of Coriolo and by the low hills covered with olives that lie between the mountains and the plains. The ground on which the battle was fought, confined within a radius of a mile and a half from the southern gate of the town, was perfectly flat and almost on a level with the neighbouring beach. On this seaward plain stood farms, mills, and small hamlets, scattered about in a manner foreign to the interior of the island, where the whole population was housed at nightfall in hill-towns of several thousand inhabitants each. These isolated houses strengthened the Royalist position on the plain. The ground was occupied by cornfields and vineyards, or near the sea by brakes of canes, seven feet high, used by the peasants for training their vines. The vineyards and cane brakes were enclosed by thick hedges of cactus, or by high white walls, which had been loopholed by the Bourbon troops. These were formidable barriers against an army of irregulars without artillery. The only way by which Garibaldi's men could pierce the enemy's line without scaling the loopholed walls and hewing through the cactus hedges was to charge along the two beaches and along the

e
le
alf
nd
is
ed
re
ns
ed
n. or
by
nd
by
r-
ly
:h
it
is
le

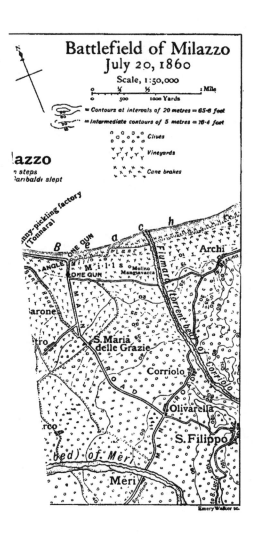

Battlefield of Milazzo
July 20, 1860

Scale, 1:50,000

= Contours at intervals of 20 metres = 65·6 feet
= Intermediate contours of 5 metres = 16·4 feet

Olives

Vineyards

Cane brakes

azzo

n steps
Garibaldi slept

Emery Walker sc.

various roads converging on Milazzo. But the roads and the beach on either side of the town were remarkably straight and were swept by the cannon of the Royalists. Against their eight excellently served pieces the Garibaldini had nothing to oppose except two useless carronades, dragged about by hand, which were brought into action only to be withdrawn after a few minutes. The one road that was not straight enough to be swept by the Bourbon artillery was a sunk lane that wound through the vineyards, hollowed out by a water-course that finally entered the side of the S. Palino road as a culvert, and issued into the sea under the main road, beneath a little bridge 500 yards from the town gate.* This bridge was chosen by Bosco to be the scene of the final stand outside the town, in case his more advanced positions were forced, and here two of the cannon were placed. Two more stood a mile in front near the 'angle' of the high-road to Messina. Beyond this 'angle' the Bourbon left wing occupied the Mills near the seashore, thus forming an advanced post which could enfilade Garibaldi's advance against their centre near S. Palino. Their right was supported by the other four guns, which were placed at Casazza and on the western beach.

These formidable positions in front of the castle were held, according to Bosco's own report, by 2500 excellent Neapolitan *cacciatori*, the flower of the army, aided by the eight guns and a squadron of cavalry. In the castle on the rock overhead was the garrison, about 1000 infantry of the line, and over forty cannon of different sorts, some of which were able to fire with effect towards the close of the day. In the peninsula behind the castle Bosco had stationed another 400 *cacciatori* to prevent a landing from

* This water-course, dry in spring and summer, is called a *fiumara* in Bosco's report and by some of the inhabitants to-day. But it is not a typical *fiumara*, as it is of brown earth only, not of white stones.

total of all arms defending
by the Neapolitan staff at

centric lines of defence, cul-
castle, Garibaldi was leading
;er in numbers than that of
if judged by the normal mili-
cavalry and until late in the
try consisted of North Italian
;tily raised and regimented in
o to 900 each, many of which,
Gaeta battalion,' had handled
last forty-eight hours and did
drill ; while even Medici's and
. a few weeks' drill, did not know
.heir Enfield rifles. But in most
vas a large proportion of veterans
nts who had deserted, collusively
·egular army ; and of officers of
me cases of remarkable talent in
,ve all, the whole force was in-
ieir cause and for their leader which
,lace of discipline, and made them
·y heavy losses without which even
ι not possibly have been stormed.

on July 20 the Garibaldini moved
f the hills of Olivarella and Coriolo.
ro was occupied without opposition ;
tta and his Lombards began their
s advanced post at the Mills ; while
[alenchini and his Tuscans, marching
d S. Marina, developed the attack on
ιe western beach.

The day began with a disaster. Malenchini carelessly led his men up to the mouth of the Bourbon rifles and batteries, which opened on them with terrible effect and fairly drove them off the field. Garibaldi, who was watching the first stages of the fight from the roof of a wine-store on the edge of the plain, sent Cosenz with fresh troops to rally the fugitives and to take over the command of the left wing. Nevertheless the Royalists, supported by cavalry and artillery operating on the broad beach, advanced and drove back the Garibaldian left and left-centre for nearly a mile. Although Malenchini and many of his Tuscans returned to the fight, it was all that Cosenz could do to hold the Zirilli farm and the western approaches to S. Pietro.

The General himself, rightly confiding in the calmness, authority, and military talent of Cosenz, had not gone to rally the defeated left wing, but had bent all his personal energies to effect an advance along the other shore, at the head of the right wing under Medici. If he could penetrate by way of the Mills and the ' angle ' of the road as far as the bridge, he would be able to threaten the rear of the victorious advance of the Royalists on the west, which was in fact a dangerous move on their part at so early a stage in the battle.

Garibaldi's method of sending his troops into action on this day was to stand well exposed to the fire at some spot by which the next detachment would have to enter the battle, and to speak, almost in a whisper, some word of encouragement to the young soldiers, of whom many were then hearing the bullets for the first time in their lives. In a small army of volunteers depending more on individual courage than on discipline, the General's exercise of his strange powers of fascination considerably increased the chances of victory. As one section of Dunne's Sicilians with their English officers and cadets filed by him into

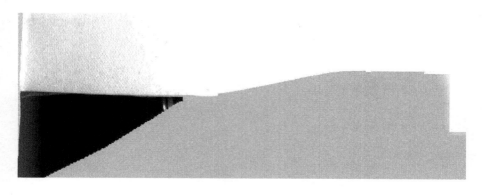

standing almost alone in the middle of the road, a conspicuous mark at which the enemy were directing their
fire.

The first success of the day was the capture of the
Mills by the Northerners of Simonetta's and of Specchi's
'battalions.' It cost a severe struggle, for Bosco was
there in person encouraging his men, and he had skilfully
placed two guns near the 'angle,' one on the high-road,
the other in the Mill Lane. The latter, after doing great
execution, was captured through the devotion of a volunteer named Alessandro Pizzoli, who, leaving his comrades
in ambush behind a wall flanking the Mill Lane, himself
sprang down a few yards in front of the cannon's mouth
in order to draw its fire. He was blown limb from limb,
and the next moment his comrades leapt down after him
and captured the piece.

Thus the Royalists were slowly pushed back on the
east flank from one vineyard and farm to another. But
the few positions gained by the red-shirts seemed to many
but little compensation for the long train of wounded continually passing to the rear, for the suffocating heat, the
thirst, the hunger, and, as the day wore on, the sheer fatigue.
Those who had no stomach for eight hours of such work
went off with the wounded and forgot to return. The
better sort of men, getting together in groups often irrespec-
tive of their proper 'battalions' fell...

...ual prowess. And more and m
the General himself appeared, now h
charges which behind him never fai
our countrymen, Mr. Patterson, a
had left his home a few weeks befor
found himself with a few of his co
and a number of men from other
the end of a cane-brake through wl
firing at them from behind a wall. T
through the tall canes which snap
the men were falling fast, the p
Suddenly the Englishman was awar
up to them, leaping off his horse, a
look dashing up the narrow ride bet
at a small opening in the wall lined
He did not once look round to see if
for he knew that none who saw h
Bourbons stood to it to the last, and
before the wall was cleared.*

By a series of such charges I
pushed back, well after midday,
outside the town. This was the b
where stood the two reserve guns co
roads that converged on that spot.
was a large facto...

cane-brakes and behind the loopholed walls, but always exposed to his shots, firing only at close quarters, making headway by rushes and rallies, by dashes down the sunk lane, here leaping over a wall and there tearing through a cactus hedge into the flank or rear of the enemy, they carried on the battle, which had now become a mere test of individual prowess. And more and more as the day went on the General himself appeared, now here, now there, heading charges which behind him never failed of success. One of our countrymen, Mr. Patterson, a lad of seventeen, who had left his home a few weeks before for love of Garibaldi, found himself with a few of his comrades from Dunne's, and a number of men from other battalions, standing at the end of a cane-brake through which the Royalists were firing at them from behind a wall. The bullets were crashing through the tall canes which snapped under the shower, the men were falling fast, the position was untenable. Suddenly the Englishman was aware of Garibaldi galloping up to them, leaping off his horse, and without a word or a look dashing up the narrow ride between the canes, straight at a small opening in the wall lined by the enemy's rifles. He did not once look round to see if his men were following, for he knew that none who saw him would linger. The Bourbons stood to it to the last, and the bayonet was used before the wall was cleared.*

By a series of such charges Bosco's *cacciatori* were pushed back, well after midday, to their last position outside the town. This was the bridge over the culvert, where stood the two reserve guns commanding the straight roads that converged on that spot. Close by, on the shore, was a large factory for pickling tunny-fish. Here the crisis of the battle took place. The General sent Missori to

* Mr. Patterson was later in the day wounded at the bridge, and Garibaldi made him lieutenant for his services that day.

piece. A score of them made a spirited charge over the bridge, and Dunne's men scrambled out of the road to let them pass. If Bosco had followed up the charge with a body of fresh infantry he might have won the battle, but his last reserves on this side of the castle had been used by Colonel Marra to support the advance of his right centre. As the cavalry rode back from running the gauntlet through the Garibaldian lines, Dunne's Sicilians emptied half a dozen saddles, firing from behind the cactus hedge that lined the road. But two men, who had not taken refuge behind the hedge when the cavalry first charged by, were still standing alone in the roadway, on the line of their retreat. Of these two one was Garibaldi and the other was his aide-de-camp, Missori, a handsome young Lombard of noted gallantry. Both were on foot, and the horsemen, unable to avenge their fallen comrades on any one else, swarmed round, eager to cut them down. Missori shot the horse of the Bourbon captain, who rose in the stirrups as it fell and slashed at the Dictator. Garibaldi parried the blow, and laying his hand on the bridle of the kneeling animal struck the captain in the neck with his sabre and killed him on the spot. Missori with his revolver shot two more of the cavalry, and the half-dozen who were still left alive galloped back through the gates of the town.*

played full upon the bridge, while on it at close quarters from the houses along the side of the port. One of his best and most popular was killed, and Corte was wounde the two carronades, the only artiller on the bridge proved that they we in a few minutes the General ordere Seeing that an immediate advanc possible, he put most of the men f the tunny-factory and some wood others kept up a fire against the the bridge and neighbouring garden fishing-boats on the beach. In parti Englishman, whose long beard and comrades of King Lear, kept his c at the bridge, suffering severe loss that Colt's five-chambered revolving were armed, leaked fire at the bree the hand that used it, and had the history of modern armaments. Du early afternoon the affair continued baldini losing men, but holding the p and resting after the fatigues of a

The Garibaldini, having now occupied the bridge, had turned Bosco's left flank and were threatening his rear. The rash advance of his right wing would have to be turned into a hasty retreat if the red-shirts could maintain their newly won position. That was indeed no easy task, for the cannon of the fortress, firing over the roofs of the town, played full upon the bridge, while the *cacciatori* below fired on it at close quarters from the town gate and from the houses along the side of the port. Garibaldi's men fell fast. One of his best and most popular lieutenants, Migliavacca, was killed, and Corte was wounded. An attempt to bring the two carronades, the only artillery of the force, into action on the bridge proved that they were perfectly useless, and in a few minutes the General ordered them to be withdrawn. Seeing that an immediate advance on the town was impossible, he put most of the men for rest and shelter into the tunny-factory and some wood stores near by, while others kept up a fire against the walls of Milazzo from the bridge and neighbouring gardens, and from behind the fishing-boats on the beach. In particular, Peard, Garibaldi's Englishman, whose long beard and fine head reminded his comrades of King Lear, kept his company of thirty men at the bridge, suffering severe losses, and demonstrating that Colt's five-chambered revolving rifle, with which they were armed, leaked fire at the breech, woefully scorching the hand that used it, and had therefore no future in the history of modern armaments. During two hours in the early afternoon the affair continued in this state, the Garibaldini losing men, but holding the position they had taken, and resting after the fatigues of the morning's attack.

report we may deduce that the name of the unfortunate Bourbon captain was Giuliani, and that his lieutenant, Faraone, got back to the town with seven shot wounds. The only question is whether the cavalry charged up the main road or the sunk lane or up both. On this there are various opinions given.

Having thus established his men on the bridge, Garibaldi left them under Medici's command and rode off to deal with Bosco's victorious right wing, which was still pressing Cosenz near the Zirilli farm and S. Pietro. For this purpose he made his way down with a few staff officers to the western beach, found a small boat, and rowed out to the *Tüköry*, a paddle-steamer of 400 horse-power, carrying ten guns, which had arrived on the scene that very afternoon from Patti. This vessel, formerly the *Veloce* of the Bourbon service, had recently deserted to him at Palermo, and now composed his whole fighting navy, over and above his transports and such help in convoy work as was afforded him by the Piedmontese warships. His aides-de-camp, watching from the shore, soon saw him swarm up the mast of the *Tüköry* to view the field. Taking her close inshore under fire from the guns of the castle, he proceeded to bombard the enemy's cavalry on the western beach. The victorious right wing of the Royalists, feeling the fire of the *Tüköry* from the west, and learning that their rear had been turned on the east, at length hastened to retreat. This incident calls to mind the obvious truth that if the Neapolitans had sent a part of the fleet to protect Milazzo, their fire would have rendered it impossible for Garibaldi to occupy or even to attack the town.

Cosenz and his men, thus relieved by the retreat of their assailants, followed up, and joining with Medici on the bridge, stretched a line across the neck of the Peninsula, and invested the walls of Milazzo. Next after Garibaldi, Cosenz had borne the burden of the day. He came of a French-Neapolitan family, whose military and patriotic traditions dated from the days of the Parthenopean Republic, of Marengo, and of Murat. But his friends said that Enrico Cosenz seemed rather to belong to some northern race, for his manners were imperturbable in their calm. He was modest and retiring almost to a fault. He has been well called Garibaldi's good angel in politics and war. This thin, quiet man in spectacles had restored the courage of Malenchini's routed troops and held them to their post all day. Now in the late afternoon he was standing close under the walls of Milazzo, in the hottest fire from the fortress, wiping his spectacles with the deliberation of Mr. Pickwick, while a breathless aide-de-camp from Garibaldi, waiting for his reply to a message, wished that he would either make up his mind more quickly, or continue his meditations in a more secluded spot.

Bosco might still have held out in the town with some likelihood of success. By his own account he had lost not more than 150 men, a fifth part of the loss confessed by the victors. But his troops were overcome with exhaustion and discouragement at the end of their brave but unsuccessful fight of eight hours under an almost tropical sun, and the fear of Garibaldi, which Bosco alone of the Bourbon officers had for a while conjured away, returned upon them like a fate. He therefore marched his *cacciatori* up into the castle to join the garrison there, leaving only a few soldiers to keep up a fire from the town walls. When about four o'clock the Garibaldini began to make their way into Milazzo, creeping in first along the port-side where the walls no longer existed,* they found to their surprise that the streets were empty. Even when they advanced into the upper part of the town, no enemy was there, although marksmen in the fortress overhead opened fire upon them and wounded Cosenz. Before sunset the whole city was occupied, and the entrances of the streets were barricaded against the castle. Garibaldi chose for his headquarters the steps of a small church beside the sea; there he sat giving

* The walls of the town have now disappeared altogether, but in 1860 they existed along the west side and at the gate facing the bridge.

4

his orders, propped up against his South American saddle, which he always took off his horse with his own hands. For a few hours at midnight he slept, as he liked best to sleep, with his head upon that soldier's pillow, which had served him when youth and love were still his, in lands where man needed only sword and saddle for the free rover's life upon the uplands.

CHAPTER V

SURRENDER OF MILAZZO CASTLE——THE CHECK AT THE STRAITS—DIPLOMATS AND POLITICIANS

'Garibaldi a une grande puissance morale, il exerce un immense prestige non seulement en Italie mais surtout en Europe. . . . Si demain j'entrais en lutte avec Garibaldi, il est probable que j'eusse pour moi la majorité des vieux diplomates, mais l'opinion publique européenne serait contre moi. Et l'opinion publique aurait raison, car Garibaldi a rendu à l'Italie les plus grands services qu'un homme pût lui rendre. Il a donné aux Italiens confiance en eux-mêmes : il a prouvé à l'Europe que les Italiens savaient se battre et mourir sur le champ de bataille pour reconquérir une patrie. . . . Cela n'empêche pas qu'il ne soit éminemment désirable que la révolution de Naples s'accomplisse sans lui.'—*Cavour to an intimate friend*, August 9, 1860 [*Chiala*, iii. 321].

THE castle of Milazzo, which Garibaldi had yet to take, rose between the two seas on a granite precipice more than three hundred feet high. Founded by the Saracens, improved by Norman and Angevin, it had been finally enlarged and beautified by the Emperor Charles V. A place of importance throughout the Middle Ages, it had in the war of the Vespers been occupied by Sicilians and French in turn. In 1675 it had successfully sustained a regular siege, and in the wars of the early eighteenth century and again in the struggle with Napoleon, it had been occupied by the British and their allies; the English cavalry barracks of fifty years back could be seen on the shore below. When Bosco held it against Garibaldi, it was, as it still is to-day, a spacious and pleasant place, unlike some of the featureless castle-prisons of the

99

Neapolitan mainland, of which the very style of architecture seems to symbolise cruelty and crime. Below the fine mediæval keep lay grass plateaus a quarter of a mile broad and long, enclosed by the outer works of Charles V. Thence the defenders could view the Calabrian coast ; the Lipari islands and the eternal smoke of Stromboli ; the gulf of Milazzo where Duilius with his grappling-irons destroyed the fleets of Carthage and made Rome mistress even of the sea ; the plain where Garibaldi had just triumphed in conflict man against man ; the bare mountain ridges stretching away towards hidden Messina ; and near at hand a profusion of cactus, fig-trees, and shrubs clinging to the precipices of the castle rock. In the silent midday heat the stronghold gives the impression, not of decay, but of long unbroken peace. Its defences, if antiquated, were in good repair, and could only be breached by siege cannon, which Garibaldi did not possess.

To defend such a place against irregular troops would have been an easy and even a pleasant task, if Bosco had taken care to lay in provisions while his communications were still open. But there was little food and that bad, the water stank, and the dirty habits of more than 4000 soldiers, who would not even take the trouble to bury the corpses of man or beast, soon rendered the whole of that large area insanitary. The Royalists had fought well in the battle, but defeat had destroyed their discipline, and when they were put on half-rations they muttered threats about opening the gate. At the first sound of mutiny the fighting Colonel himself lost his nerve and began signalling to Messina the tale of his distresses in messages on the semaphore which Garibaldi and his officers read with delight. He enlarged on the state of the provisions and water ; he complained that the enemy had in the last twenty-four hours shot one man dead on the ram-

parts besides would each for a storming party could be made
declared that a breach for a storming party could be made
in a few days. The latter proposition was undeniable as a
piece of abstract military theory, for the Windmill Hill,
whence the Garibaldini were sniping, was only 500 yards
away, and was on a level with the lower parts of the castle.
But the practical inference was *nil*, because the assailants
had no breaching cannon, and the fortress was defended
by forty pieces. 'The morale of the troops,' so ended
Bosco's tale of woe, 'is destroyed.' And so, he might
have added, was that of their commander, who could no
longer distinguish between a real danger of starvation and
imaginary dangers of storm and battery.

On July 21 Marshal Clary held a council of war at
Messina. His subordinates hated him and one another,
and the prevailing sentiment at the council was each
man's desire to throw upon his neighbour the responsibility for disasters present and to come. The sense of
the council of war appears to have been that they were
bound in honour to march at once to relieve Bosco, but
that there were not enough horses and carts for the transport service, and that a column of Garibaldini advancing
northwards from Catania would step into Messina if any
part of its garrison of 15,000 were rashly sent to Milazzo.
This fear was somewhat out of place, since Eber's column
at Catania as yet barely numbered 1000 men, and only
two or three hundred had been sent as far north as Taormina; but this trivial reconnaissance, as Clary's own despatches show, seriously affected his decision not to move
to the help of Bosco.

Once indeed, on July 22, Clary ordered three regiments to embark, and signalled to Bosco that they had
already sailed to his relief. But in a few hours he countermanded the movement, either from fear of the Garibaldini

at Taormina, or else in obedience to orders from the War Minister, Pianell.

When first the news reached Naples that Bosco's force was shut up in Milazzo, Pianell, much as he wished to suspend all hostilities, felt that he must extricate the rash Colonel before resuming the defensive. He therefore ordered a large expedition to be put on board the fleet in the bay of Naples, to sail to the relief of Milazzo. But the fleet, more liberal in political sentiment than the army, refused to take the troops on board, and the mutiny was encouraged by the Admiral, Count D'Aquila, the King's uncle. The case was brought up for discussion before the Ministers, into whose willing ears D'Aquila poured such effective arguments against a resumption of hostilities in Sicily, that they decided to send, instead of a relieving fleet and army, empty transports to fetch away Bosco and his men. Following the transports they despatched a large part of the fleet, with a Colonel Anzani on board, whose instructions from Pianell were to negotiate the capitulation both of Milazzo and of the garrison of Messina. But Clary, as soon as he was assured that the Ministry did not require him to relieve Milazzo, again assumed the part of aggrieved hero, and refused to evacuate Messina on any account.

On July 23 the approach of the Neapolitan war-vessels to the port of Milazzo caused some anxiety among the volunteers. If the town were bombarded from the sea, it would be necessary for them to retire and to lose the fruits of the victory which they had so dearly bought. Garibaldi, as usual, showed a bold face and fitted up a battery on the mole with cannon landed off the *Tükőry*. The new-comers, however, proved to be intent on more charitable thoughts. Colonel Anzani and the Dictator soon signed a treaty of capitulation by which the troops in the castle were to march out with their arms and half the battery mules. The cannon and ammunition of the castle, the rest of the mules and all the horses were to be left behind for the conquerors. Bosco had boasted that he would enter Palermo on Medici's horse, so Garibaldi had determined that Medici should enter Messina on Bosco's horse, as shortly afterwards took place.

On the morning of July 25, when the Bourbon troops were to march out of the castle, the Piedmontese fleet appeared in the offing. Admiral Persano, seeing Neapolitan war-ships lying off Milazzo, ordered his decks to be cleared for action, presumably intending to save Garibaldi from bombardment even at the cost of a rupture with Naples. When he found how peacefully matters had been settled, he contented himself with embracing the Dictator, and congratulating him in the name of Victor Emmanuel on his fresh victory for the common cause.

The Bourbon troops filed down to the point of embarkation, with the honours of war, between two lines of ragged volunteers. Although they had full opportunity to desert, and were loudly invited to fraternise and to join the army of true Italians, few except among the artillery answered the appeal. At the tail of the column walked Bosco, guarded as a prisoner, fuming and pulling at his moustache. He was hissed by the townspeople, who were beginning to return to their houses from their hiding-places in the peninsula. It was an unpleasant scene and moved the Garibaldini to sympathy for Bosco in spite of his hectoring manner, which did not desert him in this dramatic exit from before the footlights of history.

It soon became known why Garibaldi had caused Bosco to be placed under arrest during the embarkation. When Peard with a few of his fellow-countrymen and others went to take possession of the abandoned castle, they found the mules which had been surrendered under

the capitulation lying about dead on the turf, and many
of the guns spiked. They luckily detected, before they
had trodden upon it, a train of gunpowder hidden under
straw, thickly strewn with detonators and running under
the door of a magazine, which was intended to blow the
citadel and its new occupants sky-high.*

When Garibaldi, accompanied by Admiral Persano
and the Marios, came up into the castle they found Bosco's
horses, abandoned and frightened, running round and
round the grass plateaus of the outer enclosure. The
Dictator took his lasso, and amused himself and his companions by a display of the skill which he had acquired in
South America more than twenty years before.

Alberto Mario and his English wife Jessie had arrived
from Palermo in pursuit of the army. They found a
number of truants from their ' Garibaldi Foundling Hospital ' enlisted in Dunne's ranks, half a dozen of them
badly wounded. Although they had run away from the
institute they had not run away from the rifles of the
cacciatori. One little wounded Sicilian apologised to
Mario, stroking his hand as he said : '.Are you angry
with us, Signor Commandante ? So many of our brigade
are wounded and killed : *Milordo* the Colonel says that
after the battle of Milazzo no one can say again that the
Sicilians never fight.' Another boy of twelve suffered
amputation sitting in the lap of Jessie Mario, who said
that she cried more than he did. These young scamps

---

* Mr. Dolmage, who was present at this discovery, writes to me (July 8,
1910) describing the incident, and adds : ' We afterwards heard that Garibaldi had known of the slaughter of the animals and the spiking of the guns
early in the day, and that the disgrace of Bosco was the consequence. The
gunpowder train was our little find. But we never suspected that Bosco
had to do with the stupid act. It must have been the work of some under-
strapper. The Neapolitans did not always play the game properly, and
some of them were brutal enough.'

of the streets of Palermo were not the only class who behaved admirably in the hospital. Throughout the campaign,
in the ill-equipped field hospitals, without chloroform or
proper dressings, the silent endurance of pain by Italians
of sensitive and cultivated natures aroused the admiration
of British military men. The terrible, and partly unnecessary sufferings to which the patriots were exposed
by the absence of proper provision never moved them to
indignation or even to complaint; they would bear anything for Italy and for the General. In Milazzo, where
lay half the men wounded in the recent battle, there was
no straw to fill the bed-ticks which the Marios had brought
from Palermo. At Barcellona, which took in the remaining
300, the inhabitants were more active and things went
better.

Both here and later on at Naples and Caserta, 'that
excellent creature of the Lord, Jessie White Mario,' as one
of her patients called her, did her best to be the Florence
Nightingale of the campaign, though she had no staff of
trained nurses. Fanatical in her republicanism, lacking
in toleration and in charm of manner, she had the Spartan
virtues of her creed and a power of complete self-sacrifice
which she had learnt perhaps from her friend and master,
Mazzini. She was equally the friend of Garibaldi, who
knew well how much he owed to ' Jessie,' and how many
of his best followers were saved by her ceaseless exertions.
Superficially at least there was little in common between
this lady of fixed and fiery faith and the comfortable citizens
of her native island. But they too were ready to praise her
when they heard how she attended the wretched pallets
of hundreds of wounded Italians, who blessed her in their
pain, and her country for her sake.

Desiring to take advantage of the enthusiasm for his
cause prevailing in England, Garibaldi, while still quartered

4 a

in the castle of Milazzo, consulted his British companions
in arms, who had borne themselves so well in the battle,
as to the possibility of raising more of their compatriots
to come out and join him on the Neapolitan mainland.
The idea was suggested to him by Hugh Forbes, the gentleman who, wearing a white top-hat, had shared the perils
of his retreat from Rome to the Adriatic in 1849.* In the
interval between the two Italian revolutions, Forbes had
been in the United States, where he had had some peculiar
dealings with old John Brown previous to the Virginia raid.
He now appeared at Milazzo. Garibaldi fell in with Forbes'
proposal that a British Legion should be raised, but refused
to give him the command, and left him behind as Governor
of Milazzo Castle. The scheme aroused little enthusiasm
among those who would have been best qualified to carry
it out. Mr. Dolmage, who was a British officer on leave
from Malta, refused to touch it, and Dunne himself, who
had quarrelled with his countrymen when he left the
Queen's service, angrily declared that he did not want
any more of them out there. He prophesied that a whole
regiment raised at a few days' notice among a civilian
population and shipped to a strange land would contain
good elements, but that, for disciplinary reasons, it would
be more trouble than it was worth during the short period
that the war was likely to last. But Garibaldi, though
he knew that the British Legion would not come in time
to be of much assistance in the Neapolitan kingdom,
looked forward to a campaign in the Papal States, and
to the capture of Rome. He therefore sent to England
as agent for the raising of the Legion, a certain Styles,

---

* See *Garibaldi's Defence of the Roman Republic.* Hugh Forbes must
not be confused with Captain C. S. Forbes, R.N., Peard's friend, who in 1860
went in the van of the advancing army as a non-combatant, and whose book
is a well-known authority for this campaign.

who had behaved well in the battle of Milazzo, but who turned out no better than he should be, and soon fell out with the disinterested Committee who took up the project in London.

It was now evident that there would be no further fighting in Sicily. Since Marshal Clary and his 15,000 at Messina had not moved to the relief of Milazzo, they certainly would not take the field on their own account now that it had fallen. Garibaldi's way lay open down to the shore of the Straits. Medici, duly mounted on Bosco's horse, led the vanguard into the streets of Messina, and on July 28 he signed a treaty with Clary, by which the citadel was to be held by the Royalist garrison and the town by the Garibaldini. Hostilities between them were to be suspended by sea as by land, so that the citadel, which completely dominated the entrance of the harbour, might not fire a shot at the Dictator's vessels, even when they sailed out under the muzzles of the King's cannon to invade his Calabrian provinces. Such a treaty, extorted without bloodshed from 15,000 men in an impregnable fortress, was a great advantage for the inferior forces of the volunteers, who would have had much difficulty in entering the streets of Messina if Clary had resisted their approach on the mountain ridges above the town, and in the forts designed for its protection. Nor could they have remained in Messina if the citadel had been free to open fire. The terms of this treaty are a measure of the panic struck into the heart of the Royalist troops by the defeat of Bosco, and a measure also of the ardour with which the Neapolitan Ministers desired to avoid further fighting in the island. The greater part of the garrison were now withdrawn from the citadel of Messina to the mainland.

During the anxious month that followed the battle of Milazzo, the politics of Europe turned on the question whether Garibaldi could succeed in crossing the Straits. Would the naval Powers interfere to prevent him ? And even if they did not, could he cross in the face of the Neapolitan army and fleet ?

The diplomatic part of the question was destined to be settled in a few days by the secret activities of Cavour. He was now fully determined to acquire the Neapolitan kingdom for Victor Emmanuel, if possible without, but if necessary with further aid from Garibaldi. On July 14 he had still believed that he would be able, before Garibaldi could leave Sicily, to engineer a revolution in Naples by means of the agents whom he had sent there ; at the critical moment the Piedmontese fleet was to appear in the bay. Sanguine of success, he had written to Admiral Persano : ' We must at all costs, on the one hand prevent Garibaldi from crossing the Straits, and on the other excite a revolution in Naples. If this were to succeed, the government of Victor Emmanuel would at once be proclaimed there. In that case you would immediately sail with your whole squadron for Naples.' The plan presupposed some active disloyalty in the army, and some power of initiative in the inhabitants of Naples. Neither was forthcoming. A week after he had written this letter to Persano, Cavour had become so far doubtful of his ability to provoke an internal revolution, that he decided to clear the way for Garibaldi's passage of the Straits. His earnest wish to forestall the Dictator at Naples no longer blinded him to the fact that the advance of the red-shirts might prove after all the only means of deposing the House of Bourbon. He continued, indeed, until after the middle of August, to work and hope for a wholesale desertion of the Neapolitan army to the national cause, which would remove the need for Garibaldi to cross the Straits, and would place all authority at both ends of the Peninsula in the hands of the Ministry at Turin.

But meanwhile, not allowing himself to be duped by these golden hopes, Cavour entered into a conspiracy with Victor Emmanuel to open Garibaldi's way before him, in spite of the threats of European diplomacy, to which it was necessary all the while to appear subservient. The King and his Minister, while publicly requesting the Dictator to halt, secretly urged him to advance. And while not daring to dispute, through regular diplomatic channels, the proposition that he ought to be stopped at the Straits, they dissolved by a hint to England the concert of naval Powers that was being formed for that purpose. These two pieces of secret service, Count Litta's mission to Garibaldi, and Sir James Lacaita's mission to Lord John Russell, have only recently been established as certain historical facts. Their importance in the history of the crisis that made Italy is very great.

At four o'clock on the evening of July 22, Count Litta Modignani came by appointment to the Palace at Turin to receive from the King's hands a written message which he was to take to Garibaldi. Victor Emmanuel first gave him a letter requesting the Dictator not to cross the Straits—the ostensible royal message published to the world to allay the threatenings of France. But here, said the King to Count Litta, is a second note which you will at once administer to Garibaldi ' to neutralise the effect of the first.' So saying, Victor Emmanuel handed over a letter containing the following words in his own handwriting :—

' To THE DICTATOR GENERAL GARIBALDI.

' Now, having written as King, Victor Emmanuel suggests to you to reply in this sense, which I know is what

you feel. Reply that you are full of devotion and reverence
for your King, that you would like to obey his counsels, but
that your duty to Italy forbids you to promise not to help the
Neapolitans, when they appeal to you to free them from a
Government which true men and good Italians cannot trust :
that you cannot therefore obey the wishes of the King, but
must reserve full freedom of action.'

With these two missives in his pocket, Count Litta
left the royal presence. The same day he saw Cavour
and Farini, who chaffed him on the ' Garibaldian part '
he was about to play. He sailed to Palermo and thence
to Milazzo, where he arrived on the morning of July 27,
just in time to catch Garibaldi before he started to over-
take Medici and the vanguard at Messina. As soon as
they were closeted together, the King's messenger produced the two letters in their order. At the second,
delivered by Litta with sly excuses for the first, Garibaldi
burst out laughing. He rose at once and went into his

Litta hastened back to Tu
famous reply. But the world
document which he safely car
inal draft, of which the Dictat
phrase adorned with a few (
most compromising of docume
after a discreet interval of fifty

It was easy thus, while sa
sure that Garibaldi would obey
go forward as fast as he was
maritime Powers from stopping
harder task.

For the moment little was
alienated as she was from the G
the nature of its appeal to Engl
The diplomatic representatives of
to allege that if the western Powers
truce upon Garibaldi, their count

Litta hastened back to Turin, the public bearer of this famous reply. But the world knew nothing of the other document which he safely carried back, the King's original draft, of which the Dictator's answer was but a paraphrase adorned with a few Garibaldian touches. That most compromising of documents has just come to light after a discreet interval of fifty years.

It was easy thus, while saving appearances, to make sure that Garibaldi would obey the law of his being and go forward as fast as he was able. But to prevent the maritime Powers from stopping him at the Straits was a harder task.

For the moment little was to be feared from Austria, alienated as she was from the Government of Naples by the nature of its appeal to England, France, and Piedmont. The diplomatic representatives of Naples did not hesitate to allege that if the western Powers would force a six months' truce upon Garibaldi, their country would be able to hold the elections to her new Parliament, and would lend her regular army as soon as it was required for the ' inevitable ' war against Austria in Venice. Though such promises were only the result of abject fear and were unlikely to be fulfilled, they caused irritation, if not alarm, at Vienna, and postponed the season of Austrian intervention.

Napoleon, on the other hand, at that moment desired to preserve the Bourbon dynasty on the mainland as a constitutional State under French direction far more ardently than he desired a month later to preserve the Pope's Adriatic dominions. He was therefore most anxious to stop Garibaldi at the Straits ; but he was no less anxious to preserve good relations with England. Both these objects could be achieved by a naval combination of France and England to hold the Straits of Messina against the

passage of the Garibaldini, and this was proposed by the French Ministers to Palmerston and Russell. Lord John, in his English simplicity, supposed that Victor Emmanuel and Cavour meant what they said when they declared against Garibaldi's invasion of Calabria, and no doubt felt that he could best serve Italy by acting in accordance with the publicly expressed wishes of Cavour.

The British Ministers, therefore, were not indisposed to listen to the arguments of Napoleon when he proposed that England and France should send the two greatest fleets in the world to protect the Calabrian coast against the red-shirts. Details as to the number of ships to be employed were actually arranged at Naples between King Francis' Ministers, Brenier, and the French Admiral. The final consent of the British Cabinet had yet to be received, but if Palmerston and Russell fathered the scheme it would meet with no resistance from their colleagues, who, except Gladstone, were less enthusiastic than they in the Italian cause.

It was a moment full of danger, but Cavour was warned just in time of the blow which the extreme subtleness of his policy was preparing for him in the house of his friends. The warning came, it is said, through an indiscretion of one of his worst enemies. The story goes that the French Empress in conversation with Nigra, the Piedmontese representative at Paris, let drop a hint of the negotiations with England, that Nigra extracted the whole truth from her by pretending to sympathise with the project, and sent on the news to Turin.

Cavour, gravely alarmed, went straight to the British Legation and asked Hudson point-blank how to prevent Russell from being made an unconscious agent in the ruin of Italy's best hopes. Hudson, happily inspired, advised Cavour to send Sir James Lacaita, the intimate

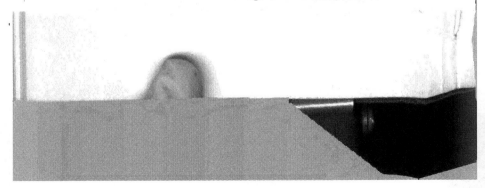

friend of the Russell family, to explain the real situation to Lord John.*

Giacomo Lacaita, a gentleman of Apulia and a lawyer of Naples, had in 1850 been Mr. Gladstone's political mentor during his famous visit.† Driven into exile for this, he became naturalised in England and was knighted as Sir James Lacaita for public services rendered to his adopted country. In July 1860, he was engaged in examining the candidates for our Indian Civil Service. On the 23rd,

* Sir James Hudson's autograph letter to Lacaita, written in 1885 to bear witness to this event, is in possession of Mr. Charles Lacaita, who has given me a photograph of it. The letter, which runs as follows, at length puts the story beyond all possible doubt :—

'FLORENCE,
'9 May, 1885.

'MY DEAR LACAITA,

'I have a clear recollection of the circumstances connected with your visit to Earl Russell in 1860, and as far as the action of Count Cavour was concerned, I can declare that he called upon me at the Queen's Legation at Turin, and pointing out the dangerous complications which must arise if a stop was not put to the negotiations then in progress between France and Naples, into which it was hoped to induce England to enter (i.e. to exercise a direct armed pressure upon Garibaldi), begged me to take such steps as I might deem practicable to prevent this mischief to the Cause of Italy.

'I told the Count that the only thing which occurred to me would be to address you upon the subject desiring you to go immediately to Lord Russell and explain to him the real bearings of the case—that I proposed yourself because you were intimately known to the family of Lord Russell as a man of honour and a Neapolitan Gentleman having a perfect knowledge of the whole case and its deplorable consequences if not promptly checked : and, moreover, because this was not a case where a Regular Diplomatic Agent could be of use, who, if he acted at all, could only do so under Protest ; to which if no attention was paid at the instant, would render the " agreement " between the Powers concerned an " accomplished fact."

'Therefore the success must lie entirely in the personal qualifications of the gentleman employed in so delicate a conjuncture.

'Count Cavour agreed in this view of the case, and said he would telegraph to the King's Minister in London to concert with you the steps to take.

'Your success on that occasion added one more to the many services you had already rendered to Italy.

'Yours sincerely,
'JAMES HUDSON.'

† Garibaldi and the Thousand, chap. iii.

the rain of an English summer's day gave him a severe
cold, and further to his distress, as he noted in his diary,
he heard that a special Neapolitan envoy, the Marquis
La Greca, had arrived in London and had been closeted
with Lord John. On the next day, Tuesday July 24,
he spent another chilly morning examining the young
men *vivâ voce*, came home exceedingly ill, and took to
his bed. He was called up by an unexpected visit from
Emmanuel D'Azeglio, the Piedmontese Minister in England,
who, in obedience to Cavour's message, came to request
Lacaita to go at once to Lord John ' and put him on his
guard against an application he would receive for intervention to force an armistice on Sicily.' In spite of his
illness, Lacaita dressed again, and disregarding the protests
of his family dragged himself into the streets to obey the
orders of Cavour, and, as it chanced, to bring about the
making of Italy.

Arriving at the Russells' town house * he rang the bell.
The servant who appeared knew him well as a friend of
the family. The conversation that followed was to this
effect :—

' Is Lord John at home ? '

' Not at home, Sir James.'

' Is he out or only busy ? '

' He's engaged, most particular, Sir James, with the
French Ambassador ; I've turned away the Turkish Am-
bassador, and I've strict orders to let in no one except the
Minister for Naples.'

' There's no time to lose,' thought Lacaita, and then
inquired :—

' Is Lady John at home, then ? '

* Lady Agatha Russell writes to me : ' I think my parents were probably at Chesham Place : they came to Pembroke Lodge Saturdays to
Mondays.'

Sir James, ill.'

' She's in bed,' took

Then Lacaita out a card and wrote upon it, ' For the love you bear the memory of your father * see me this instant,' and sent up this strange message to the lady of the house. In a few minutes he was by her bedside. He persuaded her to send down to her husband the simple message, ' Come up at once.' Thinking to find his wife suddenly taken worse, Lord John left Persigny, the French Ambassador, sitting there, rushed upstairs, opened the door of the bedroom, and found himself face to face with Lacaita. It was no time for apologies or explanations. In a flood of impassioned words the Apulian poured forth his soul to his English friend. Was 1848 to be repeated ? Then Sicily had revolted, then England and France had helped to prevent the Sicilians from invading Naples, and Sicily had been reconquered. If Garibaldi crossed now Italy would be made. If he was stopped, division, reaction and disaster would ensue as before. Did Lord John wish to be for ever loved or for ever hated by Liberal Europe ? A violent paroxysm of coughing shortened his eloquence. But he had said enough to show Lord John what Cavour wanted England to do. ' Go to bed,' he said to Lacaita, ' and don't be so sure that I am going to sign the treaty yet.' †

* *Gilbert* Elliot, second Earl of *Minto*, a great friend to Italy in public and to Lacaita in private life.

† Such as the story told by Lacaita to Villari, and published by him in various places. The story was first published in 1880 in an imperfect form in *Fagan's Life of Panizzi* (ii. 207). Lacaita was annoyed at this, and Villari therefore asked Lacaita for the real details, which Lacaita furnished. Villari's story is Lacaita's authorised version. His son, Mr. Charles Lacaita, told me this. Sir James told the story not only to Villari but to his son, and to various other people. Lady Russell's journals for 1860 are lost, but see pp. 319, 320 below, for complete evidence from Mr. Vernon's diary that she and her husband acknowledged the truth of Lacaita's story. For the remarkable personality of Lady John Russell, see the *Memoir* of her by Mr. Desmond MacCarthy and Lady Agatha Russell (Methuen, 1910).

with what excuse he could, for two hours later he sent round a messenger to Lacaita to tell him to be of good cheer. And at the Cabinet held on the afternoon of July 25 it was decided to reject the French proposal with regard to coercing Garibaldi.*

Persigny was amazed at the *volte-face* of the British Ministers, for, as he himself tells us, ' he had obtained Lord Palmerston's promise ' to join in stopping Garibaldi.† On July 26 Lord John wrote to our Ambassador at Paris a despatch suitable for publication, no reader of which would ever guess that the majestic current of British foreign policy had just been deflected from its course by one of the Civil Service Examiners. ' I informed M. de Persigny,' writes Russell, ' that Her Majesty's Government were of opinion that no case had been made out for a departure on their part from their general principle of non-intervention.'   Her Majesty's

---

* *Br. Parl. Papers*, vii. p. 40, No. 50. The Cabinet held on the afternoon of the 25th (see *Times*) is the meeting referred to. The visit of Lacaita to Lord John's house must have occurred some time between D'Azeglio's call on Lacaita on the 24th, and this Cabinet on the 25th, *viz.* either in the afternoon of the 24th or the morning of the 25th July.

---

doctrine. To come to the p
interfere alone, we should me
and protest against it.   In o
ought to be masters either to
baldi.'

Napoleon was not prepared
which England would protest,
intervention fell dead.

Garibaldi h-d -- '
French and British fleets, bu
a military operation of imme
Straits of Messina through th
fleet and to land on the Calabr
Neapolitan army. The moder
sandy cape of Charybdis, and g
castled rock, bethought him of
heroes had striven in vain to be
Half a century before, the gene
including Murat himself, had
strip of sea, two miles wide -t
h-d

Government had only come to this conclusion within the last forty-eight hours. 'That the force of Garibaldi was not in itself sufficient to overthrow the Neapolitan Monarchy. If the navy, army, and people of Naples were attached to the King, Garibaldi would be defeated; if, on the contrary, they were disposed to welcome Garibaldi, our interference would be an intervention in the internal affairs of the Neapolitan kingdom.' This was sound doctrine. To come to the point: 'If France chose to interfere alone, we should merely disapprove her course and protest against it. In our opinion the Neapolitans ought to be masters either to reject or to receive Garibaldi.'

Napoleon was not prepared to take a course against which England would protest, and the project of foreign intervention fell dead.

Garibaldi had no longer anything to fear from the French and British fleets, but he still had before him a military operation of immense difficulty, to cross the Straits of Messina through the midst of the Neapolitan fleet and to land on the Calabrian coast in the face of the Neapolitan army. The modern Odysseus stood on the sandy cape of Charybdis, and gazing across at Scilla's now castled rock, bethought him of his many devices.* Other heroes had striven in vain to become masters of this event. Half a century before, the generals of the great Napoleon, including Murat himself, had been baffled by this same strip of sea, two miles wide at the narrowest point, which had guarded Sicily from the French as safely as twenty-

* The currents in the Straits, which had given rise in the sea-ports of ancient Hellas to the fable of the Charybdis whirlpool, are so slight that they caused but little inconvenience to Garibaldi's transport operations from the Faro, although these were principally conducted in scores of row-boats, each one smaller than Odysseus' ship.

one miles of northern ocean had guarded from them a more favoured island.*

The lighthouse which gives its name of 'Faro' to the cape of Charybdis, and an old fort and battery by its side, stand at the end of the spit of sand where the north and east sides of the triangle of Sicily unite. On the sand dunes behind the lighthouse the greater part of the Garibaldian army was bivouacked during the first three weeks of August. The depth of the water round the cape, which enables the tunny-fishers to row their boats within a few yards of the pebbly shore, made it an excellent place for a great embarkation. Two salt-water lakes near at hand gave safe harbourage to the larger transports and to rafts which were being constructed to take across horses and cannon; while the flotilla of small boats which Garibaldi collected from Messina and the neighbouring fishing villages were drawn up along the beach of the sea. The mean houses of Faro village afforded useful shelter. It was on these sands that the British had been encamped fifty years before, and the remains of their trenches could still be seen. Garibaldi had three new earth-work batteries erected, where he mounted some indifferent cannon, taken from

* See Johnson, *Napoleonic Empire in Southern Italy*, for the two attempts of the French to invade Sicily, in 1806 and 1810. On the second occasion 'the King of Naples [Murat] arrived at Scilla on the 3rd of June, saluted by the ringing of bells and by salvos of artillery that were re-echoed, but with solid shot, by the British batteries on the further side. The Strait of Messina at this point appears little more than a river winding between hilly and picturesque banks. It gradually widens from about two miles across at the Faro to eight or nine miles at Messina. The troops of both armies were mostly encamped at the narrowest point, and so slight was the distance between them that from the lofty rock of Scilla, 550 feet above the sea, nearly all the British camps and intrenchments could be discovered. From the further side the view was no less remarkable and clear, and one English traveller claimed to have distinguished and recognised from the Faro through a telescope the person of the King of Naples.' Garibaldi was now using his telescope from the spot where the 'British traveller' had used his fifty years before.

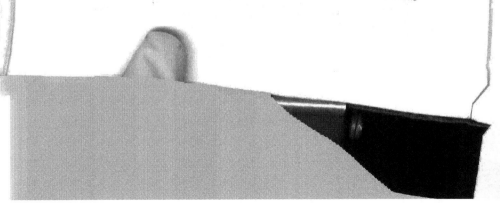

off his only warship, the *Tüköry*, and from the castle of Milazzo. With these and the three small cannon in the fort beside the lighthouse, he made pretence to command the Sicilian side of the narrow waters.

On the roasting sand between the lighthouse and the lakes the volunteers lay encamped day after day amid scenes of nature and of man very different from the rainy streets of London and the dim rooms in Chesham Place where their fate had just been decided. The crowded quarters soon became insanitary; the food and water were insufficient; on the open sands the sea mist soaked them by night and the sun scorched them by day, and there was little to relieve body or soul except constant bathing in the sea, drilling, and guessing how the General meant to carry them across. Among Garibaldi's own retinue the gaiety of the days in Palermo Palace and Milazzo Castle had given place to a more serious mood. Their chief was silent for hours together, passing about between Messina and the Faro, sometimes mounting the lighthouse to watch the coming and going of the Bourbon ships, sometimes vanishing no one knew whither, concealing even from Medici the plans that engrossed him all day long, but keeping his telescope ever directed on the Calabrian shore.

The eyes and thoughts of all men were fixed on the coast opposite, so near and yet so far, the ground whence one could march to Naples, to Rome, to Venice. The toe of Italy * has for its bone the enormous granite mass of Aspromonte, 'the rugged mountain,' of which the plateaus and spurs, clothed in forests of oak, pine, and chestnut, and cut by deep cañons each paved with a dry *fiumara* of stones washed white by flood, run down to the shores upon which the Garibaldini were so covetously gazing.

* See henceforth Map II., at end of book.

Where the last steep precipices of Aspromonte overhang the Mediterranean, a road crawls beneath them along the narrow strip of shore, joining the crowded villages of Bagnara, Favazzina, Scilla, and Cannitello. Along that road the red-shirts could watch the enemy's columns moving to and fro.

The narrowest point of the Straits was commanded from the Calabrian side by two small forts of Torre Cavallo and Altifiumara, built on the hill-side about a hundred yards above the road and the sea. If Garibaldi could capture one of these forts, his guns would command the narrowest part of the Straits from side to side, for he would then have batteries on both shores. The Neapolitan fleet would therefore be compelled to stand out of the narrows, and he could pass his army across from the Faro to the captured fort. It was on this basis that he planned his first attempt.

On the night of August 8, a forlorn hope of 200 men, picked out to capture the fort of Altifiumara, embarked in row-boats at the Faro. Garibaldi himself, always to the fore in any maritime operation, arranged and guided the flotilla into mid-channel. He then returned to the Sicilian shore where the rest of the army was embarking in steamers and fishing boats, ready to cross at dawn if a signal from the opposite shore announced the success of the enterprise. Meanwhile the 200, under cover of a cloudy night, rowed through the middle of the Neapolitan cruisers, and landed not far from the desired place. Their leader, Musolino, a Calabrian, had visited his native soil in disguise a few days before, and had arranged, as he believed, that the gates of the fort should be opened from the inside. But the alarm was given, their night attack was repulsed, and they had no course left but to escape into the mountains of the interior. At first they ascended the *fiumara* that debouches beside the fort, guided through the night by the glint of its white stones; later on they climbed the mountain walls in complete darkness, dragging each other up the steepest places by the muzzles of their guns.

During the next ten days these 200 men were the only invaders on Neapolitan soil. They wandered about the upper plains of Aspromonte at a height of over 3000 feet above the sea, suffering from intense cold by night and August sun by day, sometimes starving in the mountain desert, sometimes falling in with trains of mules bearing ample provisions sent up for them from the Liberal Committee of Reggio. Owing to the fact that the new Intendant of Reggio appointed by Don Liborio Romano was a 'constitutionalist' in tacit sympathy with the invaders, this rebel Committee acted with singular publicity, in spite of the presence of the royal troops in the town. The old Royalist militia—the *guardie urbane*—had just been disarmed by an order of Don Liborio from Naples, and the new National Guard, Liberals to a man, had been armed in their stead. The civil and local authorities, therefore, no longer gave any support to the regular army camped in their midst.

The pitiful numbers of the invading force in Aspromonte were increased by small bands of Calabrian peasants, hardy mountaineers in goat-skin sandals, knee-breeches, shirt-sleeves, and brimless sugar-loaf hats ornamented with streamers of black velvet—the romantic Calabrian costume which the opera-house and the picture gallery of that era had made as familiar to cultured Europe as the kilt of Sir Walter Scott's Highlanders. Their leader was Plutino, a local magnate jealous of the fame which his fellow-Calabrian Musolino had acquired in the province as leader of this expedition. Both Musolino

and Plutino were feudal chiefs and political leaders rather than expert military men, and the command of the expedition was made over by consent to Missori, the Lombard who had saved Garibaldi's life at Milazzo. Under his spirited leadership these few hundred men kept the Neapolitan army perpetually on the *qui vive*. Every night they lighted a blaze of bonfires along the heights, to show their friends on the Sicilian shore that the insurrection was alive in Calabria. Once they came right down to the coast, captured Bagnara, and held it until driven out by several thousand troops. The Calabrians behaved well in this first skirmish.

In mountain hamlets like Solano and Pedavoli the invaders learnt something of Calabrian local politics, the blood-feuds which under the form of Liberal and Bourbon faction-fights had devastated the villages in '48. Since that year the course of events had so far alienated or discouraged the Royalist party, that Missori's men were almost everywhere assisted and were nowhere opposed by the Calabrians themselves. This was the more remarkable seeing that the country was still occupied by the Neapolitan troops, and that for the ten days preceding Garibaldi's crossing, Missori was being hunted like a partridge in the mountains. On August 15 General Ruiz with two battalions was sent up after him from the coast, and pursued him in vain through the forest gorges, of which the fantastic magnificence had more than once attracted landscape-painters like Arthur Strutt and Edward Lear to brave very real dangers of brigandage. The Garibaldini escaped over the upper plains of Aspromonte, many miles across, where only a few huts and sheepfolds broke the monotony of the desert, and where ' the only point visible on the horizon was Etna's purple cone. It was impossible,' wrote Alberto Mario as he tramped behind scenes, 'even in the hazardous pro-, not to be at times subdued by a

After this first failure, Garibaldi was only the more anxious to cross the Straits. The 'call of the peoples' for his presence among them, of which he had spoken in his letter to Victor Emmanuel, was growing daily more insistent. Calabria, in anticipation of his coming, was already in open revolt; the liberty of the press, the sympathies of the new 'constitutional' magistracy and police, made rebellion easy in any town or village not actually occupied by the regular troops; and the lower clergy, in contrast to the bishops, often took the popular side. In the toe of Italy the presence of 16,000 troops prevented the insurrection from breaking out along the thickly populated coast-line, and confined the movement to the wanderings of Missori's bands in the heights of Aspromonte. But the province of Cosenza in Upper Calabria fell more or less into the hands of revolutionary committees in the first days of August, and the Basilicata followed suit on August 18. The movement in Calabria had been stirred up by the great local proprietors—the Plutino and Medici family, Stocco of the Thousand, and Pace of old home, whom Garibaldi had sent on to their homes to prepare the way before him. In the Basilicata a like part was played by Mignona, also commissioned by Garibaldi. The leaders of the insurrection in the provinces south of the capital showed both sense and courage, and succeeded in overawing the troops in their midst, such as the formidable garrison of Cosenza, who remained passive spectators of the rebellion. If the Northern provinces had been equally Liberal, and the inhabitants of Naples equally bold, Cavour would have

got his revolution w—out need of further help from Garibaldi.

As the moment for invading the mainland drew near, the recently enlisted Sicilian bands, considering their part in the affair completed, began to desert in hundreds from Messina and the Faro. Many of them had fought well for the deliverance of their own island, but few shared the enthusiasm of their Northern Liberators for the idea of Italian Unity. In so far as it meant protection by Piedmont against the return of the detested Neapolitans, Italian Unity was good; but in so far as it meant friendly dealings with the Neapolitans, it was nought. Now that their own island was safe, they returned to their homes. Only Dunne's regiment of six hundred and a 'Sicilian brigade' of eight hundred *Cacciatori d' Etna*, led by real enthusiasts like La Masa, Corrao, and La Porta, of whom the last two were good soldiers, shared the fortunes of the army until the end of the Volturno campaign.

If the Dictator had any doubts as to the real wishes of the Court of Turin, they were removed by another secret message which reached him at the Faro through the hands of Victor Emmanuel's aide-de-camp Trecchi, the regular medium of royal communication with Garibaldi. The King's positive orders to the Dictator were to occupy Naples, and thence to invade the Pope's territory of Umbria and the Marches.*

* Like the secret letter carried by Count Litta (mentioned a few pages above), it has only just been made known to the world after fifty years (*Nuova Antologia*, June 1, 1910, *Trecchi* papers). The text of the message in Trecchi's handwriting, dictated apparently on August 5, runs thus :—

'Words dictated by Victor Emmanuel to be conveyed to Garibaldi. Garibaldi in Naples. Will regulate himself according to opportunity, either occupying Umbria and the Marches with his troops, or allowing bands of volunteers to go. As soon as Garibaldi is in Naples he will proclaim its union to the rest of Italy as in Sicily. Prevent disorders which

... judge whether or not Cavour was a [...]. On the one hand it was a habit [...] carry on a policy of his own through [beh]ind the back of his Ministers. And [...] on principle opposed to a red-shirt [...] Papal States. He wished to keep the Marches and Umbria as a royal pre[rogative, and] not to allow it to become a new source [...] the advanced parties, who, he feared, [...] state terms to the Monarchy and attack [...] at the risk of a war with France.

On the other hand, the King's message, though in apparent contradiction to Cavour's policy, was perhaps one of the subtlest moves in the Minister's game. In order to interpret the royal words of encouragement to Garibaldi, dictated on August 5, it is necessary to understand that Cavour had already, four days earlier, determined in his own mind to invade the Papal States from the north with the regular army of Piedmont. On August 1 he had written to Nigra in Paris and to Emmanuel D'Azeglio in London disclosing to them this the key to all his subsequent policy, in 'ultra secret confidential' letters which were to be destroyed as soon as read. The grounds on which he adopted this decision, the greatest and boldest of his whole life, will be discussed in a future chapter. The policy did not take effect until September, and till then was not foreseen by the world at large. It is, therefore, enough at this stage to point out that by August 1 Cavour had secretly determined to invade the Papal States himself. He had, therefore, the less objection to the further advance of

would harm our cause. Keep the Neapolitan army in being, for Austria will soon declare war. Let the King of Naples escape, and if he is taken by the people, save him and let him escape.'

invasion of the Papal States from Naples, which would now never really take place, since the royal troops would forestall him in the Pope's territories. It was the more necessary to tell Garibaldi that he might invade the Papal States from Naples, because Cavour was at this moment putting his veto on Mazzini's plan to invade the Papal States direct from Genoa with Bertani's private army.

Bertani's Committee in Aid of Garibaldi had not yet sent out to him any large body of men. Throughout June and July the expeditions despatched to Sicily had been organised chiefly by the moderates and by the supporters of Cavour. Although Bertani had been levying and equipping volunteers ever since Garibaldi sailed in May, he had hitherto held them in reserve for a blow at the Papal States. Garibaldi had all along favoured such a design, while at the same time demanding reinforcements for himself in Sicily. On July 30 he wrote from the Faro to Bertani : ' As to the operations in the Papal and Neapolitan territories, push them on with all possible vigour.' The time had now come to strike the blow. In the first days of August Bertani had at his disposal 8940 volunteers, who, unlike the men of the earlier expeditions, were ready

Lamoricière's newly levied an
superior in numbers and not
to Bertani's volunteers, coul
rapidity which was essential i
ference was to be forestall
volunteers under the comman
and Bertani had chosen for h
military capacity, would not
under Garibaldi. Further,
find, as August advanced an
their homes, that he could nc
the Neapolitan armies on the
received strong reinforcements from
II he was expecting shortly to be
the volunteers whom Bertani h
But Pianciani was preparing to le
different part of the Italian Penin
that Garibaldi would have 6000 Sic
him across the Straits, in addition t

Cavour, however, prevented this
made. He could not allow revolu
by Mazzini and Bertani, to star

...de Umbria and the Marches respectively, while ...body were to sail from Genoa, land ...at a point north of Civita Vecchia, ...terbo to join Nicotera and the others ...Civita Vecchia, the only places occupied by French garrisons, were to be spared for the present. There were grave objections to this plan. First, Lamoricière' newly levied army of Papal crusaders, being ...bers and not wholly inferior in enthusiasm superior in ...unteers, could not be destroyed with the to Bertani' ...was essential if French and Austrian interference... to be forestalled. Nine thousand Italian volunteers ...to be under the command of Pianciani, whom Mazzini and Bertani had chosen for his politics rather than for his military capacity, would not be worth half the number under Garibaldi. Further, Garibaldi was beginning to find, as August advanced and the Sicilians dispersed to their homes, that he could not cross the Straits in face of the Neapolitan armies on the Calabrian shore until he received strong reinforcements from the North. On August 11 he was expecting shortly to be joined at the Straits by the ...unteers whom Bertani had organised at Genoa. But Pianciani was preparing to lead them off to a wholly different part of the Italian Peninsula, under the delusion that G...ribaldi would have 6000 Sicilian soldiers to take with him a...ross the Straits, in addition to his Northern followers. Ca...vour, however, prevented this fatal mistake from being made... He could not allow revolutionary armies, organised by Mazzini and Bertani, to start from Genoa direct for the Papal States. An invasion made under such conditions must inevitably provoke French interference. He therefore sent to Genoa his principal colleague Farini, to negotiate with Bertani about the destination of Pianciani's force. Saffi, ex-triumvir of Rome, was present at to Garibaldi's orders. After touching at Sicily they might go to whatever part their leaders wished, not excluding the Papal States, provided that they did not re-enter Piedmontese territory as a base from which to attack the Pope. This compromise was agreed upon by Farini for the Government, and by Bertani for the volunteers.

The clear intention of the authorities to use force rather than permit the invasion of the Papal States direct from the port of Genoa had compelled Bertani to temporise. But he had no real thought of fulfilling his part of the bargain by sending Pianciani's men to Sicily. The Government had promised to let his volunteers sail for the Golfo degli Aranci: he intended to persuade Garibaldi to come to meet them at the Sardinian port and himself to lead them thence, not to Sicily, but to the Papal States. With this object in view, he sailed to the Faro, landed there at dawn on August 12 and laid his proposal before the Dictator. Garibaldi took ship with Bertani that very evening for the Golfo degli Aranci, stealing away from the camp beside the Straits so secretly that no one knew whither he had gone nor why. But all felt that great events were in the air, and that when next they saw him there would be an end of this weari-

attempt a direct *coup de main* on
But the vigilance of the Piedr
settled the matter beforehand.
the *Washington*, bearing Garib
into the Golfo degli Aranci, on
that had transported the volu
to be found in the bay. The re
pelled by Piedmontese warships
accordance with the agreement
with the Government and was
He was wild with fury when h
frustrated. Garibaldi, on the ot
out any serious loss of temper
entertained three days before of
force the passage of the Straits of
Since he had chanced to co
home of Caprera, he went to p
repose. With the poignant aff
boy at home on his day's *exeat*
Dictator wandered amid the s
the chaos of granite rocks, call
to him by name and fed

Bertani was under the erroneous
would consent to lead the volunteers
degli Aranci to the Papal States.
of Bertani's arrival at the Faro,
to use the greater number of them
the Straits of Messina, and he himself
Bertani's proposal to go to the Papal
considering instead whether he might not
coup de main on Naples.
of the Piedmontese Government had
beforehand. When at dawn of August
bearing Garibaldi and Bertani, steamed
Aranci, only one part of the fleet
the volunteers from Genoa was
transported The rest had already been com-
in the bay. Piedmontese warships to go on to Sicily, in
with the agreement which Bertani had made
Government and was now plotting to evade.
with fury when he saw that he had been
wild Garibaldi, on the other hand, fell back with-
frustrated. of temper on the plan which he had
out any serious loss before of using Pianciani's men to
entertained three days the passage of the Straits of Messina.
he had chanced to come so near to his island
he went to pass a few hours there in
of Caprera, he poignant affection and delight of a
With the home on his day's *exeat* in the middle of term, the
wandered amid the sweet-smelling shrubs and
chaos of granite rocks, called his favourite cows up
to him by name and fed them from his hand. Then he
took ship again for Palermo, where all Pianciani's expedition was soon assembled, 6000 strong.
Even at Palermo, Bertani again implored him to lead
the men to the Papal States. but his mind was now once

5

under Nicotera, who had not been specifically mentioned in the terms of agreement between Bertani and Farini at Genoa. Garibaldi, though requiring Pianciani's men in order to effect the passage of the Straits, was still willing that Nicotera should invade the Pope's territory by land, and wrote to him to that effect. But Cavour instructed Ricasoli, as Governor of Tuscany, not to permit any such movement. After an embittered quarrel, in which Ricasoli and Nicotera behaved each with small consideration for the other, the Governor had his way, and the last of the volunteers were forcibly shipped to Sicily. Thus the whole army which Bertani had prepared against the Pope, more than 8000 in number, finally swelled Garibaldi's force in the South, and was of indispensable service to him in his occupation and subsequent defence of Naples. They were almost the last volunteers who joined him from North Italy. For Cavour, alarmed by the constant threat of the advanced parties to invade the Papal territory, and now fully determined to invade it himself, prohibited on August 13 the further levy or despatch of volunteers under any pretext, and this time, to the surprise of diplomatic Europe, actually enforced his proclamation. There were no more departures *en*

...the year, and at the Straits he already ...his crossing, much the greater part of ...Sicilians. He was a match, even in ...troops in the toe of Italy, provided his ...escape the enemy's fleet. But by all ...ion that was impossible.

CHAPTER VI

THE CROSSING OF THE STRAITS

'Che volete, Signorini ; io sono un vecchio soldato, e perciò m'attendeva che Garibaldi m'attaccasse di fronte, ed invece m'è capitato alle spalle ! '

'What do you expect, gentlemen ; I am an old soldier, and so of course I expected Garibaldi to attack me in front, and he came from behind instead !'—*General Gallotti's explanation of his defeat overheard by Arrivabene.*

'Lu curaggio è nu donu di Dio, ed io nu l'aggiu.'

'Courage is a gift of God, and I have it not.'—*Saying attributed to a Neapolitan soldier by the Garibaldini.*

BETWEEN the working of one great action and the next, Nino Bixio was heard of chiefly through his deeds of insane violence. After the taking of Palermo, 'the second of the Thousand' had distinguished himself in the Sicilian capital by his quarrel with a brother in arms, the self-sacrificing Agnetta, whom he struck in the face for an imaginary insult. Since Garibaldi would allow no duel on campaign, they did not fight it out until late in the following year, in Switzerland. Bixio came tardily and unwillingly on to the 'field of honour,' because he of all men had scruples against duelling. Agnetta shot him in the hand, crippling it for the rest of his life, whereupon Bixio said, 'I am punished in the hand that gave the offence.' He subsequently earned Agnetta's gratitude by services of real friendship.

Bixio was not present at the battle of Milazzo, for he was leading his command through the south of the island. When at the end of July all the Garibaldian columns met near the Straits, he was sent by the Dictator to suppress a

...ous anarchist rising under the western ...re, at Randazzo and on Nelson's old ...summary methods and manners soon ...s into submission at the cost of only ...s. Bixio's own soldiers were always 'He is mad, he is intolerable.' 'Very ...om do you wish to serve then?' 'What? ...Bixio, of course.' At Bronte one morning ...recently arrived from North Italy, and ...d to his ways, were late in turning out of ...into the houses after them with a horse-whip. ...troops, who had marched under him and learned to ...with difficulty saved his life from the fury of the ...who had come out to fight under Garibaldi, not to be whipped-in like hounds.

But now an action was in hand on which his rage to be up and doing for his country could be spent to better purpose.

The Dictator had been away in Sardinia and Palermo for nearly six days, and no one at the Straits knew when ...whether he would return. The suspense on both shores ...rrible. On the morning of August 18 he suddenly ...ared in the Faro camp, gave his orders, left for ...a, and an hour afterwards was seen driving through ...eets in a three-horse carriage along the southern road. ...ovements were still as mysterious as ever, for he was ...travelling away from the scene of active operations ...e Faro. But in fact the camp and flotilla beneath the ...house were to serve during the next twenty-four hours ...as a decoy to fix the attention of the enemy's ships ...regiments on the narrow waters of Scilla and Charybdis, ...ile the real crossing took place at the broader part of the ...aits, thirty miles to the south.

On the afternoon of August 18, Garibaldi's carriage reached the hamlet of Giardini, which stretches along the beach between the wall of mountains and the sea, at the southern foot of Taormina rock. Here Bixio's men from Bronte and Catania had been secretly collected during the last two days. Here the *Torino* and *Franklin* had safely arrived, after steaming round the whole island from the Faro in order to avoid the Neapolitan cruisers in the Straits. The captain of the *Torino*, a man of peace, who objected to the use of his transport vessel for an enterprise so hazardous as an attack on the Calabrian coast, had been silenced and placed under arrest by Bixio. The troops, 3360 in number, were already on board the two steamers when Garibaldi drove up. When all was ready, it was found that the *Franklin* had sprung a leak. The hole could not be found, and Bixio proposed that they should start with the *Torino* alone, but, when Garibaldi took the matter in hand, the hole was soon found and stopped. To judge by the space which he allots to this operation in his Memoirs, the Dictator recalled it with more interest than all his historic achievements during the next fortnight. That he should cause 15,000 soldiers of tyranny to lay down their arms seemed to him no more than an inevitable fate, now that Italy's hour had struck; but to find and calk a hole in a ship which had baffled the other seamen, was an action of which a man had good right to be proud.

At nightfall the two vessels steamed out from below the rock of Taormina. The distance to Melito, the point chosen for the landing in Calabria, is thirty miles, and if at any point in the crossing the unarmed transports had fallen in with a Neapolitan warship they could have been sent to the bottom. But the enemy were all away at the narrows, watching the camp and flotilla at the Faro. The voyage was unbroken by anything more terrifying than the voice of Bixio from the *Torino* continually shouting through his megaphone to the silent Garibaldi in the *Franklin*.

When dawn revealed Ætna's cone and the long ranges of Sicilian mountains at her feet, the Calabrian coast lay close ahead. Again, as at Marsala, Bixio ran his vessel aground on the shallows. But the men of both the steamers were taken off in the ships' boats and landed on the desolate beach called Porto Salvo, a mile from Melito village.

There were no houses near, but an old chapel with a cupola rose amid the cactuses and aloes at the edge of the sea sand. The flat country behind, though it bore olive groves and scraps of cultivation, was arid for the most part, stripped and scarred each winter by the torrents from Aspromonte. The mountains themselves here stand back a mile or two from the coast, but the Garibaldini as they landed saw the pillar rock of Pentedatilo raising its five grotesque fingers against the dawn.*

Garibaldi spent the whole morning of the 19th in a vain attempt to salve the *Torino*. He was waiting also for Missori's men to come down from the mountains near San Lorenzo, whither he had sent them a message to announce his landing. In the afternoon Neapolitan war vessels appeared from the direction of Messina, destroyed the grounded and derelict *Torino*, and fired, not without some effect, into the red-shirts on shore. The *Franklin* had returned safely to Sicily. Towards evening the vanguard of Missori's men appeared on the neighbouring mountains, and the night of August 19–20 was spent in bivouac not far

* Pentedatilo had been a favourite place of Edward Lear's during his painting tour in Calabria which was cut short by the revolution of 1848. Very few others have visited Pentedatilo before or since; Calabria is out of fashion now even with painters, though safer and no less magnificent than of old.

from Melito. For thirty-six hours many of the troops had neither food nor drink; some of them who were inland-bred dug holes in the sea-shore and lapped the water that oozed up, in the desperate hope that Neptune would lose his salt by filtering through the sand.

On August 19 the telegraphs and semaphores in the Neapolitan kingdom had been wagging all day with ominous rumours from the south, and before midnight the Ministers at Naples knew that there had been a landing in force a dozen miles beyond Reggio. There were now some 16,000 Royalist troops in Lower Calabria. General Vial, their commander-in-chief, had his headquarters at Monteleone, too far removed from the scene of operations. His regiments were scattered along fifty miles of the road between Monteleone and Reggio. His lieutenants, Melendez and Briganti, were guarding the supposed points of danger opposite the Faro, but at the moment of Garibaldi's landing there were no troops south of Reggio, and in Reggio itself only some 1000 men, chiefly of the 14th line. When, forty-eight hours later, Garibaldi fell upon the city, the numbers of its garrison had not been increased by a single man. The news of the landing at Melito ought to have caused an instantaneous move in that direction on the part of each of the columns scattered along the coast road, but neither Vial, Melendez, nor Briganti stirred until it was too late to save Reggio, in spite of a stream of indignant telegrams from Pianell at Naples. The War Minister had been anxious to avoid fighting in Sicily, and had perhaps not sent enough troops to guard the Straits, but his telegrams show that he did his best to make the generals fight Garibaldi when once he had landed.

Old General Gallotti, in command at Reggio, was the most complete dotard of them all. When informed of the landing at Melito, he said that Garibaldi had taken to the mountains, and that Reggio could not be attacked from that side, but only in front from the sea. He therefore made no preparations to defend the city. He forbade the energetic Colonel Dusmet to take up a good position near the castle, and compelled him instead to bivouac in the middle of the Cathedral Square, a mere trap for those who occupied it, unless the entrances to the city were strongly guarded. These, however, were confided to the National Guard of Liberal *bourgeoisie*, whose loyalty was more than doubtful. Gallotti himself remained in the castle with a garrison. The castle of Reggio is a tall, grim building, flanked by round towers, somewhat similar in strength and appearance to the Bastille of old Paris, though on a smaller scale. But unlike the Bastille it does not rise clear above all possible assailants. For Reggio was built on the side of a hill, and since the castle is only half-way up the hill, its battlements can be commanded by sharpshooters at the top of the town.

On the 20th the invaders marched from Melito along the coast. The General walked with his sabre over his shoulder, talking and singing with the men. All were hungry but in high spirits. Near Reggio they rested again, and at midnight advanced to the attack. Garibaldi with Missori's men entered the upper town by way of the hills, through Spirito Santo. Bixio with the main column kept through Sbarre, and came in by the principal the high-road streets below the castle. His men stumbled upon outposts at the entrance of the city.

 ' Chi va là ? '
 ' Garibaldi. '
 ' Avanti ! '

It was the National Guard standing aside to let them pass. They hurried on through the sleeping streets. In the middle of the town they came upon other sentries.

5a

' *Chi va là ?* '

' Garibaldi.'

Bang!

They had come upon the loyal troops at last.*

A fierce struggle raged in the great Cathedral Square until the morning. Colonel Dusmet and his son, not yet of age, fell gallantly fighting in front of the Royalists. Bixio's horses received nineteen wounds, and their rider two in the arm to which he paid no attention till Garibaldi sent him to bed the next night, saying, ' I suppose the balls that reach you are made of puff-paste.'

The odds were all against the 14th line, and Garibaldi's column was pouring in upon their rear from the upper town. As day broke the red-shirts possessed themselves of all Reggio except the castle, which was provisioned for a month and could easily be defended against its present assailants.

Later in the same day (August 21) Briganti approached Reggio from Villa San Giovanni with about 2000 men. Garibaldi led his troops out into the country just beyond the northern suburbs and took up a position to cover the town. After the exchange of a few shots in a feeble re- connaissance, Briganti fell back, leaving Reggio to its fate. Garibaldi afterwards wrote that if the attack had been pressed, the Royalists might very possibly, with the help of the garrison in the castle, have recovered the town, and that in that case his own position would have been desperate. Indeed the troops in the castle had clamoured to be led out to attack him in the rear and join hands with the relieving force. But Gallotti had refused to allow a sally. Hitherto the Royalist garrison in Reggio, with the exception of Gal- lotti himself, had behaved well, but after Briganti's retreat they felt themselves deserted and began to lose courage.

* Such was the account Tedaldi gave me of his own experience.

When sharpshooters placed by Garibaldi in the upper part of the town commenced picking off the men on the battlements, panic set in, and the castle, which might have held out for weeks, was surrendered within twenty-four hours. The taking of Reggio had cost the victors about 150 in killed and wounded.

On the same day another important event took place to the north of the Straits. Garibaldi had left Cosenz in command at the Faro with instructions that he was to carry his troops across the water at the moment when the Dictator himself attacked Reggio. There was a good chance that Cosenz would be able to cross in safety because the Neapolitan war-vessels had now, too late, left the narrow waters and gone south to attend to Garibaldi after his landing at Melito. Before sunrise on August 21, to the sound of the distant firing from Reggio, the flotilla of row-boats put out from Faro, carrying between 1000 and 1500 volunteers ; they struggled successfully against the currents of Charybdis, made a wide detour to avoid the cannon-balls from the fort of Scilla, and landed the same morning on the strip of flat shore beneath the wall of wooded mountains at Favazzina. The Neapolitan warships, hastily summoned back from Reggio, sank and captured a large number of the boats as the fishermen were taking them back empty to the Faro.

A few minutes after Cosenz and his men had landed at Favazzina, they were attacked while crossing the coast road by Neapolitan troops from Scilla on one side and from Bagnara on the other. The enemy were repulsed chiefly by the Genoese carabineers, the pick of Garibaldi's original 'Thousand,' and the whole force proceeded straight up the sides of Aspromonte by precipitous tracks through the brushwood. At noontide the greater part had reached the hamlet of Solano, 2000 feet above the sea. Overcome by heat, thirst, and fatigue they took their siesta in the houses, believing that all the Royalist forces were far below them on the level of the shore. From the precipice edge or Solano they looked back down the gulf of an enormous ravine below, but the village is itself closely overshadowed by other heights, covered with chestnut woods, and in these a few hundred Neapolitan troops were lying concealed. They were a detachment of Ruiz' men who had not yet gone down off Aspromonte from their vain pursuit of Missori's column. Though inferior in numbers to Cosenz, the Royalists seized their advantage, surprised the sentinels and burst into the village. The Garibaldini had an hour's hard fighting before they could drive them out. Two little companies of French and English volunteers distinguished themselves in the scuffle under the leadership of De Flotte and of Goodall. De Flotte was killed in the street at the head of his men. He was a French Republican exile, who had played a part in Paris in '48, and narrowly escaped Cayenne after Napoleon III.'s *coup d'état*. He had been loved by all his companions in arms, English, Italians, and French; and Garibaldi, when he heard of his death, mourned for him as a true soldier of liberty. They buried him where he fell, high up among the granite gorges and the chestnut woods, far from his fierce, gay city and the Boulevard lights.

After repulsing this attack, Cosenz' column mounted another 1500 feet to Forestali on the higher plains of Aspromonte. There they received a message from the Dictator bidding them march westward and join him above Villa San Giovanni. Their sufferings on the plateaus of Aspromonte were severe. Starved and sunbaked all day, at night they were soaked with the dew and chilled with the intense cold of the mountain, so that Goodall and other useful soldiers were put out of action.

The movements of Garibaldi and Cosenz are a model of combined action from two separate bases. Each had enabled the other to succeed, by distracting the attention of the enemy's naval and military force. And now they were about to join hands at a spot above and in rear of the enemy's main line of defence.

On August 22, the morning after the fall of Reggio, the Dictator and Bixio moved northward to attack the forts and regiments commanding the narrowest part of the Straits. Again Bixio kept the coast road and Garibaldi the hills. On the evening of that day the Dictator joined forces with Cosenz above Piale and Villa San Giovanni. After this junction he had with him about 5000 men, and was for a while superior to the enemy both in numbers and position. Down below, between him and the sea, lay rather more than 3000 troops under Generals Melendez and Briganti. The greater part of this force was in Villa San Giovanni on the coast road, under the command of Briganti; but Melendez with 1200 men occupied Piale village, a mile up the hill-side. Garibaldi was above them both at Campo Calabrese, where Murat had pitched his tents when he threatened Sicily with invasion. These seaward heights now occupied by the red-shirts bore no resemblance to the wooded and precipitous mountains below which Cosenz had landed. It is a tumble-down land of broken mud banks on which vineyards, fruit gardens, cactuses, and houses maintain an ever precarious existence. The landscape on this part of the Calabrian shore is more weird than beautiful, but the view thence of the Straits, of Sicily and of Ætna—*Mongibello*, ' the fair mountain,' as the Calabrians call it—filled the Garibaldini with delight as they waited for the surrender of their foes. An artillery duel between the Neapolitan ships and the batteries at the Faro was watched by both armies as from the seats of a theatre, of which the lower circles were occupied by the Royalists.

On the 22nd Melendez and Briganti might still have retreated to Scilla, for it was only during the following night that the Dictator cut off their retreat by pushing his advance guard down to the coast at Cannitello. But they let the hours slip by in the vain expectation of reinforcements from the north. Besides the men whom they had with them, there were more than 10,000 Royalist troops in Lower Calabria, and they naturally supposed that Vial would lead these to their rescue. But the commander-in-chief had no advantage except in point of age over his dotard lieutenants. A pleasure-loving and idle young man, raised by personal influences at Court to a command for which he had no qualifications, Vial had too much of the heartless flippancy of the Neapolitan to be serious over even the gravest situation. He continued to linger and amuse himself at Monteleone, saying that he 'would give Joe a ducking'* if he tried to cross the Straits. When he heard that 'Joe' had crossed, and was taking Reggio, he still lingered with the greater part of the troops under his command fifty miles from the scene of action. At length, driven to the front by furious telegrams from Pianell, the War Minister, he sailed from Pizzo on the morning of August 22, taking with him one of his best battalions. He landed alone at Villa San Giovanni, interviewed Briganti and Melendez, and ordered them to hold out while he set this battalion ashore at Scilla and led it to their rescue. He then returned to Scilla, but as a sea had momentarily arisen which made the landing of troops difficult, he hailed the excuse to sail back with the battalion to Pizzo and Monteleone, leaving his lieutenants to their fate with-

* 'Avrebbe pescato Peppariello.' (Peppariello = Giuseppe Garibaldi.)

out even warning them that he had changed his plan and run away.

Meanwhile, Melendez and Briganti were expecting aid not only from Vial, but also from General Ruiz, who had at length descended from Aspromonte to the coast road, and was hurrying along it to their rescue. Like Vial, Ruiz came on alone in front of his column to take stock of the situation. He visited Melendez and Briganti up at Piale and then went down to the main road again to bring up his column from Altifiumara. But on his way back through Villa San Giovanni he could not fail to observe that Briganti's men were in a state of complete lemoralisation. Red-shirts were going about among them 'ith impunity in cafés and at street corners, exhorting em not to prolong a useless and fraticidal contest; d it was only too evident that the men were listening. ere was little of active disloyalty or of political Lib- 'ism among the rank and file.   But they had in August ll motive or encouragement to fight. They were at terrified and fascinated by the name of Garibaldi, after the taking of Reggio regarded him as uncon- ble. During the last two months, ever since the of the Constitution, they had been forced to march the tricolour flag,—the flag, as it seemed to them, r enemies. They witnessed, in every street down they passed, the enthusiasm of the populace for olution and the open disloyalty of the new civic es, who had proclaimed ' Long live the King ' as us cry. Their own officers were visibly shaking , muttering their doubts to each other, or pre- with private thoughts of which the character oo evident. Their General, Briganti, was known iation. The enemy, it appeared, ore than half a friend, since no one prevented his emissaries from entering their lines to talk sedition in the open street of Villa San Giovanni.

As Ruiz rode through the town noting what he saw, he judged that Briganti and his troops did not mean to fight, and that he had best save his own men from sharing in their surrender. A few miles further north, at Altifiumara, he met his column hastening up, ordered it to turn right about, and before nightfall on the 22nd had led it back to Bagnara. Like Vial, Ruiz was pursued by indignant telegrams from the War Minister at Naples to the effect that Melendez and Briganti were preparing to die at their posts, while he basely deserted them. But he knew better, and rather than face Garibaldi again, resigned his command. His successor, Morisani, on the morning of the 23rd began to march back once more to the relief of San Giovanni, but was met and turned back for good and all by a messenger from Melendez himself, who declared that it was now too late.

In this fashion Melendez and Briganti, lured by false hopes that Vial and Ruiz were marching to their relief, had let slip the opportunity to escape out of their untenable positions on August 22. At daybreak on the 23rd they saw that retreat was no longer possible. During the night Garibaldi had drawn the net round them by sending down detachments from Campo Calabrese to Cannitello. They were completely surrounded with a semicircle of sea on one side, and a semicircle of red-shirts on the other. As the sun rose the Garibaldini began to descend upon them from the hills. The Neapolitan rifles and cannon opened fire, but the advancing host made no reply. The slow, ordered, noiseless approach of their enemies affected the nerves of the Royalists, as Garibaldi had intended that it should. They opened negotiations. A Garibaldian *parlementaire* with the white flag in his

hand was shot dead, but General Briganti himself came out
to apologise. He explained to the Dictator that he would
have been a Liberal himself, but that he had two sons in
the Neapolitan army and so felt gratitude to the Bourbons.
'Otherwise,' he said, 'I would join you.' He asked to surrender with the honours of war. Garibaldi gave him and
Melendez till three o'clock to surrender unconditionally,
and allowed them to send out a messenger, who, as already
related, stopped the further advance of Morisani to their
rescue.

Meanwhile, the Garibaldian army halted on the hill-
side and watched the confusion growing hour by hour
among their enemies below. When the appointed time had
run out the advance was resumed. As the red-shirts drew
the circle close upon them, the Royalists threw away arms
and knapsacks and fled in a mob along the northern road.
They were turned back by a volley, and crowded together
like driven sheep in the centre of their position. Garibaldi
rode almost alone into their midst. 'Soldiers,' he said,
'you as well as my companions are the sons of Italy;
remember that. You are at liberty. Whoever wishes to
remain with us may address himself to General Cosenz,
your countryman, who is charged to enlist you. But whoever wishes may go home.' At these words they rushed at
him with cries of joy, and much to his disgust began kissing
his hands, arms, and feet. Three thousand five hundred
men, four field pieces, and the fort of Punto del Pezzo with
its artillery were the prize of this bloodless victory. Very
few of the men chose to enlist under Cosenz, but as they
scattered to their homes they spread the news that Garibaldi's custom was to send off his prisoners free, and this
knowledge greatly incre   the readiness of the troops
under Vial and Ruiz to   , the example set at Villa San
Giovanni.

army, among whom Garibaldi himself was one of the foremost. As soon as the batteries of these forts had compelled the Neapolitan navy to sail out of the Straits, Medici's regiments at Messina were brought safely across to the mainland.

The race to Naples had now fairly begun. It was led by Garibaldi and his staff, many hours ahead of the van of their army, accompanied by Jessie and Alberto Mario, and by some English gentlemen who liked fatigue and had the luck and money to hire horses that could keep the pace. There were more than 10,000 of the enemy close ahead, but no one feared that they would resist when overtaken. Basilicata and Upper Calabria were already rising in arms. The Dictator and his companions set out to ride unchallenged along the great trunk road that stretches for 250 miles through mountains and forests and fever-stricken plains from the foot of Aspromonte to the foot of Vesuvius.

THE MARCE

' O, how con
To the spirits of j
When God into tl
Puts invincible m
To quell the migh
The brute and boi
Hardy and indust
Tyrannic power, b
The righteous, anc
He all their ammu
And feats of war,
With plain heroic
And celestial vigoi
Their armouries ai
Renders them usel
With wingèd expe
Swift as the light
.... errand on the wicke
Lose their defence, distr

THE Calabrian Liberals were
such a deliverer. The Garil
to admire in the inhabitants
all the facile enthusiasm at
they had crossed the Straits
among ' a staid, manly, and a
The Calabrians of those
to

CHAPTER VII

THE MARCH THROUGH CALABRIA

> ' O, how comely it is, and how reviving
> To the spirits of just men long oppressed,
> When God into the hands of their deliverer
> Puts invincible might
> To quell the mighty of the earth, the oppressor,
> The brute and boisterous force of violent men,
> Hardy and industrious to support
> Tyrannic power, but raging to pursue
> The righteous, and all such as honour truth !
> He all their ammunition,
> And feats of war, defeats
> With plain heroic magnitude of mind
> And celestial vigour armed ;
> Their armouries and magazines contemns,—
> Renders them useless,——while
> With wingèd expedition,
> Swift as the lightning glance, he executes
> His errand on the wicked, who, surprised,
> Lose their defence, distracted and amazed.'
>
> MILTON. *Samson Agonistes.*

THE Calabrian Liberals were not altogether unworthy of
such a deliverer. The Garibaldini, who had seen little
to admire in the inhabitants of Eastern Sicily in spite of
all the facile enthusiasm at Messina, declared that when
they had crossed the Straits they soon found themselves
among ' a staid, manly, and athletic population.'

The Calabrians of those days were not unaccustomed
to war. For sixty years past they had from time to time
conducted guerilla campaigns for and against the Bourbons.
Some towns had always been on the side of reaction, like

147

Waterloo, forty years of obscurantist inquisition into every household by spies and police officers had left the restored Bourbons but few zealous adherents, and had made every man of spirit and intelligence their active enemy. In 1848 the Calabrian peasants had upheld the national cause with a valour that distinguished them among the populations of Southern Italy. In the reaction that followed, the leaders of the movement—doctors, professors, and landed proprietors—had gone into prison and into exile. Their day was now come. Francesco Stocco of the Thousand, the principal landlord of the Catanzaro district, reappeared among his own people, with the wound which he had received at Calatafimi yet unhealed. In 1860 feudal devotion was still strong in Calabria, and helped much to make the rising effective. Even in exile Stocco had been regarded as the real leader of the country, like a Highland chief living across the water after 1745. And now that he was among his people once more, they answered to his call as to that of a tribal king, who interpreted the will of Garibaldi the racial deity. Fortunately Stocco was a simple and disinterested man and used his authority well. *

* Plutino at Reggio, Morelli at Cosenza, Pace at Castrovillari, played the same part as Stocco at Catanzaro. The late Achille Fazzari (ob. 1910) was another younger Calabrian leader in 1860. A few months before he died, he sent Dr. Ashby and me in a boat from his house at Capanello, near Staletti, to visit the great sea-cave, a Cathedral choir of granite hollowed

mountain shepherds of
the fruit-bearing hills
plain of Maida, gathered
They pitched their cam
plateau of Campo Lung
prepared there to cut of
men. Vial still lay a
blocked his road to the
him from the south. Pi
retreat on the capital, b
sea, and he had only
used it to effect his
board with him a tho
bequeathed to General
should march back by la
leaving Otto with 10,000,
Calabria.

From the semaphore stat
leone, the grass-grown site of
could watch through his tele
Calabrians on the table-land
the high-road by which alor
Seeing himself thus cut off h
Dictator and begged for a fre
honours of

On August 26 the citizens of Catanzaro proclaimed the Dictator's government, while the town was still occupied by the Bourbon garrison. When it marched out next day towards Nicastro, it was surrounded and disarmed by the people of that region two days before the arrival of the Garibaldian vanguard. Meanwhile, the mountain shepherds of Aspromonte, and the farmers of the fruit-bearing hills that overlook the fever-stricken plain of Maida, gathered to a head under Francesco Stocco. They pitched their camp, several thousands strong, on the plateau of Campo Lungo, above the bridge of Angitola, and prepared there to cut off the retreat of Vial and his 12,000 men. Vial still lay at Monteleone, while Stocco thus blocked his road to the north, and Garibaldi advanced upon him from the south. Pianell had at length ordered him to retreat on the capital, but the only path left open was by sea, and he had only one steamer lying off Pizzo. He used it to effect his own escape to Naples, taking on board with him a thousand of his men. The rest he bequeathed to General Ghio, with instructions that they should march back by land. A thousand more disbanded, leaving Ghio with 10,000, the last Royalists in Lower Calabria.

From the semaphore station on the heights of Monteleone, the grass-grown site of an ancient Greek city, Ghio could watch through his telescope the bivouac of Stocco's Calabrians on th table-land of Campo Lungo, close above the high-road t which alone he could hope to retreat. Seeing himself 1 s cut off he sent a flag of truce to the Dictator and be d for a free passage to Naples with the honours of war On August 26 Ghio's messenger found

Volturno, became ; nd of Garibaldi, spent several years with him on Caprera, and receiv a as guest at Capanello in 1882, a few months before the hero's death.

horses and walked seven miles through the deep sand and
marshes of the plain, wading through rivers above the
knee. He thus arrived in time to welcome Medici's men
as they landed on the beach below Nicotera. Thence he
sent back Ghio's officer to Monteleone with a demand for
the unconditional surrender of the ten thousand.

At dawn on the 27th the Dictator posted over the
hills to Monteleone, by way of Mileto, where he rejoined
the vanguard of his army coming up from Rosarno by
the great trunk road. Mileto, situated half-way up the
long rise out of the plain to the heights of Monteleone,
was famed for the numbers of its clergy and of its brigands. The wealthy Bishop had fled, but the priests and
people welcomed Garibaldi and his men. In the middle
of the main street was to be seen a dried pool of blood
and the charred remnants of some large animal. On
that spot, two days before, the Bourbon troops had detected their general, Briganti, attempting to ride through
Mileto in civilian disguise. It was he who had so recently surrendered at Villa San Giovanni. They fell
upon him with cries of ' Traditore,' and emptied their
rifles into his body, which they stripped and mutilated in
beastly fashion, while others killed and burnt his horse.
All this took place in the open street of Mileto, beneath
the eyes of the regimental officers, who drank shame to

edge of the green and
whence the moral and
below seems to have b
ever since the ancient
ponium upon this plea
other travellers before
panorama of the Medi
nearer at hand the lon
city with its hospitable
life, its unexpected trea
Garibaldi himself, the fi
that is remembered in
in its civic life. For six
true to the cause of fr
of those
weeks past their town had be
the day before they had narr
hands of the soldiery who had
had been saved only by the
Marquis Gagliardi, the patriot
Garibaldi was among them,
arms crossed and head bowed
at the crowd below. ' Unwo
passing between him and the
pathy of

eral and a traitor, others because he was a Royalist,
ers because they wanted his boots.

Horrified, but encouraged by this evidence of the utter
oralisation of his enemies, Garibaldi, after a *siesta* in a
n at *Mileto*, drove on to Monteleone the same day,
g to receive the surrender of these wretched men.
e *afternoon* of the 27th his carriage mounted to the
f the green and prosperous table-land of Monteleone,
the moral and material squalor of the towns down
eems to have been banished by decree of nature,
ce the ancient Greeks founded their city of Hip-
upon this pleasant sward. The Garibaldini, like
vellers before and since, were enchanted by the
of the Mediterranean, Stromboli, Sicily, and
hand the long outline of Aspromonte; by the
its hospitable inhabitants, its free and cheerful
xpected treasures of statuary and architecture.
mself, the first to arrive, was given a welcome
embered in Monteleone as the greatest event
fe. For sixty years its inhabitants had been
cause of freedom, and for more than forty
: had been subject to cruel

on earth can alter them.' But it was the ...nce and not the words that dwelt most in the memory of some present.

There was, however, one cause for disappointment. Ghio's ten thousand, who had marched out of the town shortly before Garibaldi's arrival, were allowed by Stocco to march past him unchallenged. It appears that Sirtori had sent Stocco a message which he interpreted to mean that the Neapolitan troops had joined the national cause and were to be treated as brothers in arms. They were therefore allowed to file across the long bridge of Angitola, and below the wooded precipice of Campo Lungo under the eyes of Stocco's army, who stood at ease and cheered them as they passed. But Ghio's men were, in fact, still bearing arms against Garibaldi, and he had declared for nothing short of their unconditional surrender.

The mistake, whether due to Sirtori or to Stocco, called for instant remedy. If Ghio's men recovered their morale, or fell in with Caldarelli's troops in Upper Calabria, they might yet occupy one of the thousand strong mountain positions that barred the road to Naples and seriously delay the Dictator's advance. In any case he did not want 10,000 more added to the Royalist troops collecting for the defence of the capital. He therefore left Monteleone on the 28th at a hand gallop to ride down the fugitive army. He was partly accompanied and partly pursued by the mounted portion of his staff and by some English ladies* and gentlemen in a carriage. There were as yet no cavalry, so the rest of his men, with Stocco's bands well to the fore, were to come on behind as fast as their legs would carry them.

The country through which the race now ran, with its ever-changing views of mountain, plain, and sea, was rich in memories of the last sixty years of feud between revolution and reaction. First, they left behind them

* Jessie Mario and Corte's wife.

o, hanging on a cliff over the beach, with its squalid
castle where Murat had been shot, an eagle trapped
filthy cage and torn to pieces by vermin. At the
of La Grazia they passed a battle-field of '48. Then
d wound among low, fruit-laden hills, skirting the
na of Maida. On that seaward plain, half-covered
ushwood and cut by sandy streams and white
the British infantry, set ashore by our fleet in
6, had in half an hour of volley-firing proved
iority of the line-formation over the French
hich had carried all before it since the revolu-
s began.* The grand mountains looking down
le-field from north and east had been the scene
brian rising against the French that followed
h victory, when the methods of the reactionary
rified our officers, that many of them were
ven back to Sicily and swore never again to
devilry on the mainland.† Following up
he Amato, Garibaldi turned into the heart
ains, where far other political sentiments
ong the peasants, and, under his influence,
of warfare. Those blood-feuds of Bourbon
e marchings of foreign armies on the soil,
that was passing away, as the flag of

urier, who was in the battle, wrote: 'Avec nos
s égales, être défaits en si peu de minutes! Cela
révolution.' For the great effect of the lesson
tactics, see Mr. Oman's article, published by

is describes the character of the war between
labrian peasants: 'Ceux que nous attrapons,
quand ils nous prennent, ils nous brûlent le
Moi qui vous parle, Monsieur, je suis tombé
irer, il a fallu plusieurs miracles. J'assistai
de savoir si je serais pendu, brûlé ou fusillé.

saw with special delight that the Dictator was wearing the conical hat of Calabria. He and his friends had no baggage and no change of clothes ; each had one travel-stained red shirt, which was sometimes washed at the mid-day *siesta*, and put on again to dry as they rode forward under the scorching sun. In this guise the small group of horsemen climbed the steep ascent out of the Amato valley to the ancient town of Tiriolo, that hangs on the edge of the mountain-wall, 2000 feet above the Tyrrhenian and Ionian seas. Besides this simultaneous view of the two parts of the Mediterranean, the riders admired the gorgeous Calabrian costumes of the women which, then as now, were seen at their best in the neighbourhood of Tiriolo. Thence the trunk road runs northwards for a two days' journey to Cosenza, at an average height of over 2000 feet, through an endless succession of oak and chestnut forests, above the flanks of deep, wooded gorges, down which even in August and September the clear water went leaping and gurgling to the sea. In these altitudes Garibaldi overtook Ghio's army. On the evening of August 29, five miles beyond Tiriolo, he suddenly came in sight of the tail of the enemy's column winding round the flank of the mountain a few hundred yards in front. Since he had only half a dozen companions with him, he turned aside for the night into the neighbouring village of S.

close beneath still highe
village of Soveria-Mann
flat corn-land around, G
of Ghio's army of 10,00
without rearguard or
placed or out-posts occ
The men were disconsol
the officers were doing
they intended to proceed

Ghio had in fact aba
because he had learnt
miles to the north, was
of Upper Calabria. The
travelled, led by their feud
had already on August 27
General Caldarelli at Cosenza
to retreat with arms in their
had next proceeded to occ
that if Ghio crossed the wa
into the district of Cosenza
the south, Caldarelli would t
unite with the new-comers t
royal cause. On the summit
3000 feet

felt nothing.

t dawn he started on again to seize his prey. While sing sun flooded the peaks and valleys with light, lowed the road along the crest of a wooded ridge, opened out after six miles into the high cultivated nd of Soveria. At the farther end of this plateau, neath still higher mountains to the north, lay the of Soveria-Mannelli. In its long street and on the -land around, Garibaldi saw bivouacked the whole army of 10,000 men, packed like sheep in a fold, rearguard or advance-guard, without sentinels out-posts occupying the surrounding heights. were disconsolately cooking some stolen lambs; were doing nothing; there was no sign that ed to proceed with their march. l in fact abandoned the idea of further retreat, had learnt that the pass of Agrifoglio, five of Garibaldi. Under his direction trenches were dug and trees felled across the road up which Ghio would have to march. But Ghio, on being informed that Caldarelli had come to terms and that the summit of Agrifoglio pass was thus fortified against his own retreat, determined to proceed no further, but supinely to await the arrival of Garibaldi at Soveria.

There, throughout the morning of August 30, band after band of Stocco's Calabrians came in from Tiriolo and the south, exhausted with their forced march, but eager to be led into action. As fast as each arrived on the plateau, Garibaldi led them up into S. Tommaso village and the other hills to east and north of Soveria. Down below, the Bourbon troops still sat cooking their lambs, and watching Garibaldi's encircling movement with the fixed indifference of despair. In the course of the morning Mario, Peard, and the ex-priest Bianchi from the camp at Agrifoglio, severally entered the village and demanded the surrender of Ghio's army. They were received with courtesy by the General, and by some of the troops, while others were with difficulty restrained from shooting them. Soon after midday Garibaldi found himself at the head of 2000 of Stocco's Calabrians and a few of Cosenz' red-shirts ranged in a circle round the village below. He gave

several thousand of the the Calabrian bands of Sto of whom, thus armed, came in the Volturno campaign. Garibaldi for the first time s to mount a hundred caval hussars had trudged all the and sabres through the dust. were made over to them at sprang into the saddles with reared on the Magyar plain They seemed to the onlooke from tired tramps into knight joyfully into the forest in sea some glorious way to die.

In the midst of these sce in the squalid street of Sove Naples and handed a letter Alexandre Dumas, who had in his yacht. He wrote tha view with Liborio Romano, of the King and by far th Naples.* 'Liborio,' wrote Du together with at least

llow-Calabrians
see the coming
were dug and
would have to
Caldarelli had
Agrifoglio pass
determined to
the arrival of

ʒust 30, band
1 from Tiriolo
d march, but
ch arrived on
ımmaso village
overia. Down
; their lambs,
ıent with the
ıf the morning
ɪrom the camp
and demanded
e received with
he troops, while
shooting them.
ɪlf at the head
of Cosenz' red-
ɪelow. He gave
ıntly and slowly

10,000 rifles and twelve cannon, and without more ado disbanded, each to his home or to a life of brigandage.

Several thousand of the rifles were distributed among the Calabrian bands of Stocco, Pace, and Morelli, many of whom, thus armed, came on to Naples and took part in the Volturno campaign. The captured horses enabled Garibaldi for the first time since he had crossed the Straits to mount a hundred cavalry. Hitherto his Hungarian hussars had trudged all the way, trailing their huge spurs and sabres through the dust. But when the enemy's horses were made over to them at Soveria, the gallant gentlemen sprang into the saddles with the alacrity of a cavalier race reared on the Magyar plains to horsemanship and war. They seemed to the onlookers to be suddenly transfigured from tired tramps into knights of old romance galloping off joyfully into the forest in search of dragons and giants and some glorious way to die.

In the midst of these scenes of confusion and triumph in the squalid street of Soveria a messenger arrived from Naples and handed a letter to Garibaldi. It was from Alexandre Dumas, who had recently gone to the capital in his yacht. He wrote that he had obtained an interview with Liborio Romano, now the principal Minister of the King and by far the most influential person in Naples.* 'Liborio,' wrote Dumas, ' is at your disposition, together with at least two of his fellow-Ministers, at the first attempt at reaction on the King's part. At this first attempt which will set him free from his oath of fidelity, senger as fast as horses could carry him, again leaving his army days behind upon the road. Two fears drew him on to the capital at his topmost speed : the fear that anarchy, massacre, or civil war would break out before his arrival ; and the fear that Cavour and Victor Emmanuel would seize the reins of power in Naples, and so bring to an end his Dictatorship and with it his chance of invading the Papal States.

Meanwhile, the other detachments of his army scattered along the road between Scilla and Tiriolo were toiling after the vanguard by forced marches. It was the hottest period of the year, cooled by occasional thunder-storms. There was no proper commissariat, and the food of the country was scarce, especially for the rearguard who followed where Ghio's 10,000 and their own main body had already swept the villages clean. Fruit was in season, and in some places on the route abundant ; few of Garibaldi's followers could, like their leader, be satisfied with a bunch of grapes, a cigar, and the thought of Italy as a substitute for a day's rations. Everything taken was paid for at a good price, and grape-thieves were liable to be shot. Once at least the corpse of a red-shirt, laid out between the vinevards and the road, warned the passing

usual Garibaldian short rati
the hungrier Saxon race ;
muted for imprisonment.

The liberated population
welcome, and profuse of al
had to offer ; but in those
civilisation in Calabria and
meagre kind.* Hunger, expo
march made the race to Nap
cal tests of patriotic endura
mother of the Cairoli anothe
of typhus contracted on the
were left behind disabled. B
suared in the march, admir
restraint of the Italian volunte

The Dictator, at first on
carriage, was forging on ahe
Five miles above Soveria, on
of Agrifoglio which divides U
he was greeted with wild del
had blocked the pass there ag
he galloped along the well-er

were condemned to be shot for plundering on the north bank of the Volturno, where they had been left on the usual Garibaldian short rations, an intolerable torture to the hungrier Saxon race; but their sentence was commuted for imprisonment.

The liberated populations were enthusiastic in their welcome, and profuse of all the hospitality which they had to offer; but in those days the material resources of civilisation in Calabria and Basilicata were of the most meagre kind.* Hunger, exposure, and the ceaseless forced march made the race to Naples one of the severest physical tests of patriotic endurance. It took away from the mother of the Cairoli another of her boys, Luigi, who died of typhus contracted on the road: and many stronger men were left behind disabled. Both French and English, who shared in the march, admired the endurance and self-restraint of the Italian volunteers.

The Dictator, at first on horseback, later in an open carriage, was forging on ahead with a few companions. Five miles above Soveria, on the top of the water-shed of Agrifoglio which divides Upper from Lower Calabria, he was greeted with wild delight by the Calabrians who had blocked the pass there against Ghio's army. Thence he galloped along the well-engineered road which leads

* Those Garibaldini who had the fortune, good or ill, to be received into the houses of the hospitable Calabrians, had to be prepared for an evil which I will veil for the English reader in the decent obscurity of Luigi Cairoli's

down the side of a forest gorge o   lpine pro]
Carpanzano and Rogliano, and thence he pushe
the same afternoon to Cosenza. The capital
Calabria is built on the steep sides of three
hills above the meeting-place of two mountain
in one of which, the Busento, Alaric the Goth lies
At nightfall on the last evening of August, Gariba
welcomed into the streets of the city lit up in his hon

There were memories at Cosenza. Here, sixteen
before, one of Italy's forlorn hopes had perished :
attack of a handful of idealists, led by Ricciotti and
brothers Bandiera against the Bourbons in the pleni
of their power, had here come to its tragic, premedita
end, in order to teach Italians by example a lesson whi
many had since learnt, how to die for their countr
Garibaldi well remembered how the news had reache
his penurious household in Montevideo, and how Anita
and he had named their second-born after Ricciotti.*
The most sacred place in Cosenza was a nameless slab
in an aisle of the Cathedral under which the bodies lay.
The victors of 1860 all went to do it honour. Garibaldi
himself had not time to visit the other scene, four miles
distant in the mountains, where the execution of the
Bandieras had taken place. But after he had passed
on his way, when, some days later, the main body of his
followers began to arrive at Cosenza, nothing could restrain them from marching out, regiment after regiment,
to see the water-washed stones in the torrent bed below
Rovito, where their forerunners had dropped one by one
before the firing-party, with the forbidden name of Italy
upon their lips. There the regiments stood bareheaded,
while Nino Bixio addressed his men in words of fire.

During the short night that Garibaldi spent at Cosenza

* See *Garibaldi's Defence of Rome*, chap. ii.

Papal States, but which Cavour and Garibaldi had between them diverted to Sicily and the south.* When the Dictator learnt from Bertani that 1500 men lay ready to his hand at Paola, with transports at their disposal, he sent Türr down to the coast to take over the command and carry them forward by sea from Paola to Sapri. In this way a force that Bertani had raised in the interest of the advanced Mazzinian party passed under the control of Türr, the most Cavourian of Garibaldi's lieutenants. Bertani, concealing his chagrin, attached himself to the person of the Dictator, and began, after they had travelled together for a few days, to recover the influence which he seemed recently to have lost. Meanwhile Türr rode down from Cosenza to Paola, took command of the troops collected there, and carried them by sea to Sapri, where they arrived on September 2, twenty-four hours before Garibaldi himself. In this way these 1500 men from the rear became the vanguard of the advance on Naples, owing to their good fortune in finding transports while the others had to march by land.

At three in the morning of September 1, Garibaldi with Cosenz and Bertani left Cosenza in an open carriage, pursued and gradually overtaken by a second carriage containing Peard with an English party. All morning their wheels ploughed through twenty miles of sandy high-road along the desolate banks of the Upper Crati. On each side the mountains shut in the long valley bottom,

* See p. 140 above. They had crossed from Sicily to Tropea, marched

a flat surface two miles broad over
and rapid river spreads itself uncorrec.
irregular channels, hidden from the eye
wood, trees, and reeds of the marsh. 1
the watery jungle is called, unreclaimed by
beginning of time, seems fantastically out o
sole occupant of a broad and well-watered
looks, when first seen from distant hills, to
Val d'Arno or Upper Tiber. But the sand
deterred Greek, Roman, and modern Italian .
introducing civilisation or agriculture into the up₁
of the Crati. Even the hills around were thinly i.
and notorious for brigands. At length, at noon, th.
road led the travellers up out of this gigantic ditch
the heights of Tarsia and thence to Spezzano Alb.
where the Albanian colonists, like their kinsmen of 1
dei Greci, near Palermo, three months before, greeted
Dictator even more warmly, if that were possible, th.
the Italian villages along the road. From the hill
Spezzano, Garibaldi—and his army, when it followed
during the next week—gazed over the plain of Sybaris,
bounded on three sides by peaked mountains, and on the
fourth by the Gulf of Taranto. The view resembles that
of the Campagna from Tivoli, save that there is no Rome.
Like Anio and Tiber, the lower reaches of the ancient
Crathis and its tributaries still wander through the vast
plain to the sea; but there is no city, no civilisation, and
no history save the knowledge that somewhere in that
comfortless expanse, now breeding death at night, stood
once Sybaris, mother of luxury. The site is unknown;
Sybaris has disappeared as completely as Sodom and
Gomorrah, though not by any catastrophe of nature.
Only her name is left as a proverb of degeneracy, but whether
the Sybarites deserved such eternal censure more than

»ut of place as the
itered valley, that
lls, to be another
ie sandy soil had
Italian alike from
o the upper valley
'e thinly inhabited
it noon, the trunk
;antic ditch on to
»ezzano Albanese,
kinsmen of Piana
;fore, greeted the
re possible, than
?rom the hill of
hen it followed
)lain of Sybaris,
ains, and on the
íiew resembles that
there is no Rome.
;es of the ancient
through the vast
;o civilisation, and
»mewhere in that
h at night, stood
site is unknown;
as Sodom and

swarming with birds like an English park. Thence he mounted to Castrovillari one of the pleasantest towns south of Rome, a rival in importance to Cosenza, and a great centre of revolution that year under the leadership of Pace. Castrovillari stands in the midst of a fruitful plateau, raised half-way between the plain of Sybaris below and the limestone peaks of the Monte Pollino, which tower above to a height of 7000 feet. The old town with its mediæval churches and palaces is built in pleasing disorder round the edge of some precipitous cañons which here cleave the plateau. But already in 1860 the old town was falling into disrepair in favour of the more cheerful modern streets, long, straight, and spacious, in which stood Pace's house, the centre of the insurrection, and on this night the headquarters of Garibaldi.

Next morning (September 2) he passed on across the luxuriant plain that lies close at the foot of Monte Pollino, rivalling Tuscany in wealth of vegetation, and thence passed at once into the regions of naked limestone, the heart of the mountains which divide Calabria from Basilicata. At the top of the first pass he entered the Campo Tenese, a meadow 3000 feet above the sea, and several miles in extent, enclosed on all sides by mountains. Here in a snowstorm in 1806 the French had put the army of the Bourbons to rout. At the far end of the Campo Tenese Garibaldi climbed another pass,* and thence descended

out of Calabria into the Basilicata. Th
he reached in the new province was
Rotonda, where he found the National G
paraphernalia of revolutionary authority a
as if it had been Paris, or Cosenza at the lea

At Rotonda a change took place in Garil
of travelling. Hitherto he had kept to the
road the whole way from the Straits of Mes
now, close in front of him on that road, were Gen
elli's troops, retreating on Naples with arms in tl
according to the agreement which they had m
the revolutionary committee of Cosenza. If
ceeded farther, he would find himself at Castellu
the midst of these demoralised Royalist troops.
intentions were doubtful, perhaps even to thems
At one moment Caldarelli sent a message to Gari
at Rotonda saying, ' This army of yours puts itself at y
orders ; ' at the next he was promising to his soldiers ı
victory of the Bourbon cause through the intervention ꞇ
Austria. The Dictator's friends wisely persuaded him noꞇ
to trust himself defenceless among these men, who might
shoot him as readily as one of their own generals, but to
go round by the mountains and the sea to Sapri, where he
would find Türr's 1500 men newly come from Paola. With
them he could march up to Lagonegro, present himself
there in force upon the line of Caldarelli's retreat, and
negotiate with him under more favourable conditions.

So on the night of September 2, the General and six
companions, including Bertani and Cosenz, left the high-
road at Rotonda and, mounted on mules, rode towards the
coast through the western mountains. Near Laino they
entered the trackless gorge of the Lao River, and followed
it down by the light of the moon for several miles. ' Here
we are,' cried Bertani, ' seven of us on seven mules, going

t to the great trunk
s of Messina. But
were General Caldar-
arms in their hands,
hey had made with
enza. If he pro-
f at Castelluccio in
list troops. Their
ven to themselves.
essage to Garibaldi
s puts itself at your
to his soldiers the
the intervention of
persuaded him not
e men, who might
n generals, but to
to Sapri, where he
from Paola. With
ro, present himself
relli's retreat, and
le conditions.
e General and six
enz, left the high-
rode towards the
Near Laino they
ver and followed

of Italy than this unvisited riviera, where the precipitous ridges run out one beyond another and sink into the waves.* The rugged coast is best seen from a boat, but Garibaldi, exhausted by the night's ride, lay asleep in the prow, while his friends covered him with a sail to protect him from the rays of the noonday sun. Only as they entered the bay of Sapri they all stood up to gaze on the beauty of the scene, and to honour the memory of Pisacane, who, in 1857, had run into this bay to raise the Italian flag upon the mountains.† On the beach where his forerunner had landed under the shadow of doom, Garibaldi stepped ashore on the full tide of victory, welcomed as '*fratello Garibaldi*' by the people of Sapri, who three years before had frowned on Pisacane and his more questionable following. Here also the Dictator found Türr's troops, who had sailed in the day before from Paola.

There is a fine beach, but no artificial landing-place at Sapri. Only there may be seen in the clear water the ruins of an ancient pier. It runs out from the foundations of a palace built long ago by some magnate of Imperial Rome, who discovered the beauty of the little bay, and carried thither the whole apparatus of ancient luxury, leaving less adventurous pleasure-seekers at Puteoli and Baiae. Some modern Lucullus will imitate him ere long. Meanwhile Garibaldi landed there and spent the night in a straw hut upon the beach.

* There is not ...

Next day the Dictator and Türr's
Milanese, marched up all morning fro.
cipitous forest paths to a shoulder of Mo1
thence descended on the Lagonegro hi,
which Caldarelli and his men were retreat1
here runs at an average level of over 20.
point where Garibaldi dropped down on it f1
was the wayside tavern of Il Fortino. Here,
ber 4, he was overtaken by Piola, an officer o.
montese navy, whom Depretis, his Pro-Dictator
had sent on commission to persuade him to pe
immediate annexation of the island to the domi.
Victor Emmanuel. Türr and Cosenz, the soldiers in .
ance on the General, eagerly seconded Piola, begging
chief to allow Sicily to be annexed on condition that De,
should for the present continue to govern it as V1
Emmanuel's lieutenant, and that supplies of men and mo1
should continue to be sent from Sicily to the Garibaldi.
camp. Garibaldi yielded to their entreaties, and ha.
actually dictated to his secretary the words, ' Dear Depretis,
have the annexation made whenever you like,' when Bertani came in upon them from the other compartment of the
tavern and caught his Cavourian rivals in the act. ' General,'
said the agitator, ' you are abdicating ; ' and in spite of
all that Türr and Cosenz could say, Bertani in a few minutes
persuaded him to rely for the further liberation of Italy
not on the co-operation of Cavour and the Piedmontese
Government, but on the men and money which, so Bertani
declared, would be supplied in unlimited quantities by
Sicily and by the provinces of Naples as fast as they
were liberated. The half-written letter was torn up and
another was sent, bidding Depretis delay the annexation
yet awhile.

Bertani's triumph at this unlucky pothouse of Il

the way for the struggle between Gari-
di and the Government of Turin, which during the
uing months marred with unseemly altercation the
mn act of the Making of Italy. Depretis was right, if Garibaldi could
time had come to annex Sicily, he had refused to
have seen it. When in June have prevented him
w annexation because it would been right and Cavour
1 crossing the Straits, he had could have no object in
1g. But in September he except to keep himself
1er delaying the annexation, and Venice, or otherwise
to attack the cities of Rome of Victor Emmanuel's
1wart and embroil the policy Fortino he had known
sters. It is possible that if at Il vading the Papal terri-
Cavour was on the point of invaded Bertani's advice and
; himself, he might have rejected with the Piedmontese
nted to work hand in hand
mment.

eanwhile, the military business in hand was to catch
relli and his three thousand. On September 3,
leaving Lagonegro, Caldarelli had again assured
1ldi's emissaries that he and all his men intended
;ert to the side of the nation. He had, however,
ued his retreat on Naples, and had passed through
tino a few hours before Garibaldi struck into the
t that point. On September 5 he was finally over-
near Padula, where Pisacane had three years before
feated by the Royalist troops under Ghio. There

At Casalnuovo, on September 5,
by Mignona, Governor in his name o1
Basilicata, which had declared for him 1
night before while he was engaged in cros
The 'Lucanians,' as the men of Basilicat
selves in memory of classical times, sent
nona a good will offering of 6000 ducats (2
and raised a 'Lucanian brigade,' which fo.
baldi to Naples. Thence 900 returned hom
remaining 1200 took part in the Volturno campai

From Casalnuovo the Dictator raced on in
carriage through the Province of Principato
As he drew nearer to the capital its corrupting i
became ever more apparent in the moral degra
of the people, and warlike volunteers were no
forthcoming. But south of Naples there were no
of reactionary feeling. All along the road the people
the local authorities vied with each other in the frenzy
their enthusiasm, which was compounded of joy at delive.
ance from a cruel and inquisitorial tyranny, interestec
subservience to the rulers of the hour, and good human
devotion, in which also superstition had a part, for the
person of the almost mythical Garibaldi.*

For several days, however, these semi-divine honours
were paid to the wrong person. Peard, 'Garibaldi's
Englishman,' as he posted along the road from Sala Consilina to Eboli, was universally taken for the Liberator
himself. He was accompanied during this strange ad-

* One Garibaldi legend, seriously told and believed a few years later,
was to this effect. Once when his army was in need of water, Garibaldi
fired a cannon at a rock and water gushed out. This adaptation of a Bible
story to modern conditions is a curious example of the growth of hagiology.
If Garibaldi and his educated followers had been professional traders on
popular superstition, it would have been easy in the 'sixties to have set up
a Garibaldian Lourdes in South Italy, and to have worked profitable cures
with red-shirts.

Fabrizi, who was commissioned by the Dictator to su[rvey] the military positions in advance. These men, having the capacity of non-combatants passed through Caldarelli, column prior to its disbandment, had kept the high-road the whole way from Cosenza, and had thus gained fifty miles on Garibaldi, who had been forced to go round by the coast. In the afternoon of September 3, while the Dictator was sailing into the bay of Sapri, Peard was entering Auletta amid a scene of tremendous enthusi- asm. The people,' he noted in his diary, 'thought I was Garibaldi, and it was thought that it would do good to yield to the delusion. It became a nuisance, for deputa- tions arrived from all the neighbourhood to kiss my excel- lency's hand, and I had to hold regular levées.' The town was illuminated and *Te Deum* sung in honour of his arrival.

Next day, while the real Garibaldi was weaving and un- weaving the web of his uncertain policy in the tavern at Il Fortino, Peard and Fabrizi, accompanied by National Guard, brass bands, and people of Auletta, ascended to the hamlet of Postiglione, where they found every one 'mad with excitement. At the Syndic's, one of the priests (there were numbers of the fraternity present) went on his knees,' writes Peard, 'and called me a second Jesus Christ. I was not prepared for so excessive a bit of blas- phemy.' Postiglione hangs on the side of Monte Alburno, commanding a view of the plain of Eboli with the gulf and mountains of Salerno beyond. Somewhere in that plain or in those mountains, as Fabrizi and Peard well knew, Francis II. must fight for Naples, or else abandon his capital without a blow. Twelve thousand of his soldiers lay in Salerno and on the pass of Cava behind it; * the plain

* See Map IV., end of book.

plains of Eboli, the steep wall of mountains behind Salerno would still form a natural barrier, protecting the approaches to Naples.

Peard and Fabrizi determined to take advantage of their strange situation to spread such reports as would strike panic into the enemy's headquarters and lead to the abandonment of these all-important positions. In pursuance of this design they hastened on to Eboli on the evening of September 4, at some risk of being caught there by the enemy's patrols or arrested by the local authorities, who had not yet come within the sphere of the advancing revolution. But the pseudo-Garibaldi brought the revolution with him wherever he appeared. 'Within half an hour of our arrival,' wrote Commander Forbes, Eboli 'was brilliantly illuminated, the entire population besieging the Syndic's, brass bands banging away in every direction, and the crowd roaring them-

telegraph, who appeared t
between a file of the Nat
the Neapolitan general com

and Garibaldi's movemen
announcing Garibaldi's pr
ing to four or five thousa
he had close at hand.
Caldarelli's brigade had
marching with the nationa
were inaccurate, but they
both at Salerno and in th
with Peard, wired the sam
Naples closely connected
The belief, erroneous in fa
gone over of their own acc
one to expect that the tr

tried to persuade some of the leading men that Peard was not Garibaldi. 'Oh! you're quite right to try and keep your secret,' they replied, 'but you know it won't do, we know.' The gigantic Englishman did not, in fact, resemble the Nizzard at all closely, but his greater height and longer beard in no way impaired the belief of the people that they had the hero among them.

Peard and his Italian companions of the jest decided to turn the absurd situation to serious account. Shortly before midnight they sent for the official in charge of the telegraph, who appeared trembling before the 'Dictator' between a file of the National Guard. He reported that the Neapolitan general commanding at Salerno had an hour before wired for information about Caldarelli's brigade and Garibaldi's movements. Peard dictated the reply, announcing Garibaldi's presence at Eboli and exaggerating to four or five thousand the number of troops that he had close at hand. Above all, he announced that Caldarelli's brigade had changed sides and was now marching with the national forces. All these statements were inaccurate, but they appear to have been believed both at Salerno and in the capital. Gallenga, who was with Peard, wired the same reports to private friends in Naples closely connected with the Court and Ministry. The belief, erroneous in fact, that Caldarelli's men had gone over of their own accord to the invaders, led every one to expect that the troops at Salerno would do the same, unless they were withdrawn before Garibaldi could reach them from Eboli. Thus the misleading reports circulated by Peard and Gallenga, and the presence of the supposed Garibaldi at so short a distance from Salerno, were among the influences which induced Francis II. not to fight for his capital. This decision was taken beyond of September 5, when the com-

mander-in-chief at Naples telegraphed to Marshal Afan
de Rivera at Salerno, ordering all the troops at Salerno
to retreat by way of Cava to Nocera.

Meanwhile, the pseudo-Garibaldi and his party, not
knowing that their bluff would succeed in scaring the
enemy away, escaped unnoticed from Eboli in the
small hours of the morning. Peard returned as far as
Sala Consilina to meet the real Garibaldi, who heartily
approved what he had done. When they heard that the
Royalists had evacuated their positions, Peard hastened
forward again at Garibaldi's request, and entered Salerno
in triumph at five in the morning of September 6. The
whole town turned out to welcome 'the Dictator,' who received deputations in public all the morning, detected by
no one in authority or out of it, except by a single officer
who whispered him in the ear.

In the course of the morning the Piedmontese vessel
Authion appeared off Salerno and set ashore Evelyn
Ashley, son of the good Lord Shaftesbury, and private
secretary to Lord Palmerston. The young man, to the
intense delight of his chief, had gone out to spend his
holidays with Garibaldi instead of with the partridges.
A few days before, Ashley had presented himself to Cavour
in Turin, with a letter of introduction from the British
Prime Minister, and had asked where he could find Garibaldi. 'Garibaldi! Who is he?' said Cavour, with a
twinkle in his eye. 'I have nothing to do with him. . . .
He is somewhere in the Kingdom of the Two Sicilies,
I believe, but that is not, you know, at present under
my King.' However, Cavour put Ashley on board the
Authion, and sent him to search for himself. He took with
him Mr. Edwin James, Q.C., and at Naples fell in with
others of his fellow-countrymen, with whom he continued
to coast southwards. Off Salerno they saw flags and

the shouting of a vast multitude in the town. On being informed that it betokened the arrival of Garibaldi, the Englishmen landed, only to find that it was in reality by this time exceedingly anxious to be relieved his task of impersonation. He asked his compatriots and meet Garibaldi and hasten his coming. On the English party met hundreds of disbanded Royalist troops, unarmed, starving, and in the last state of misery, dragging themselves home along the road, or lying prostrate by the wayside. Garibaldi had shared with them all the money he had at hand, but their condition was pitiable. Arrived in Eboli, Ashley found the Dictator, who greeted him warmly as England's emissary, and allowed him to follow his staff as a non-combatant, on the sole condition that the new-comer should wear his simple livery, in order to be safe from maltreatment in the confusion of the times. And so our Premier's secretary donned the red shirt.

At five in the evening of September 6 the Dictator and his staff entered Salerno in a string of open carriages, two days' march in front of his nearest troops, the 1500 under Türr, and many days in front of the rest of the army. Outside the town he was met by the Syndic, the National Guard, and his English precursor, now deposed. *Viva Garibaldi!* he cried, taking off his hat in mock homage to Peard, and every one joined in the cry with shouts of laughter and applause. Darkness fell as they forced their way one step at a time into Salerno, amid the delirium of 20,000 people, who seemed desirous to tear the real Garibaldi in pieces. The town was illuminated, and all the heights far away towards Amalfi and Sorrento were ablaze with fires of joy.

On the same evening the last of the Bourbons and his queen were leaving the Palace of Naples by the water-gate and taking ship for Gaeta.

CHAPTER VIII

THE ENTRY INTO NAPLES

‘ Venu è Galubardo !
Venu è lu più bel ! ’
Neapolitan Song of 1860.

THE flight of King Francis from Naples on September 6 was but the final catastrophe in a process of dissolution which had set in with the news of the fall of Palermo and the consequent proclamation of constitutional rights in June. Freedom of press and person had effectively and instantly broken up the machinery of repression. The police had, in Liborio Romano's conjuring hands, been turned in a few days into an instrument of Liberalism. The King had handed over the civil administration to his enemies, and had gained nothing in return except the diplomatic support of France that failed him at every crisis. At home the constitution won over to him a few individuals, but no class or party. The decadent nobility of the capital, the peasants of certain districts in the northern provinces, and the bulk of the army remained loyal, not because of the constitution, but in spite of it. Every one else was looking to Piedmont. The perfidy of his ancestors divided King Francis from his people. Remembering the fate of the constitutions of 1820 and 1848, the citizens refused to enroll themselves on the electoral lists, because in case of reaction the appearance of their names on the register might be used against them as evidence of treason. And when Garibaldi in August came marching up through the constituencies, all talk of holding elections for Parliament ceased.

The King suspected his Ministers, though most of were passively loyal. Above all and with good reason he hated Don Liborio Romano. But Don Liborio, like Lafayette in the autumn of 1789, was the man of the hour with whom neither Court nor people could dispense: he had at his beck and call the police, the National Guard of respectable burghers, and the camorra of criminals. So King Francis had to endure him throughout all July and August, first as Police Minister only and then as Minister of the Interior also. In the latter half of August, Don Liborio held confidential interviews on the subject of coming events with the Dictator's friends in Naples, with the Piedmontese admiral, Persano, and with the King's uncle, the Count of Syracuse, who had already openly declared for a change of dynasty. Persano wrote to Cavour that Don Liborio was helping the cause of national unity ' so far as he was permitted by his very delicate situation ' as Minister of Francis II.

His object, however, was not actively to compass the destruction of his master, which he regarded as already certain, but to prevent the fall of the dynasty from involving in its ruin the public peace and safety. For this reason, as well as for the satisfaction of his own vanity, he had accepted office in June, and for this reason he determined to remain in power during the days or hours that must elapse between the fall of Francis II. and the establishment of any new form of government. If he forced the King to accept his resignation, the camorra would, he believed, break loose in the great city, which contained a larger proportion of criminally disposed persons than any other in Europe, the Royal troops would begin to fight with the National Guard, and disasters of the most appalling character might occur. The respectable part of the citizens took the same view, begging Don Liborio and his colleagues to retain office under the Crown at any sacrifice to their own dignity or honour. And those who knew best the Naples of those days were the least inclined to deny the claim afterwards put forward by the discredited politician that he saved the capital from destruction.

Meanwhile, the Cavourian agents were striving in vain to precipitate a revolution. Villamarina, the Piedmontese Minister at Naples, and Admiral Persano, who arrived there with his fleet from Sicily at the beginning of August, lent their aid to Finzi and Visconti Venosta, to Nisco, D'Ayala, and Nunziante in their attempts to win over the army and incite the civilians to resolute action. But the army remained loyal, in spite of the propaganda of the popular general, Nunziante, among his old companions in arms, and in spite of the blandishments of the Piedmontese Bersaglieri. Some companies of the latter were allowed to land off Persano's ships and to show themselves in the streets, partly in order to encourage the population to revolt and partly in order to fraternise with the Neapolitan troops, who replied by breaking their heads.

The citizens were more sympathetic but not more active than the soldiers. The Neapolitans did not see the use of doing at the risk of their own skins what Garibaldi was coming to do for them. Moreover, the Mazzinian 'Committee of Action,' which contained the bolder and more energetic spirits, had resolved to wait for the Dictator's arrival, fearing that if they rose before he appeared on the scene, Naples would fall at once into the hands of Cavour; while the Cavourian 'Committee of Order,' which would fain have seen a revolution effected while Garibaldi was still on his way, consisted of 'moderate men,' unfitted by nature to initiate a revolt.

The motives of Cavour's policy throughout August are relatively clear to those who will read them in the light of two established facts : first, that he had, in the last days of July, persuaded Russell to permit Garibaldi's passage of the Straits ; and secondly, that he had as early as August I made up his mind to invade the Papal provinces with the Piedmontese army. His desire was, without more delay, to possess himself of Naples and so to forestall a Garibaldian Dictatorship; while at the same time he would invade the Papal States, and so link up the north and south of the Peninsula in one free monarchy. It was only because he feared that the revolution in Naples would perhaps miss fire without the help of the guerilla, that he had persuaded Russell to let him cross from Sicily to the mainland. Even after he had taken this step as a measure of insurance in case of his own failure, he continued to work for the overthrow of Francis II. through his own agents, and since time was needed for this experiment, he was not sorry to see the Dictator kept waiting three weeks at the Straits. That is the reason why in the first days of August he wrote to Admiral Persano, ' Do not help the passage of General Garibaldi on to the continent, but rather try to delay him, by indirect means, as far as possible.'

When the Dictator had safely crossed and was beginning his march through Calabria, Cavour caused arms to be landed at Salerno and distributed among the rebels of the south, 'in order to open out the way for Garibaldi's advance.' But at the same time he made a last effort to obtain possession of Naples for his own party, writing to Villamarina on August 27, ' Do all you can to avoid a Garibaldian Dictatorship, on which you count too much.' He instructed Persano to accept the Dictatorship if it was offered to him. Even now Cavour shrank from the one sure method of avoiding the Garibaldian regime in Naples, which he so much dreaded—namely, an open declaration of war by Piedmont on King Francis—because, as he told Villamarina, that would ' compromise us altogether with Europe.' By ' Europe ' he meant most of all Napoleon, with whom he was at that moment secretly negotiating for leave to attack the Papal territory.

A few days later he saw that he had lost the race for Naples. On August 30, while the Dictator was receiving the surrender of Ghio's ten thousand at Soveria, Cavour wrote to Villamarina acknowledging defeat and bidding him abandon all thought of forming a Government at Naples independent of Garibaldi. ' You must act frankly in unison with him, trying only to get the fleet and the forts into our hands.'

Although Cavour failed actually to overturn Francis II. before the arrival of Garibaldi, the prestige of the Royal family and of the Royalist party was rapidly melting away throughout the whole of August. The National Guard, the police, the citizens, and the Piedmontese agents were all in a tacit conspiracy against the King and his soldiers, and whenever any of the latter gave vent to their feelings by rioting in the streets, their bad discipline was pointed to as proof that Francis II. intended to destroy the constitution by military force. A series of half-hearted reactionary plots were unearthed by Don Liborio's police, and their details published to the further discomfiture of the King. In one of these conspiracies his uncle, the Count of Aquila, was supposed to be implicated. Aquila had been for a few weeks an ardent constitutionalist, but he had rejoined the ultra-Royalists in the hope, it was said, of displacing his incompetent nephew in their affections. On August 14 the Ministers succeeded in driving him

exile, under cover of sending him on a foreign mission.*

On August 20 Don Liborio presented to the King his Memorandum, in which he tried to persuade his to retire from the Kingdom ' for some time,' leav- regent ' a Minister who would inspire public con- .' In this way alone, wrote Don Liborio, could orrors of civil war' be averted, seeing that mutual ' the h nce between the people and their prince ' has become confide y difficult but impossible.' Four days after Francis not onl eived this broad hint from his principal Minister had re of State , he was made the target of a public letter from his uncle of Syracuse, in which the Count exhorted his nephew to sacrifice his throne on behalf of the glorious idea of Italian unity. Such language from a prince of the blood produced a very general impression that all was now lost. Syracuse had shown the letter to Persano in his flag-ship five days before it appeared.

The ever-shifting intentions and intrigues of the King and his many rival counsellors during the last fortnight of Bourbon rule in Naples are known to us at present chiefly through the narratives of Liborio Romano and of General Pianell and his wife. These represent the con-stitutional party alone, and even so are inconsistent with each other on several important points. Unless other documents come to light, the historian will never be able to trace confidently and in detail the story of those days of cowardice, treachery, confusion, and panic. Only the main outline of events is clear.†

* What led at last to the decision to send him off was the arrival of three cases of revolvers and one case of pictures of him waving his hat, which had fallen into the hands of the Government.

† Pianell's own narrative unfortunately stops at the end of the month. His wife's goes on longer and is a contemporary journal; but on the other hand, she could only record what her husband told her each day. The

It was agreed by all parties in the Palace that the presence of the King himself in the field was necessary if the demoralised troops were ever to face Garibaldi again. It was also common ground that the Capital should be spared and should not, like Palermo, be made the scene of conflict. The main division of opinion between constitutionalists and reactionaries arose on the question whether the King should go south to defend the Capital in the plains of Eboli and the mountains of Salerno, or whether he should abandon Naples and retire north with all the loyal troops in the Kingdom behind the line of the Volturno. In the latter case he could base his new position on the strongly fortified towns of Capua and Gaeta, which might prove for him what the quadrilateral had been to Austria in 1848—a rock of refuge on which the rebels would vainly waste their strength, until the time was ripe for a Royalist counter-attack and a triumphal return to the Capital. Against Garibaldi, who had no siege guns and no siege science, the plan had a fair likelihood of success, as subsequent events showed. It was a political as well as a military move, for the retreat northwards would mean the abandonment of the tricolour in favour of the old white flag of the Bourbons, the burying of the constitution and a frank return to reaction on the *Bomba* model. The removal of the soldiers from the Capital northwards would enable them to indulge their loyalist sentiments freely in a more favourable atmosphere. Don Liborio and his colleagues would remain in Naples, while the Queen-Dowager and her reactionary clique were already at Gaeta waiting for the King. The reactionary peasants of the Volturno

Pianells are more trustworthy witnesses than Don Liborio, yet modern histories have relied almost entirely on Don Liborio alone. Whitehouse's excellent book was written before the publication of the Pianell papers. What we most want is some analogous narrative by a member of the *camarilla* or reactionary Court Party.

district were already threatening the lives of the local
Liberals. The Papal border and the Papal army were
near the rear of Gaeta.

It may therefore be supposed that the advice to retreat behind the Volturno originated from the King's
secret advisers of the ultra-Royalist party. As early as
August 27 his constitutional Ministers found that he was
meditating such a retreat. But his purposes wavered
from day to day and from hour to hour, and only the sound
of the approaching footsteps of Garibaldi could bring him
to the point of a resolve.

On August 29 his Ministers for their part urged him
to go south and head the troops at Salerno in defence of
the Capital and the constitution, though it is difficult to
suppose that they wished him a complete victory.

On the same day the reactionaries, headed by Count
Trapani, another of the King's uncles, were hatching a
plot to arrest the Ministers. The loyalist proclamation
which was to have been published as the watchword of
this *coup d'état* was seized overnight by Don Liborio's
police, and produced at the council-board by the indignant
men against whom it had been aimed. King Francis, red
with mingled anger and embarrassment, gasped out that
he agreed with much in the proclamation, and gave his
Ministers to understand that he was to some extent in
the confidence of the conspirators who had plotted their
arrest. The Ministry, who had already attempted to
resign, now pressed with somewhat greater earnestness
for leave to be quit of the Royal service. But even now
the King refused to part with them, on the ground that
he could find no one else willing to form a Cabinet, and
when their friends of the National Guard warned them
that anarchy would break loose in the streets as soon
as their resignation became known, they consented, all

except Pianell, to continue awhile longer in office. Affairs remained in this suspended condition until the night of September 4, when Peard's telegrams, the supposed presence of Garibaldi at Eboli, and the reported desertion of Caldarelli's troops brought the King's irresolution to an end, and gave him the requisite energy to carry out his plan of retreat to Gaeta.

Accordingly on September 5 Francis II. announced his approaching departure to the Ministers, the Mayor, and the officers of the National Guard, to whom he committed the charge of keeping order in the Capital during his absence. He spoke without bitterness, of which there seems to have been singularly little in his mild and foolish nature. He excused himself for going : but ' your Joe, I mean our Joe, is at the gates,' he said to these men, whom he well knew to be preparing in their hearts an enthusiastic reception for Garibaldi.

On the same day he and his brave Bavarian Queen went for their last drive in the streets of Naples. They sat in an open carriage, like simple private citizens, and the passers-by, who took off their hats to them in silence, observed that they were laughing and talking together as usual. The clumsy shyness of the King's demeanour to his wife, which had distressed her in the early months of their marriage, had now to a large extent passed away. A few yards from the Palace, at the busy entrance of the Chiaja, their equipage was brought to a stand by a block in the traffic, and they were forced to wait some moments close to a gang of workmen who were taking down the Bourbon lilies from over the shop front of the Chemist to the Royal Family. Francis pointed out to Maria Sophia the too significant nature of the men's task, and husband and wife turned to each other and laughed.

Next morning, September 6, the walls of Naples were

...ded with the King's proclamation of farewell to his people. In restrained and dignified language he protested against the way in which he was being driven from his capital, in spite of his constitutional concessions, and ...ced that he hoped to return if the luck of war and favoured his claims. In the course of the day ...n part of the army marched out of the town by the Capua road, indignantly refusing D'Ayala's invitation to fraterni...e with the National Guard and desert to the side of Italy. A garrison of six or ten thousand was left behind to guard the fortresses of the Capital, but their commanding officers were strictly ordered by Francis II. to remain neutral and to shed no blood. Nothing was said to them about surrender or evacuation, although if they were attacked they could only hold the forts by shedding blood, which would transgress both the letter and the spirit of the King's commands. It is probable that he had not clearly thought out what he wished them to do. But it may fairly be said that he adhered in an honourable manner to his decision not to inflict the horrors of war on Naples, and the rumour that he ordered the castles to bombard the town, after he had gone, was pure fiction.

At four in the afternoon the constitutional Ministers were summoned to the Palace to take their leave of the King. There was no party in the State that wished them to accompany him to Gaeta. They found him courteous and cheerful, buoyed up by excitement at a great change and by relief after long tension. He said to Don Liborio, half in jest, half in earnest, 'Don Libò, look out for your head,' referring no doubt to his own prospective return. 'Sire,' was the unabashed reply, 'I will do my best to keep it on my shoulders.' The Ministers were not invited to say farewell to the Queen.

Shortly before six in the evening Francis and Maria

Sophia walked down arm-in-arm from the Palace to the dock which lay close under their windows. Both were composed and cheerful. The Queen left her wardrobe behind, saying to her maids, ' We shall come back again.' The hundreds of Neapolitan grandees and officials who had fattened on the Court for twenty years past were notable by their absence. But the faithful Captain Criscuolo received his sovereigns on board the *Messaggero*, a small ship of 160 horse-power and four guns. As she steamed through the crowded port of Naples, she ran up a signal for the rest of the fleet to follow, but not one vessel stirred. The captains were already in league with Persano, and the prevailing sentiment of the men and still more of the officers favoured United Italy.*

The little ship, shunned by all her fellows, carried the last of the Bourbons for ever out of sight of Vesuvius and the Bay. At dusk she passed the island of Nisida where Gladstone had visited *Bomba's* victims. A few minutes later, off Procida, she met another section of the fleet, signalled again, and was again disobeyed. All night she ploughed her solitary way under the stars, through a tranquil sea.

The interregnum of twenty hours that followed the King's departure was outwardly the quietest, but inwardly the most anxious day that Naples had passed for several weeks. Knowing that Bourbon garrisons were still in the four great castles—Nuovo, S. Elmo, dell' Ovo, and Carmine —the population stayed indoors until something decisive occurred. Fortunately the authorities took the right steps. Liborio Romano still continued to act and to sign himself

* Some Spanish vessels escorted the *Messaggero* for a very short distance. Two other small vessels, the *Delfino* and *Saetta*, and the sailing frigate *Partenope* were the only ships of the Royal Navy which later on joined the *Messaggero* at Gaeta. The remaining thirty-five vessels of the fleet passed over to the national cause.

as 'Minister of Police and the Interior,' though under which King seemed uncertain. His continued presence head of affairs helped to preserve public confidence ...ce. He sent at once for the Mayor, Prince d'Ales- and for De Sauget, the General of the National and agreed with them that Garibaldi must enter as soon as fitting preparations had been made Guard. reception, and as soon as he had troops enough Naples de to ensure his safety against the Bourbon garri- for his at his s ithin an hour of the King's departure two officers son. W National Guard were sent off to Salerno on what of the N the only railroad south of the Capital; it ran was there along the coast past Vesuvius, turned inland by Pompeii and ended at Vietri two miles outside Salerno.* On their way the two officers met a number of Bavarian mercenaries retreating northwards from the abandoned positions of Salerno and Cava. At Salerno, which they reached by ten at night, they found the streets lighted up, and groups of people still cheering 'disturbedly.' Garibaldi had made his entry, and had gone to rest. The envoys reported to Cosenz the flight of the King and announced the intention of the Mayor and the commander of the National Guard to come from Naples early next morning.

Garibaldi, when he awoke on September 7, telegraphed to Don Liborio: 'As soon as the Mayor and commanding officer of the National Guard arrive from Naples, I will come to you: I am waiting for them first.'

Don Liborio wired back: 'To the invincible General Garibaldi, Dictator of the Two Sicilies—Liborio Romano, Minister of the Interior and Police.

'Naples awaits your arrival with the greatest im- patience to salute you as the redeemer of Italy, and to place in your hands the power of the State and her own

* See Map IV., at end of book, for environs of Naples.

destinies. . . . I await your further orders and am, with unlimited respect for you, invincible Dictator,

'LIBORIO ROMANO.'

This exchange of telegrams barely preceded the arrival at Salerno of the Mayor and General, who were at once ushered into the presence of Garibaldi. He was surprised to hear from them that Naples did not expect him that day, and expressed annoyance at the suggestion of any need to erect triumphal arches and to make official preparations for his entry. More serious arguments for delay were the presence of the Bavarians on the railway line between Salerno and the Capital, the garrisons in the four castles with cannon trained on the heart of the city, and the absence of Garibaldi's own army. His nearest force, Türr's 1500, were still forty-eight hours behind, and the rest of his 20,000 men were scattered along the roads of Basilicata and Calabria at distances varying from four to fourteen days' march. His staff officers, Bertani, and the emissaries from Naples, all besought him to wait at least till Türr's force came up, and till the departure of the Bavarians for Capua was completed. But Garibaldi, hearing some talk of difficulties and dangers in the Capital, swept all this aside. 'Naples is in danger,' he said, rising to put an end to the conference. 'We must go there to-day; we must go this minute.' His friends were horror-struck, but they knew better than to resist. His decision was approved by the event, and indeed hesitation on his part might have dispelled the illusion of his invincible power and compromised his peaceful occupation of the city. And thus he was able to enter, as he wished, not like a conqueror surrounded by an army, but as a deliverer welcomed and protected by the people.

After despatching a telegram to the Capital announ-

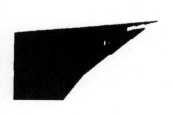

cing **their** arrival for midday, **the** Dictator and his party
drove **out** of Salerno, at exactly half-past nine on the morn-
ded **Friday** the 7th of September, amid another scene of
enthusiasm.* At the terminus station of Vietri they
a special train, which was soon packed to over-
first by Garibaldi, his staff, and personal friends,
n by a score of the so-called National Guard of
and th and any one else who could wedge himself through
Salerno, r climb on to a carriage-roof. During the journey
a door rator was calm and quietly radiant; so was that
the Lib e soldier, Cosenz, who smiled behind his spectacles
other fin
at the thought that he would in a few hours see his mother,
from whom he had been separated by twelve years of exile.
The rest of the company in the train, which included Palmerston's secretary in his red shirt, W. G. Clark the Public
Orator of Cambridge University, Captain Forbes, R.N.,
and Edwin James, Q.C., were for the most part in boisterous
and noisy spirits. The Italians kept singing over and over
again :—

> ' Siamo Italiani,
> Giovani freschi,
> Contro ai Tedeschi
> Vogliam pugnar.
> Viva l' Italia !
> Viva l' Unione !
> Viva Garibaldi !
> E la libertà ! '

At Nocera the enemy's Bavarians, entrained for Capua,
were shunted to let the victors pass. A little before they

* ' At half-past nine we heard the roar of *vivas* in the street, and, coming
to the window, saw Garibaldi himself passing in the direction of Vietri. One
of the crowd, while cheering in the most frantic manner, suddenly fell in a
kind of convulsive fit. I asked our landlady, a vivacious, black-eyed Calabrese
damsel, whether he had not been drinking the General's health. " No,"
she said, " it is joy. Ah," in a tone of reproach, " you English, who have
always been free, cannot imagine the delight of deliverance." And she
made a gesture as if she were about to fly.'—W. G. CLARK.

reached Pompeii, Garibaldi, who sat by the window ⊂
the side towards the mountain, said, ' Look out, we sha
soon see Vesuvius.' When its cone and streamer hov⟨
in sight, Cosenz was visibly moved by the familiar form o⌈
the mountain of his boyhood.

It was a day of scorching Southern sun. Beyond
Pompeii the train made slow progress even for an express
south of Naples, for between Torre Annunziata and Portici
the line was occupied by tens of thousands of the inhabitants of that densely populated coast. Fishermen who
left their nets on the beach, swarthy fellows naked to the
waist who had been winnowing corn on the flat roofs of
the houses, priests and monks leading their flocks, men,
women, and children in countless multitudes, rushed
shouting on to the line, and swayed to and fro round the
train in their attempts to see and touch Garibaldi.

In his carriage the Mayor of Naples and the staff officers
were arranging the route which was to be taken in the
streets of the Capital. It was decided to go by the centre
of the town and not by the quay-side, lest they should need-
lessly provoke the Bourbon garrison by dragging the triumphal procession under the muzzles of the cannon at the
Carmine and Castel Nuovo. Beyond Portici the train
was stopped by a naval officer who forced his way into the
carriage in a state of frenzy, crying out to the Dictator :
' Where are you going to ?   The Bourbon troops have
trained their cannon on the station of Naples.' Garibaldi
replied unmoved : ' Bother the cannon ! When the people
are receiving us like this, there are no cannon,'* and ordered
the train to proceed. As they went forward again the
Commandant of the National Guard questioned the young
officer, and it soon appeared that he was referring only

* ' Ma che cannoni ! quando il popolo accoglie in questo modo non vi son
cannoni.'

to the cannon in the Carmine Castle close to the station, a danger which they had already taken into account.

In 1860 there were only two short railways in the whole Neapolitan kingdom, connecting Capua and Vietri respectively with the Capital.* At that time both these lines terminated in a small junction some few hundred yards nearer to the sea than the present Central Station of Naples. On the morning of September 7 the timid silence of the streets was broken by Count Ricciardi, who drove along the Toledo, standing up in his carriage with the Italian flag and shouting out to the citizens that they should assemble at the station to greet the Dictator, who would arrive there at midday. But most men preferred to wait and see if Ricciardi's prophecy would be fulfilled before they committed themselves in face of the garrison, and it was a crowd of relatively moderate proportions that assembled at the appointed hour and place. Don Liborio, however, and the National Guard were there to represent the official world. An hour and a half passed by, till at 1.30 the train was seen to approach, and the Liberator stepped out on to the platform.

As fast as the news that he had come spread through Naples, the whole city awoke as from sleep; myriads seemed to spring out of the ground, and before Don Liborio had finished reading an address of welcome to which no one even pretended to listen, an irresistible multitude stormed the station, swept aside every official barrier, swamped the lines of the National Guard, and took Garibaldi to itself. Don Liborio was whirled off on the flood and could not fight his way to the coveted seat in the Dictator's carriage. Cosenz, who had an equally good right to be

* The first of these had a branch line from Cancello to Nola and Sarno, and the second a still shorter branch to Castellamare.

next his chief, was borne down another eddy, but ~~ a horse and rode off to see his mother. After a few minute fierce battling, Garibaldi found refuge in an open carriage into which Bertáni and half a dozen of his old fighting companions managed to climb after him, 'such fine old heads with whitened beards, and all with their red shirts covered with purple stains, like English hunting-coats which have been through sundry squire-traps,' as a lady wrote who watched the simple procession pass. At the back of the carriage clung a Neapolitan artist named Salazaro holding over their heads an enormous tricolour with the horse of Naples on one side and the lion of Venice on the other. In this fashion, without official escort or guard of any kind, 'did a son of the people,' to use Garibaldi's own words, 'accompanied by a few of his friends who called themselves his *aides-de-camp*, enter the proud Capital acclaimed by its 500,000 inhabitants, whose fierce and irresistible will paralysed an entire army.'

According to the official plan, Garibaldi was to have entered Naples by the centre of the city in order to avoid the forts. But outside the station, in what is now the Corso Garibaldi, the mob turned to the left instead of to the right, and in another minute they were passing under the muzzles of the loaded cannon of the Carmine. The soldiers were seen looking out at the carriage and its occupants, whom they could have blasted to pieces by moving a finger. Garibaldi stood up, folded his arms, and looked them straight in the face. Some of them saluted and no one fired a shot. It is true that they were only acting in accordance with the pacific orders of the King, but it is a matter of deep congratulation that no one in that unscrupulous and ill-disciplined force was tempted loyally to disobey.

The mob had now reached the water's edge, and as

the carriage turned to the right round the corner of the Carmine its occupants were greeted by the most amazing sight and sound. For a mile long, the broad quay-side was packed by as many of the half-million inhabitants of Naples as could find standing room, and all at first sight of Garibaldi broke out in one protracted yell of welcome. Along the north side of the quay, lined by tall commercial buildings, every window was astir with faces and waving arms and fluttering handkerchiefs. On the other side, where lay the great port crowded with shipping of all nations, every mast was loaded with sailors shouting or singing songs of welcome in chorus. In middle distance, far overhead, the tyrants' castle of S. Elmo looked down upon the scene.

When the procession first left the station, Garibaldi had 'sat for the most part apparently unmoved, but from time to time he lifted his hat, and smiled, as it were, with the eyes rather than the lips.' But as they began to pass along the quay, he 'stood up,' writes Zasio of the Thousand, who was with him in the carriage; 'his head was uncovered, and his face in token of reverence (*in atto riverente*) betrayed deep emotion.' The carriage moved at a foot's pace on the long, open quay, and before it reached the shadow of the Castel Nuovo his bared features seemed to his companions in the carriage to have bronzed visibly under the scorching rays of the sun. 'Did you ever see such a triumph?' asked Bertani of Zasio. 'No, not seen it,' replied the veteran, 'but I have often *dreamt* of it for the chief.'

At length they reached the Castel Nuovo, sinister of aspect with its tall round towers of black tufa. Here again they might have been blown to pieces, but here again the enemy's sentinels saluted, and the guard turned out to do him honour. Thence he was carried along the side of the Palace, also occupied by a Bourbon regiment.

The Foresteria, an annexe of the Palace used for t
entertainment of Court guests, was the goal of the pr
cession. It stood on one side of the Largo San Frances
di Paola, an immense open space which was packed tigh
with spectators.* From the windows of the Foresteri
Garibaldi looked out sideways on the front of the Palace
a few yards off with the enemy's soldiers in the gateway,
and straight below him on the heads of the vast multitude,
whom he addressed as follows : ' You have a right to
exult in this day, which is the beginning of a new epoch
not only for you but for all Italy, of which Naples forms
the fairest portion. It, is, indeed, a glorious day and
holy—that on which a people passes from the yoke of servitude to the rank of a free nation. I thank you for this
welcome, not only for myself, but in the name of all Italy,
which your aid will render free and united.' His speech
showed clearly that it was of the union of Italy that he
was thinking as much as of the liberation of Naples.

From the Foresteria he was taken to the Cathedral,
where he was again almost smothered by the embraces
of men and women. His fighting friar, Sicilian Pantaleo,
conducted the service, and the terrified canons showed
him the relics of St. Januarius, on the virtues of which he
maintained a judicious silence. †

Thence he was taken to the Palazzo d'Angri, now
chosen as his permanent headquarters. It is a fine private
mansion, standing conspicuously, half-way up the mile-

* The Foresteria is now (1911) the Prefettura, and the Largo San Francesco di Paola is called Piazza del Plebiscito.

† Next day (Sept. 8) he attended the popular religious festival of Piedi-
grotta, which had always been attended by the Monarchs of Naples : he had
said at the Straits that he would be at Naples in time for that feast, and he
kept his word. On September 19 the Blood of St. Januarius duly liquefied
for the benefit of the Dictator's Government, following precedent, since it
had liquefied for the benefit of the atheist French Republicans in 1799.
Garibaldi was not present at the performance.

from the yoke of servi-
I thank you for this
the name of all Italy,
united.' His speech
nion of Italy that he
tion of Naples.
en to the Cathedral,
red by the embraces
ar, Sicilian Pantaleo,
ified canons showed
e virtues of which he

lazzo d'Angri, now
It is a fine private

the King returned. Men and women waved swords which
they would never wield in earnest, and brandished daggers
which they were more accustomed to employ. As the
night wore on, the various cries of *Viva Garibardo, Gallibar,
Galliboard* were finally shortened into *Viva 'Board.* When
the voice gave out, a single finger was held up in token of
the union of Italy. Even after the first rage was spent
the Saturnalia continued intermittently for three days
and nights in the thousand noisome alleys which composed
the Naples of that era.

But in the Toledo, while the crowd on the first evening was shouting under the Palazzo d'Angri for the Dictator to reappear, a red-shirt stepped out on the balcony
and laid his cheek on his hand in token that his chief was
sleeping. 'Egli dorme,' whispered the vast multitude

CHAPTER IX

GARIBALDI'S MISTAKES IN NAPLES—THE CHECK BEFORE CAPUA

'Tra qualche anno, di tutti questi piccoli guai, che ora ci preoccupano tanto, chi si ricorderà ? D'una cosa sola ci ricorderemo tutti, e per sempre : ci ricorderemo che in questi due anni s'è fatta l' Italia ! '—*Manzoni's saying in the winter of* 1860. (*Venosta*, 607.)

'In a few years who will recollect all these little troubles which now obsess our minds ? One thing only we shall all of us remember for ever : we shall remember that in these two years Italy was made.'

ON September 8, the day after Garibaldi's entry, the Bourbon commandant of the castle of S. Elmo sent word that he could no longer restrain his men from bombarding the city at their feet. 'Very well,' said the Dictator, 'let them fire, and we will fire back.' He had on that day no military force in Naples except the National Guard, who were only fit for policing the streets, but his fearless tone quelled the enemy's soldiers. They did not open fire, and in the course of the next three days handed over all the four castles to the National Guard. None of the outgoing regiments would listen to the invitations to desert that were showered upon them, but marched off scowling at the people, full of zeal to join their King and comrades in the last stand behind the Volturno. The loyalty of the army to the Bourbons, even stronger among the rank and file than among the officers, defeated the calculations alike of Garibaldi and of Cavour, who had each confidently expected that if the revolution succeeded at all, the army would come over wholesale to aid in the wars of liberation for the rest of the Peninsula.

The loyalty of the soldiers was a measure of their professional feeling and of their isolation from the community at large, to whom they had been related not as defenders of the fatherland or representatives of the national honour, but as the tyrant's body-guard kept to repress the citizens. Therefore they were left untouched by the tide of popular sentiment for United Italy, and while one-half of them rallied round Francis II. at Capua and Gaeta, the other 50,000 disbanded and went sulkily to their homes or took to the hills as brigands.

In the north of the kingdom, where a part of the population itself was reactionary under clerical influence, there ensued a state of sporadic civil war of which the worst horrors had been spared to the southern provinces. On September 8 news reached the Dictator from the district of Ariano to the east of the capital that Generals Bonanno and Flores with 4000 Bourbon troops had there roused up the Royalist peasantry, who were robbing, massacring, and raping in the houses of the Liberals. The first 1500 of Garibaldi's army who arrived in Naples on the 9th were allowed only a few hours' rest before they were sent off again to quell the insurrection. Türr, who went in command, took them by train to Nola, there put them into carts and carriages and drove with the utmost speed to the scene of operations. Bonanno, in spite of his superior numbers, agreed without a blow to disband his force. It appears that conversations with comrades returning to their homes from Calabria had so much discouraged his men that he no longer dared rely upon them to fight.

Türr acted not only with vigour but with clemency. He shot two of the ringleaders of the peasant massacre, though the local Liberals who had suffered begged him

the newly acquired shipping of the port. Some of the regiments in the rear were brought by sea from Paola and some from Sapri, while others marched. The last division under Medici reached Naples on September 15 and the following days. In the course of a quarrel at Paola for the first passage on board a steamer, Nino Bixio had broken the heads of several of his companions in arms with the butt end of a musket ; as usual he repented of his savage rage and made friends with the victim whom he had nearly killed.

Cavour was agreeably surprised by the Dictator's first acts in Naples. On the evening of his entry, before he lay down to rest, he had issued a decree generously handing over the whole Neapolitan fleet to King Victor Emmanuel, and placing it forthwith under the orders of Admiral Persano, to the detriment of his own power and

out by poetic passion, t
of his own defence of the
element was the stronge
in good or evil at all
lover's passion for Rome
and the other extremists
their own political ends
delaying annexation unt
fatal to Cavour's contin
the prestige of the mo
to the position of accepti
the hands of the revoluti
Garibaldi and the Maz
as to the practicability o
believed that the French
this matter, and that t
seriously challenged, wo

the sage Cosenz, proved to all the world that no thought
lurked in Garibaldi's mind of any ultimate settlement for
Sicily and Naples except union under the monarchy
of Victor Emmanuel. But he intended to postpone that
union until he could proclaim the King of Italy on the
Capitol, and he publicly announced that he would march
on Rome over the last ruins of the Neapolitan army on
the Volturno.

The desire to march to the deliverance of the Holy
City was inspired in his mind not by political calculation
but by poetic passion, by the memories of antiquity and
of his own defence of the Janiculum in '49. The romantic
element was the strongest in his nature and ruled him
for good or evil at all the great crises of his life. The
lover's passion for Rome was fostered in him by Bertani
and the other extremists, who saw in it a means towards
their own political ends. It was to them a method of
delaying annexation until it could be effected on terms
fatal to Cavour's continuance in office and dangerous to
the prestige of the monarchy, which would be reduced
to the position of accepting the crown of Italy as a gift at
the hands of the revolutionary leader.

Garibaldi and the Mazzinians were alike under a delusion
as to the practicability of taking the city of Rome. They
believed that the French people were on the Italian side in
this matter, and that the tyrant, Napoleon III., when
seriously challenged, would be forced to withdraw his
garrison from Rome for fear of revolution in France. They
were equally wrong about prince and people : in reality
the clerical and anti-Italian feeling of the France of that
day was the main reason why Napoleon could not utterly
desert the Pope, for whom at heart he had little love.

Until, in the latter half of September, it became apparent that the Bourbon forces rallied behind the Volturno

were strong enough to check Garibaldi's advance on Rome, Cavour was at his wits' end for ways and means to prevent a complication which must involve Italy either in civil war or in war with France. Knowing that he had lost all influence of his own with the Dictator, Cavour turned in every direction to find others who could remonstrate with better chance of success. At his instigation Kossuth wrote to Garibaldi, congratulating him on his triumphs in the cause of freedom, and imploring him not to embroil Italy with France in a quarrel under the walls of Rome, that could only redound to the advantage of Austria at the expense of Hungary and of Venice.

Cavour even commandeered the services of the English to remonstrate with their favourite. Lord Shaftesbury wrote from London to tell Garibaldi that he gave thanks to God for his success, and to conjure him not to imperil it by attacking the Pope too soon. Even Edwin James, the barrister on a holiday, had been set on to use his influence with the Dictator in favour of immediate annexation. Persano implored Admiral Mundy, for whom Garibaldi had conceived a great affection since the events of Palermo,* to persuade his friend not to advance on Rome. Lord John Russell had instructed Elliot, the British Minister to the deposed King, to remain at Naples, and if possible to dissuade its new master from attacking Venice. Elliot and Mundy therefore arranged an unofficial meeting between themselves and Garibaldi in the cabin of H.M.S. *Hannibal*. It took place on September 10. Bertani, who followed the Dictator about like his evil genius, had to be asked twice to quit the cabin before he would leave his victim alone with the two Englishmen. His fears on this occasion were groundless, for Garibaldi, though cordial and patient, was impervious to all representa-

* See *Garibaldi and the Thousand*, chap. xvii., *passim*.

tions of the dangers into which his further advance would plunge Italy. He repeated in a tone of enthusiasm that he would first crown Victor Emmanuel in Rome, and that then the task of liberating Venice would devolve upon the King.

The conduct of Bertani in Naples was unworthy of his former great services to Italy. He who had once done so much to bring together Garibaldi and Cavour, now worked only too successfully to divide them. He became the mouthpiece of self-seeking politicians like Rattazzi and his friends, who, hoping to step into Cavour's ministerial shoes, were not ashamed to write that ' Garibaldi was the only person who could strike him down.' Urged on by such counsellors, Bertani daily inflamed the Dictator's hatred against ' the man who had sold Nice,' regardless of the fact that the man was now, in consequence, liberating the Papal Marches.* Garibaldi published a letter stating that he could never again work with Cavour, and then sent a note to Victor Emmanuel asking him to dismiss his great Minister. Bertani indeed advised Garibaldi against this last step, not because he wished Cavour to remain in office, but because he rightly foresaw that the request would be refused, and Cavour's position strengthened.

Unlike Rattazzi, Bertani was at least disinterested ; he was not seeking Cavour's place, but the union of Italy. He had impaired his health and his mental balance by working day and night on his sick-bed at Genoa, organising half the forces by means of which Garibaldi had reached Naples. He had brought on Italian unity by such giant strides that year, that he could not believe it necessary to call a halt. He had by his rival activities

* On September 11 the Piedmontese regular troops crossed the Papal frontier and Persano started with his fleet from Naples for the Adriatic to bombard the Pope's fortress of Ancona.

compelled Cavour to invade the Papal States himself, and he could not see that, although, thanks to Cavour's manipulation of Napoleon, Umbria and the Marches were fair game, France still threw her shield over the city of Rome. On September 19 he persuaded the Dictator to send round 300 men under Cadolini to land at Terracina in the Papal States in order to prepare the way for the advance of the main Garibaldian army on Rome. The orders for this foolish expedition were actually given, but were rescinded at the advice of Sirtori. Garibaldi's military lieutenants, Sirtori, Cosenz, Türr, Medici, and Bixio, were all opposed to the extravagant counsels of the civilians Bertani, Crispi, and Mazzini.

For Mazzini, too, was in Naples. He arrived on September 17 and remained, not in hiding, but in obscurity. A stranger, who met him one evening in a private house without knowing at first who he was, describes him as ' an old man with a sweet voice saying wise and noble things ' to a group of Garibaldian officers who listened to his words with profound respect. When he touched actual politics, he was less happily inspired. He wrote on September 23 to Garibaldi, saying that he preferred not to come to see him in the crowd at the Palazzo d'Angri, but that he hoped the Dictator would offer these terms to Victor Emmanuel —immediate annexation of Naples in return for the dismissal of Cavour and war with the Austrians in Venetia. The Dictator would probably have been better pleased if Mazzini had stayed away, but since he had come, he would listen to no suggestion for sending him back, and when the scum of Naples shouted ' death to Mazzini ' under his windows, Garibaldi protected him and rebuked the rioters.

To the men who were making Italy, Mazzini's arrival in Naples was an exasperating addition to the dangers of the gamble on which their country's existence was staked; so long as he continued to play a part, and a mistaken part upon the whole, in political affairs, it was impossible for all men to give the father of Italian Unity his meed of thanks, and to be always remembering that but for his work in the 'thirties and 'forties there would have been no 1860. Throughout this year when his life's work was being brought to fruition by others, Mazzini was in a state of melancholy resignation, for although he felt confident that the union of Italy was at hand, it was not the idealist Italy which he had striven to evoke. He sought no thanks for himself from the country which he had made, and dreamt of no apotheosis, but only of a speedy end to life in his English land of exile, now grown dear to him. 'Unity,' he writes to Mrs. Taylor, ' you may consider as settled, and so far, so good. The rest is all wrong. And as for myself, don't talk of either prosperity or consciousness of having done, etc. All that is chaff. The only real good thing would be to have unity achieved quickly through Garibaldi, and one year, before dying, of Walham Green or Eastbourne, long silences, a few affectionate words to smooth the ways, plenty of seagulls, and sad dozing.'

Except that there was less unanimity on behalf of the national cause, the attitude of the people of Naples after the entry of Garibaldi closely resembled that of the people of Palermo three months before. In Naples as in Palermo, devotion to the person of the Liberator was deep and genuine, and did not grow less on closer acquaintance. The southern populations found him far more simpatico than they found other Northerners, and when he retired in November and left them to the Piedmontese officials, they soon wished him back again. But so long as he was with them, though they were never tired of cheering him, they were annoyed by his policy of postponing the annexation, in which alone they saw a sure way of safety. The reason why the Neapolitans shouted ' death ' under the windows of Mazzini was that he opposed immediate and unconditional annexation. They wished Victor Emmanuel to come at once to give them security and peace.

The impatience of the Neapolitans with the *interim* government of the Dictator was increased by faults of administration. Many common convicts were let out of prison on the ground that they were political prisoners, and stabbing and crime grew more rife than ever. The moderate Ministers whom Garibaldi had chosen on his first entry found themselves overridden by the Dictator's secretary, Bertani, who treated them as cyphers and carried on the most important acts of government without consulting them. On September 22 the Ministry sent in their resignation; five days later it was accepted, and their places were taken by more passive tools of the omnipotent ' Secretariat.' The despotism of Bertani and of Crispi, who succeeded him on September 30 as secretary without altering the policy pursued, would have been endured gladly if it had meant order and a peaceable transition towards the approaching regime of Italian Unity. But it seemed rather to tend to anarchy and maladministration. The hopes of the reactionaries revived, and seditious correspondence was set on foot between Naples and Gaeta. Neither Garibaldi nor Bertani had any conception of the proper limits to which a Provisional Government should confine its work, and many of their decrees made important changes in the principles of law, finance, and State machinery, which should have been left to the mature decision of the future Italian Parliament.

Europe was justly shocked by a Dictatorial decree giving a pension to the mother of Agesilao Milano, the idealist fanatic who had attempted to assassinate *Bomba*, though it is possible to plead, in mitigation of Garibaldi's offence, the flattery long bestowed on Milano's memory by eminently respectable persons in England as well as in Italy.

A more innocent act of patronage was more loudly blamed in Naples. The Dictator nominated Alexandre Dumas as honorary Director of the National Museum and excavations. Dumas, who really loved the Italian cause and had, in his swaggering way, done more for it than was pleasing to the Government and the fashionable classes of his own country, was ungratefully accused by the Neapolitans of dipping his fingers into their public purse. It was true that if he had not undertaken the duties of the Directorate for nothing, it might have been given as a paid post to some native. The appointment of a foreigner was unwise, apart from all question of the novelist's equipment as an archæologist. But Dumas was subjected to much undeserved abuse.

All these political questions and quarrels revolving round the central problem whether or not annexation should be immediate and unconditional, found their solution in military events against which there was no appeal —the check of Garibaldi before Capua and the success of Victor Emmanuel's troops in the Papal States.

In return for the supreme sacrifice of his capital, King Francis had obtained a new position of strength, geographically and politically suited for a successful rally of the Royalist element in the army and the kingdom. Gaeta afforded a secure base of operation, and in the event of defeat a last stronghold which could hold out for months

even against a regular army with siege guns. The main line of defence was the northern bank of the lower Volturno, a deep, muddy river, fordable at widely scattered points known as *scafe* or 'ferries.' The only bridge was that which led into Capua. The celebrated Monsieur Vauban, whose creations so often baffled William III. and retarded Marlborough, had designed the defences of Capua, and they had been modernised and enlarged by a Russian military architect as. late as 1855. The bastions, well furnished with cannon, proved strong enough to oppose a final limit to Garibaldi's career of victory. This impregnable *tête de pont* of Capua enabled the Bourbon troops to cross the river whenever they wished, and to debouch on the cultivated plain on the south bank, which was admirably suited for the operations of regular troops against ill-disciplined levies.*

Behind these strong barriers raised by art and nature the Royalists rallied round their King. There were no longer any constitutional Ministers, any officers or privates of doubtful loyalty to create an atmosphere of division and distrust. The white flag of the Bourbons was again unfurled, the tricolour and the constitution were stowed away together and reactionary passions were no longer discouraged and concealed. In the course of September some 50,000 soldiers assembled in the lines, some of them from distant parts of the kingdom, all having come voluntarily and out of genuine devotion to a fallen cause. The privates were still the most enthusiastic grade in the service, but disloyal officers were no longer to be found in the camp. The fighting spirit shown by the Bourbon troops in the battles of September and October, after the Capital had been surrendered without a blow, contrasts strangely with the manner in which they had fled and disbanded in August,

* See henceforth Maps IV. and V., end of book.

when the royal cause had been in a far less desperate condition. The change was partly due to the presence of the King in their midst, and to the fact that they no longer had half-hearted friends within and a hostile population around. But there always remains something inscrutable to Northerners in the vagaries of the Southern temperament.

The Volturno region was not only militarily but politically well chosen. The peasants were the most reactionary in the kingdom, and the friendly border of the Papal States was close in the rear. It was suggested in high quarters that Lamoricière, who commanded the Pope's army of foreign crusaders in Umbria, should make a forced march southward, unite with King Francis' troops and carry him back in triumph to Naples. On the advice of Persigny, the French Ambassador in London, King Francis telegraphed from Gaeta to ask for the Pope's consent to this plan.* But the invasion of the Papal States by the armies of Victor Emmanuel from the north gave the Pope's generals plenty to do at home.

The Bourbon position on the Volturno was by no means merely defensive. It threatened Naples, which was divided from Capua by no more than eighteen miles of flat ground, well supplied with country roads concentrating on the Capital. Garibaldi's nominal attack on Capua soon became no better than a defence of Naples conducted with great difficulty and peril before the gates of Capua.

To the 50,000 Bourbon regulars gathered behind the Volturno, Garibaldi by the end of September opposed some 20,000 volunteers. Besides his own field army, there were 'insurrectionary bands' and private regiments

* Did Napoleon know of his Ambassador's advice? I doubt it. I suppose that as he did things behind the backs of his Ministers and Ambassadors, they took similar liberties with him.

enlisted throughout all the provinces under l
ship. When his forces were paid off in Nove:
stated officially that as many as 50,000 name
on the muster rolls, but Garibaldi himself de
only a third of those enrolled ever came near
of actual conflict. Sicily held seven out of the
sand, and besides those who were engaged in g
and patrolling the Capital, and the southern
thousands of ne'er-do-weels drew pay for traili
and sabres in the cafés of Naples and paradin
selves along the streets in uniforms of many colours.

The force actually at the front, varying during S
ber and October from 15,000 to 20,000 men, was
composed of Northern volunteers. But there were
them 3000 Calabrians and Lucanians and about as
Sicilians; the city of Naples, so Türr reported in the m
of October, had sent exactly eighty of her half-m
inhabitants to join the army protecting her on the
turno.

Dispassionate observers of the Garibaldini in that autu
agreed that they contained 'the cream and the dregs'
the nation. When the Thousand sailed for Sicily in M
there had been no dregs, but the process of adulteration ha
been continuous ever since, the bad element increasin
in exact proportion to the success already achieved, unti
after the occupation of Naples the red shirt covered as
much heroism and baseness as has ever been concealed
by cloth of any colour. Garibaldi's lifelong dream of the
levée en masse of regenerated Italians, which was to sweep
French and Austrian back across the Alps, wrecked itself
on the realities of human nature and the stern requirements
of effective military organisation. Instead of the 150,000
men for whom he had hoped, he got 50,000, out of whom
perhaps not more than half could look the enemy in the

face. But of these several thousands were of really heroic mould, and it was these few who saved Italy on the Volturno.* The further supply of the best sort of fighters had been cut off by Cavour, who since the middle of August had stopped the exodus of volunteers from Genoa and the North. By cutting off the supply of men, Cavour secured his object of rendering Garibaldi too weak to attack Rome, but in so doing he nearly caused him to lose Naples.

Garibaldi's headquarters were established in the Palace at Caserta. This monotonous and gigantic edifice is at least more pleasing than Versailles, in imitation of which it was built by Vanvitelli, architect to Carlos III., *Bomba's* great-grandfather. It has been reared upon the plain, but a mile behind it, at the end of the long Palace garden, rises a steep mountain range of white limestone, on the top of which can be seen in the distance the ruined castle and hill-town of Old Caserta.† Out of the mountain-side spouts

---

* Mr. W. G. Clark gives the following account of his twofold impression at Caserta :—

'When I reached the railway station, I found a train of empty trucks and cattle waggons just starting. A number of the red-shirted gentry demanded that a carriage should be attached to it for their use. The station-master declared that he had none, whereupon they threatened, hustled, and collared him, and finally carried him off to the Palace to answer to some one for his contumacy. . . . The train started without waiting for the issue of the dispute. I got upon a truck with a number of common soldiers (Garibaldians), whose behaviour presented a very favourable contrast to that of their officers. One provided me with an inverted basket to sit upon, another compelled me to accept a cigar, a third insisted upon my taking a cartridge as a keepsake. One of them had been an artist, he told me, and had abandoned his easel at Milan to carry a musket in Calabria. Never, surely, was there such a motley army as this. It contains men of all ranks, and of all characters. There are men of high birth and gentle breeding, there are also outcasts and vagabonds ; there are generous and chivalrous enthusiasts, there are also charlatans and impostors, and unhappily it is not always the former who fill the highest places.' From the mass of other evidence which I have read, I should not say that the officers were badly selected in the better regiments.

† See Map V., at end of book.

and tumbles a force of water conducted from t
away into that arid region by the great aquedu
vitelli, which spans the Maddaloni valley with a
worthy of Imperial Rome.   Below the cataract
the water glides more gently towards the Pal;
basin to basin, between groups of classical statues
groves of evergreen.   At such pains was this artifi
brought to the King's country seat by the first a
popular of the Neapolitan Bourbons, who reali;
highest ideal˜of kingship as understood under the
régime : for he did not forget to send on the water to
the plain and to supply the Capital.   Carlos III. di
year before the French Revolution began, and h
scendants failed to adapt themselves to the new era.
so now, among these groves so long reserved for pr
the Garibaldini were encamped, poaching the Royal pl
ants, much to the subsequent scandal of Victor Emman
lackeys, who thought that the sacred birds ought to h
been kept till their master arrived to shoot them.

While the advanced guard over against Capua h
Santa Maria and Sant' Angelo in Formis, the reserve w
bivouacked in the courtyards and gardens of Caserta Palac
and on the great parade ground that lies between it an
the station.   As in the Palace at Palermo, Garibaldi and hi
staff occupied some of the smallest rooms they could find
The Dictator enjoyed this much of kingly pomp, that
wherever he appeared, in the field or in the street, any
band that perceived him at once struck up 'Garibaldi's
hymn.'   And he was now attended by a body-guard of red-
shirts, whom it amused him to arm with a set of pompous
halberds from one of the State rooms of the Palace.   The
principal duty of the body-guard was to save him from
the hundreds of petitioners who besieged his door day and
night, clamouring for offices and pensions and for revenge

upon their private enemies. Rival committees, mutually
denouncing each other as Bourbonists with the envenomed
sycophancy of the Levantine, revolted the soul of Garibaldi.
He passed them on as far as might be to Bertani in Naples,
and was glad to spend all the hours of daylight on horseback upon the mountains, whither they could not follow
him. But when he returned to Caserta each night, he
found them still at their posts before his door.

His habit of retiring at nightfall and rising before dawn
saved him from prolonged contact with this human plague.
At Caserta he was always up and about before his staff.
Once, indeed, shortly after midnight, while Nullo and
Zasio were still sitting on in the outer room, having held
festival over some simple luxuries of the camp, their chief
came out from his bedroom, fresh from sleep and booted
for the day. He nodded and smiled to them as he passed
out, and they could only look at each other foolishly enough
and murmur, ' He gets up too soon.'

Thus abroad betimes, he proceeded every day to visit
the outposts, travelling from Caserta to Santa Maria by
train or by carriage, and thence riding along the lines
to the village of Sant' Angelo, built at the foot of the mountain out of the ruins of Roman pleasure-villas. Thence
he would climb on foot to the summit of Monte Tifata or to
the ruined chapel of San Nicola a few yards below, where
once a temple of Jupiter had overlooked the rich Capuan
plain.* Monte Tifata, the most westerly spur of the mountains that lie between the Caudine Forks and Capua, is also
one of the highest peaks of the group. It rises almost two
thousand feet sheer out of the seaward level. Half its

* On some days he took another route, riding up Monte Tifata direct
from S. Leucio by the charcoal-burners' path through the woods which clothe
the eastern slopes. It is possible to ride up this path, but on the steeper and
barer western side towards Sant' Angelo the mountain can only be ascended
on foot.

flanks are clothed with forest, and half are nak
with shrubs and flowers breaking out betweei
rocks. Arrived at its summit, Garibaldi felt
sycophants and political tormentors of every k
he spent many happy hours in the Septembe
watching through his telescope the movements (
and of the enemy's columns. On clear days he
view of every winding of the Volturno from the
Cajazzo to the sea, and of each ribbon of road on
plain stretching on all sides of Capua. It was froi
Tifata that Hannibal had watched, week after w
the glint of sunshine upon armour which might
to him some cautious move of Fabius in the plain
when they two matched wits and Capua was the
And now from the same rocks Garibaldi in his tur
watching the red and blue pieces in the game of ch
which he had challenged the Bourbon Generals.

The proper strategy for the Royalists to adopt w
have been the very opposite to the delay by which Fa
restored the fortunes of Rome. They should have
tacked in the middle of September, while Garibal
position at Santa Maria and Sant' Angelo was still a skelei
line. Marshal Ritucci, the commander-in-chief at Capt
unlike the generals of Sicily and Calabria, was neither
coward nor a fool, but he failed to grasp the need for ii
stantly taking the offensive. Overawed by Garibaldi'
unbroken record of victory, he preferred Fabian tactics
being sure that he could hold Capua against him. No
doubt he calculated that when the Dictator's advance
was shown to be permanently checked, his political hold
on Naples and South Italy would relax and his volunteer

* Ancient Capua was on the site of modern Santa Maria, where the
amphitheatre still remains. The inhabitants of Capua moved to the
present city on the banks of the Volturno in the ninth century A.D.

forces melt away. And there was talk of help in a few months' time from Austria or the Pope. Ritucci's plan was well laid, but he had forgotten Cavour. It was the Piedmontese and not the Austrians, Victor Emmanuel and not Lamoricière, who arrived to decide the well-balanced struggle on the banks of the Volturno.

CHAPTER X

CAVOUR INVADES THE PAPAL STATES WITH THE ARMY OF PIEDMONT

'Su le dentate scintillanti vette
　Salta il camoscio, tuona la valanga
　Da' ghiacci immani rotolando per le
　　　　Selve croscianti.

'Ma da i silenzi de l'effuso azzurro
　Esce nel sole l'aquila, e distende
　In tarde ruote digradanti il nero
　　　　Volo solenne.

'Salve, Piemonte !　A te con melodia
　Mesta da lungi risonante, come
　Gli epici canti del tuo popol bravo
　　　　Scendono i fiumi.

'Scendono pieni, rapidi, gagliardi
　Come i tuoi cento battaglioni e a valle
　Cercan le deste a ragionar di gloria
　　　　Ville e cittadi.'

　　　　　　　　　CARDUCCI.　*Piemonte*.

'Over the glittering, jagged summit
　Leaps the chamois, sounds the avalanche
　Off the cruel ice-beds rolling
　　　　Through crashing forests.

'Out from the silence, out from the encircling blue,
　Floats in the sun the eagle, and extends,
　In circles slowly earthward borne, his dark
　　　　And solemn flight.

'Hail, Piedmont ! hail ! to thee with melody
　Sad, from afar resounding, like the songs,

The heroic songs of thine own mountaineers.
Thy rivers fall.

'Down fall thy rivers, rushing, rapid, full,
Like thy battalions, in the plain below
Seeking the hamlets and the towns astir
With thoughts of glory.'

THE States of the Church, stretching across the Peninsula from sea to sea, opposed a geographical veto to the Union of Italy which Garibaldi's successes in the south had brought into the region of practical politics. At the moment of his entry into Naples the whole of Central Italy from Ancona to Civita Vecchia, from Perugia to Terracina, was still in the most literal sense subject to priestly rule. In the Papal territories priests were the legislators and the administrators, not, like William of Wykeham or Wolsey, lending their abilities to the State at the invitation of the lay power, but acting in their own right divine. Both in theory and in practice priests were the sole judges of what might be published, said, or done by the millions of laymen who chanced to be subjects of the Pope. There was no longer, as in 1848, any attempt at reform from within or concession to the laity. 'We are advised to make reforms,' said Pio Nono (Pius IX.) to Odo Russell, the British Resident at Rome ; ' it is not understood that those very reforms, which would consist in giving this country a Government of laymen, would make it cease to exist. It is called the " States of the Church," and that is what it must remain.'

While many of the parish priests, as soon afterwards appeared, shared the desire of their flocks to be ruled by the King of Italy instead of by the Pope, the Roman *curia* was implacable. At no period was the spirit of priestly intolerance and interference exercised with greater impolicy than in these years and months when the threatened

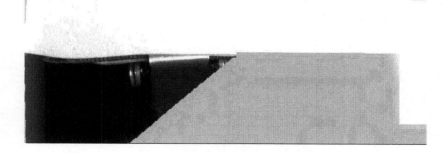

theocracy had its last chance of making terms with the modern world. Up to the very day of reckoning the hierarchy seemed to find a pleasure in reminding every layman in Central Italy that he belonged to an enslaved class and must submit to any humiliation or injustice that the Church was pleased to impose. On August 22, 1860, Odo Russell sent home to Lord John an official despatch narrating a characteristic incident of Papal rule :—

' A respectable tradesman of Civita Vecchia died some days since, and five young men, friends of the deceased, wishing to show the respect and affection they bore towards him, applied to the Ecclesiastical Authority for permission to carry his coffin themselves instead of allowing it to be carried by the religious Confraternity on whom funeral functions usually devolve.

' The request was granted at Civita Vecchia, but it appears not approved in Rome, for after four days the young men were arrested in the night at their houses by Papal Gendarmes and conveyed to prison, and the next day they were sent to the State Prisons of Soriano beyond Viterbo, where they will in all probability remain for some months and then be released without trial. The charge brought against them is interference with Ecclesiastical Customs and Privileges.'

This system of government was perpetuated no longer by the submissiveness of the Pope's subjects, but by the presence of foreign armies. The troops of Napoleon III. held down Rome and the Patrimony of S. Peter. An army of Austrians in the pay of Pio Nono maintained order in Umbria and the Marches. In the summer of 1859 these Eastern Provinces had nominally been evacuated by Austria, but the very same officers and men who had composed the former garrison had been encouraged by the Government of Vienna to go back 6000 strong and enrol themselves in the Papal service.

Thus the newly liberated Romagna was threatened

from the south by the Papal forces, of which these Austrians were the main strength, and from the north by the official army of Austria in the Venetian territory. Cavour had no time to lose. He must overwhelm the Pope's army in Umbria and the Marches and make Italy one by joining hands with Garibaldi in Naples. If he delayed it was clear that Austria, as soon as she had recuperated her strength after her losses in the war of 1859, would reconquer North Italy in alliance with the Pope. Cavour, well aware of the necessity for invading the Papal States, knew that the indispensable condition of success in an enterprise so repugnant to the interests of Austria was the passive consent of the ruler of France.

The French Emperor had no goodwill for the Austrians who were maintaining the Pope's temporal power on the eastern seaboard of Italy, although he still found himself compelled to do similar police work in the west. Napoleon's throne depended on the support of the Pope's followers in France, and the Pope's temporal power in Rome depended on Napoleon's bayonets, so each must perforce accommodate the other. But the chain of their mutual dependence was galling, and only made them hate one another the more. Napoleon, half a Liberal and wholly a man of the modern world, detested the obscurantist Government of which he was the unwilling protector ; while the Pope and the *curia*, after the Franco-Austrian war of 1859, recollected that the Third Napoleon was the nephew of the First, and thenceforward chose to regard him as the embodiment of the European revolution. They entertained high hopes of a Bourbon restoration in France, and began to talk of the present occupant of the Tuileries in the language which Cardinals and Papal Secretaries now sleeping in silent Roman cloisters had used in their day about Queen Elizabeth and Henry of Navarre. The French

Ambassador reported with amused indignation that, according to His Holiness' Irish Chamberlain, Napoleon III. was in league with the Devil and often consulted Him on political affairs.

Pio Nono considered that Napoleon had deprived him of the Romagna by the war of 1859, and that he was preparing at the earliest opportunity to rob him of Umbria and the Marches.

'*Caro mio Russell*,' he said in his 'mild and benevolent voice' to the British Resident, 'you are mistaken if you take the present crisis in Italy for a national one. What is being done now will be undone again in time. Piedmont is an instrument in the hands of the Emperor Napoleon, who thinks it is his duty to carry out the ideas of his uncle. What his ultimate objects are I know not, but whatever he establishes will end with him as the Kingdoms of his uncle ended with the Empire. The Italians are not a bad people, but they are easily led astray by foreign agents, who revolutionise the country for their own wicked purposes; when they have suffered more they will repent and return to us.'

Misled in this fashion by the false historical analogy of a bygone period, when France had imposed the revolutionary system on Italy from without, the Pope and his advisers persuaded themselves that no genuine national movement existed in the Peninsula, and looked forward to another 1815, another fall of Napoleon, and another restoration of the old Italian world. Even so shrewd a man as Cardinal Antonelli, who shared but few of the illusions of his rivals around the Papal throne, declared that he was waiting for 'the 1815 of the Second French Empire,' after which the Pope would enjoy his own again in the Romagna and elsewhere. The second French Empire has indeed since then met with its Waterloo, but it is not the Pope or the *ancien régime* that has arisen on its ruins.

The Pope, having quarrelled with his bread and butter in the shape of Napoleon's protection, was easily persuaded in the early months of 1860 to entrust his fortunes to the Belgian fanatic De Mérode, whose grand design it was to enlist an army of crusaders gathered from all parts of Europe which should be strong enough to defend the Papal territories, and so enable the Holy Father to dispense with the degrading patronage of the French usurper. Cardinal Antonelli, indeed, who saw what was possible in this life as clearly as any other worldling in Europe, argued that a mistake was being made ' in trying to turn the Holy See into a military power.' But his warnings were drowned in the clamorous joy of the church militant over the energy and zeal of his Belgian rival. Antonelli was forced to bide his time and allow the fatal experiment to be tried. The hour belonged to Monsignor de Mérode, priest and War Minister. All through the spring and summer of 1860 the quiet *piazze* of old Papal Rome resounded with the clash and tramp of regiments under arms, and the cries of officers drilling recruits in all the languages of Catholic Europe, while the French garrison, no longer the heroes of the sacristy, stared at the ' crusaders ' with mingled envy and contempt.

By September De Mérode's new army numbered not less than 15,000 men. Of these the weakest regiments, with the exception of one or two battalions, were the native subjects of the Pope, enlisted for the sake of the pay, without zeal for the cause, despised by their foreign companions in arms, and conscious that they were traitors to their own country. The foreign troops were, on the average, superior in quality. Six thousand Austrian veterans and several hundreds of Irish recruits were landed, enrolled, and drilled at Ancona. In Rome there were more Irish, besides French, Belgians, and other nationals. They were essentially

crusaders, not mercenaries. The Irish, as was justly observed, could have obtained far better terms in the Queen's service, and had come solely out of religious zeal. Peasants straight from the soil of Ireland, they were riotous and difficult to manage, but by the influence of their priests rather than by the enforcement of strict military discipline, they were at length reduced to order, and presented a soldierly appearance in their green uniforms.

But the troops who attracted most attention in this strange army were the French and Belgians of good family, who assumed the title of 'Papal Zouaves.' They were the men of the *ancien régime*, strayed into the wrong century, who had at last found a cause for which they could fight. They involved the whole army in the atmosphere of their own extreme Legitimist principles. Napoleon III. was to them a usurper and a Jacobin. They proclaimed a Royalist restoration as imminent, and cheered for 'Henry V.' of France under the windows of Napoleon's officers in Rome. In all this they were encouraged by the party now supreme at the Vatican, who spared the Emperor no insult. De Mérode in March had visited France and returned with a kinsman of his own, the retired French General Lamoricière, once a Republican, now a Legitimist and Clerical, but always openly hostile to the Napoleonic Empire. This man was put in command of the army of crusaders, as if to show that the Pope no longer valued Napoleon's friendship, and had no more need for his protection. If Cavour had been dictating the Papal policy by telepathic suggestion he could not have wished for anything better. The defenders of the Temporal Power behaved with the light-hearted insolence of some king in ancient Greek tragedy whom God has maddened that He may destroy him.

The invasion of the Papal States in September, 1860, was the crowning act of Cavour's life, and the greatest example of his political genius. He was hemmed in on all sides, and he laid all his enemies at his feet by this one stroke. It destroyed the league of reactionary Italian powers that threatened the newly formed Kingdom in the North, it liberated the populations of the Centre, it garnered Garibaldi's harvest in the south, it decided the rivalry between himself and the Dictator before it could grow into a fatal quarrel, it restored the prestige of the Monarchy as at once leading and controlling the revolution, and it made a United Italy stretching without a break from the Alps to Palermo. But proportionate to the possible advantages were the dangers of the course. It was a defiance of Austria, of the whole Catholic world, and of the whole diplomatic world except England. At best Napoleon might be persuaded to wink at an invasion of Papal territory, but he could not fight against Austria in defence of the sacrilege, because his political supporters, his soldiers, his ministers, his ambassadors and his wife, would all be on the side of the Pope. And if Austria chose to attack, Piedmont alone could not resist her armies on the Mincio. Knowing all this, Cavour decided to take the risk. Perhaps no other statesman fully alive to the facts would have dared a venture so hazardous, and certainly none could have carried it through with such perfect nerve and skill.

Two men may claim to have advised Cavour before the event, Prince Jerome Napoleon and Ricasoli. As early as June 30, while Garibaldi was still in Palermo, Prince Jerome had written urging Cavour to break with Naples and the Pope, but to be careful first to take the Emperor into his confidence, and to explain to him without reserve the true necessities of the Italian situation.

Cavour waited for two months, until Garibaldi was at the gates of Naples, before he followed the Prince's advice. But he spoke of the invasion of the Papal States, when it actually took place, as 'the plan of Prince Napoleon,' and he gratefully acknowledged Jerome's services in keeping his Imperial cousin friendly to the Italian cause, and neutralising the hostile influence of the Empress and the Ministers.

The necessity for action was also impressed upon Cavour in a series of vigorous letters from Ricasoli, Tuscany's 'iron baron,' whose fortitude and patience had carried through the annexation of his province to the territories of Victor Emmanuel. In July, 1860, Ricasoli wrote to Cavour again and again, pointing out in impassioned language that the popularity and the prestige of the Monarchy was passing over to Garibaldi and the advanced parties who stood behind him, and that nothing short of a war of liberation waged in Central Italy by the Piedmontese regular troops could recover for the King the moral leadership of the national movement. Ricasoli never tired of repeating his formula, 'Our real Garibaldi should be Victor Emmanuel.'

On the first of August, Cavour announced his decision to invade the Papal States, but only in the strictest secrecy, to his representatives at London and Paris. During the whole month the world knew nothing of his intention.

At the end of August, Napoleon III. was at Chambéry, enjoying the Alpine scenery of his new Province of Savoy, recently acquired by the bargain with Cavour, as the fruits of the Italian alliance. The place, the time, his holiday humour, the constant news from Rome of fresh insults cast upon him by the Pope and the 'crusaders,' all combined to induce this halter between two opinions to lean for one moment to the Liberal side.   And that one moment in Cavour's hands sufficed.

On August 28 there arrived at Chambéry two Piedmontese emissaries—Farini, the second man in the Cabinet of Turin, and Cialdini, the brilliant officer known as 'the Garibaldi of the regular army.' In a secret conference with Napoleon they informed him of Cavour's intention to invade Umbria and the Marches. The Patrimony of St. Peter, containing the city of Rome, was to be left to the Pope and the French garrison, provided that Napoleon would confine his own troops to that province and leave Lamoricière with his Austrians and his Legitimist French crusaders to try conclusions in Umbria with Cialdini's Bersaglieri. 'The Emperor,' wrote Cavour, 'approved of it all. Indeed he seemed greatly to relish the idea of seeing Lamoricière sent to . . .' The Piedmontese emissaries reported that Napoleon discussed the military chances of the campaign in the most friendly manner, 'laying down the limits of the plan of operations for our army,' and finally dismissed them with the words, ' Faites vite '—what thou doest do quickly.

The southward march of the Piedmontese battalions could be truthfully represented in either of two aspects —liberty or order. Cavour and his agents in explaining matters to the Emperor were careful to lay most stress on the restoration of 'order' as against Garibaldi. When the interview took place at Chambéry the red-shirts, still in the full career of victory in Calabria, had not yet received their check on the Volturno, and Napoleon had grave reason to fear that they would soon be knocking at the gates of Rome unless Cavour interposed the shield of the Piedmontese army. It was to the interest alike of Napoleon and of Victor Emmanuel that the Italian monarchy should ' absorb the revolution ' before it came up north and involved

the whole politics of Italy and France in complications that might end on either side of the Alps in civil war, Republican uprising, or Legitimist restoration.

' Not being able to forestall Garibaldi at Naples,' wrote Cavour to his Minister at Paris, ' we must stop him elsewhere—that is to say, in Umbria and the Marches. An insurrection is on the point of breaking out there, and as soon as this occurs, in the name of order and humanity Cialdini enters the Marches and Fanti enters Umbria. They pitch Lamoricière into the sea, occupy Ancona, but declare Rome inviolable.' The name of ' humanity ' was invoked in reference to the brutal conduct of the Pope's foreign mercenaries, who had repressed the insurrection of Perugia the year before with unnecessary slaughter. Cavour's emissaries represented to Napoleon that it was obligatory to invade the Papal States in order to prevent a repetition of such horrors on a greater scale. An insurrection, they declared, was inevitable in Umbria and the Marches—and truly enough the inhabitants of Urbino rose and held their hill city for three days before Victor Emmanuel's troops crossed the frontier to their rescue. Napoleon, in his official version of the Chambéry interview, declared that he had only promised his acquiescence because Farini had undertaken on his side that the Piedmontese ' would only enter the Papal States after an insurrection and to re-establish order.' Whatever Napoleon really said or tried afterwards to unsay, he left no doubt in the mind of the two Italians that he would not actively resist the invasion.

Three days later, to make assurance doubly sure, Cavour sent another emissary—Count Arese, the old Italian friend of Napoleon during the period of his connection with the *carbonari* thirty years before. Another tried friend of the adventurer now safely seated on the throne of France was Dr. Conneau, who had aided him in his romantic and perilous escape from the castle of Ham in 1846. In the midst of priests and reactionaries and courtiers, the Emperor never entirely forgot Arese and Conneau or their liberal doctrines, which had once been his own. These two intimates of Napoleon were, at this crisis of Italian history, working in league with Cavour. Arese's instructions were to seek out Napoleon and repeat the arguments of Cialdini and Farini, of which Cavour sent him the following notes for his guidance :—

'Describe to him the Italian situation after Villafranca and Nice. Underhand war continued after Villafranca by enlisting of Austrians at Rome and Naples. Alliance as good as formed between the Pope, Austria, and Bourbons. Feeling of danger of this league very strong in all Italy. After cession of Nice impossible to hold Garibaldi back. Confess that the Government has tolerated and even supported him. But it has energetically prevented Mazzinian expeditions. Impossible to allow ourselves to be distanced by the demagogues at Naples. Once annexation made we will try not to attack Rome or Austria. Emperor will save Italy if he prevents an attack on us before next spring. If necessary we will fight alone against Austria. Sure the Emperor will not allow the only ally of France (viz. Piedmont) to be destroyed by coalition. Explain that it is not at Turin but at Paris that we are blamed.'

These arguments prevailed once more, and the Emperor repeated to Arese his undertaking not to defend the Marches and Umbria with French troops.

The history of these negotiations clearly proves that but for Garibaldi's successes in the South, Cavour would have had no chance of obtaining Napoleon's passive consent to the invasion of the Papal States. Garibaldi's part in the making of Italy was not confined to the geographi-

cal area of the regions which he liberated with his own sword, for the influence of his victories in 1860 was the ruling fact in the dealings of Cavour with Napoleon and with all Europe, to whom he was able to say, ' If you won't take Victor Emmanuel, you may get Garibaldi.' Hudson's comment when he heard that the Piedmontese were about to invade the Papal States was, ' We see now what the Garibaldi expedition has produced.'

Thus reassured from the only quarter whence he could hope to obtain assurance—except from England, whose approval could be taken for granted without the asking— Cavour staked the fortunes of his country on the hazard. An ultimatum launched at the Pope's Ministers on September 7, requiring the disbandment of the foreign mercenaries, ' who suffocate in Italian blood every expression of the national will,' was followed up on September 11 by the invasion of the Marches and of Umbria, and the sailing of Persano's fleet from Naples for the waters of Ancona. Half the regular army was left on the Mincio, to protect Milan and Turin against a blow by the Austrians. The guard left was all too feeble, but Cavour trusted that the ' internal condition of the Austrian Empire ' would deter the statesmen of Vienna from moving, or would ruin them if they moved. He had already made arrangements with Kossuth and the Magyar leaders for a Hungarian rising to be armed and financed by Italy in case of war between her and Austria. But his hope was that peace would be preserved with Austria until, early next year, he could face Europe with the *fait accompli* of United Italy.

The news that Victor Emmanuel's Bersaglieri were marching gaily along the high-roads of Umbria and of the Marches, hailed with ecstasies of joy by the inhabitants, and taking in the Papal fortresses at the rate of one a day,

dispelled in an hour the foolish dreams of De Mérode and his party. Now was seen how little confidence they had at heart in the 'crusaders' for whose sake they had thrown away the friendship of Napoleon. At once the whole tribe turned to the man whom they had been insulting for months past, and demanded as a matter of course that he should send the armies of France to save them from the Piedmontese. The demand of the priests was supported by Napoleon's own Ambassador at Rome, the Duc de Gramont, and by his Foreign Minister, Thouvenel, both of them strong reactionaries and neither of them as yet informed of the promise which he had given at Chambéry. He yielded to the clamours of the Catholic world so far as to break off diplomatic relations with Turin, and to protest that he 'opposed' Cavour's act of aggression. But he refused to 'oppose by force,' although the Papal Ministers, in their agony, added those two little words to the obscure message which De Gramont had been authorised to give them from his master. The priests were accused of deliberate deceit in this matter by the French diplomats, but it must be admitted that De Gramont's over-sympathetic personal attitude at the time made it very natural to attach a war-like meaning to the message, which otherwise could have no purpose except to save the Emperor's face.

8

CHAPTER XI

THE BATTLE OF CASTELFIDARDO AND THE FALL OF ANCONA

'Ho ! maidens of Vienna ; ho ! matrons of Lucerne ;
 Weep, weep, and rend your hair for those who never shall return ;
 Ho ! Philip, send, for charity, thy Mexican pistoles,
 That Antwerp monks may sing a mass for thy poor spearmen's souls.'
                                                    MACAULAY. *Ivry.*

THERE were 33,000 men in the Italian army that crossed
the Papal border, vowed like the Frenchmen at Ivry to
deliver their countrymen from foreigners brought in by
priests. Lamoricière, who had only half his opponent's
numbers, could not hope to win unaided, but he might
prolong the defence until France or Austria came to the
rescue of the Pope. He held all the fortresses in Umbria
and the Marches, including the formidable defences of
Ancona. The task imposed on the North Italian army
by Cavour was to destroy Lamoricière, to take Ancona,
and to reach Naples all within a few weeks, under penalty
of an Austrian attack upon Italy's rear. It was a race
against time.

General Fanti was the Italian commander-in-chief.
One of his two corps, under Cialdini, crossed the ' Rubicon '
whence Garibaldi had been recalled ten months before,*
and made straight along the Adriatic coast towards Ancona,
capturing on his way the Papal fortresses of Pesaro and

* *Garibaldi and the Thousand* end of chap. vi.

Fano with their small garrisons.* The other corps under General Della Rocca, accompanied by Fanti himself, entered Umbria by the upper Tiber valley at the point where Garibaldi long ago had crossed it in his flight with Anita and the remains of the army of the Roman Republic. From Borgo San Sepolcro the deliverers followed down the poplared banks of the river, amid the blessings of the Umbrian peasants, until they reached the foot of the hill on which Perugia stands. The slaughter perpetrated there in June, 1859, by the Papal troops under Schmidt, was now avenged by the liberation of the city and the capture of the foreign bully and his 1500 men, after a sharp fight at the Sant' Antonio gate. Della Rocca sent Schmidt away by night under an escort, lest the Perugini should effect their purpose of tearing him to pieces.

From Perugia a detachment under General Brignone was sent to capture the garrison of Spoleto. The town was not defensible, but the *Rocca* or mediæval castle on the hill above was in good repair. It contained a Monsignore, the clerical governor of the district, and a garrison of 800, of whom 300 Irish and a few score Franco-Belgians were the fighting elements. The castle could, however, be commanded by the artillery and riflemen whom Brignone sent to occupy the wooded mountain on the other side of the gorge, beyond the Lombard aqueduct. For twelve hours of September 17 the North Italians bombarded the *Rocca* of Spoleto, and in the afternoon attempted to storm its gate. Almost all the small column of assault were killed or wounded. Both Irish and North Italians here, as a few weeks later at Ancona, displayed the ferocious self-sacrifice of men fighting for ideas. The assault was repulsed for that day, but when night fell the castle was crumbling beneath the bombardment, the ammu-

* See henceforth Map VI., at end of book.

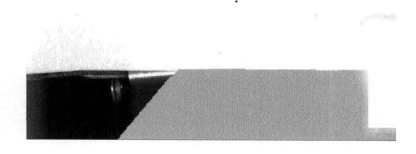

dressers of Umbria should remain enslaved and without
fatherland ? It is a strange thing, this crossing of sea and
land by these Irish, to die for a Monsignor-Governor of
Spoleto, bayed in the last lair of his tyranny. It was to
this that generations of England's greatest warriors and
statesmen had brought it in their Protestant zeal. Thus
does religious bigotry everywhere defeat its own end:
Cromwell had planted the Pope's power firm and broad in
Ireland, but Gregory XVI. and Pio Nono had destroyed
it in Italy.

Meanwhile Lamoricière, knowing that his field-force
could not give battle on equal terms either to Fanti in
Umbria or to Cialdini in the Marches, had determined to
shut himself up in Ancona. His arrival there with his
whole army would strengthen and encourage the garrison
to hold out until Austria or France should come to the
rescue. This plan might well have succeeded had a less
enterprising General been in command of the North Italian
column on the Adriatic coast. But Cialdini was not called

a forced march by Je
fidardo and Crocette,
tember 16, prostrated
If the enemy had been
they would scarcely h
defend themselves. B
to arrive with half his
on the other side of th
they had not marche
almost as much exhaus
under Pimodan was no
17th Pimodan came up
ment before nightfall.
upon the scene. And
18 the two armies were
hills on either side of t
well and recovered fro
marches.

The best that I ..

did not proceed any further along the coast to Ancona, because he feared to be caught under its walls between the formidable garrison within and Lamoricière coming from without. He decided to go round inland by Jesi and Osimo and stop Lamoricière near Loreto, and he was therefore obliged to make great demands on the speed and endurance of his men.

Two battalions of the Bersaglieri, trained to the quick, springy step that distinguishes their corps, led the way in a forced march by Jesi to Osimo and thence on to Castelfidardo and Crocette, which the vanguard entered on September 16, prostrated with heat, hunger, and exhaustion. If the enemy had been able to attack them that evening, they would scarcely have had the physical strength to defend themselves. But Lamoricière was only beginning to arrive with half his force in Loreto, three miles away on the other side of the Musone valley. His men, though they had not marched so fast as the Bersaglieri, were almost as much exhausted, and the other half of his army under Pimodan was not due until the next day. On the 17th Pimodan came up, but too late for any united movement before nightfall. Cialdini's troops had now all arrived upon the scene. And so on the morning of September 18 the two armies were still watching each other from the hills on either side of the Musone valley ; both had rested well and recovered from the exhaustion of their forced marches.

The best that Lamoricière could now aspire to do was to creep into Ancona by the track along the coast, at the expense of his baggage and probably of some part of his army. He no longer hoped to march in by the high-road through Camerano, for the North Italians were planted across it, 16,500 strong to his 6500. Cialdini, who was holding the line of hills from Osimo to Crocette, had not

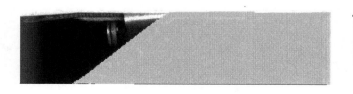

in Castelfidardo, fully expecting to be attacked by way of the bridge and the high-road. At dawn he visited the troops at Crocette and put all in preparation for defence. With a beating heart he watched the sun suck up the mists out of the Musone valley, hoping that when the bottom was clear Lamoricière's columns would be revealed in the act of crossing. But the valley was empty. The enemy were still on the hills above. After giving orders for his men to pile arms and breakfast, he rode back to Castelfidardo, saying to his staff that after all there would be no battle that day.

But meanwhile in Loreto the crusaders, gathered together under the dome of the huge church of the pilgrims, were kneeling round the famous shrine in the centre of the building, the ' Virgin's house ' which, as many of them believed, had been carried in the hands of angels from Palestine to Italy. They were preparing in a very sober mood for a desperate service. Pimodan's force, 3000 strong, was to cross the ford which had escaped the know-

House. Some m   e l
followed up across   e
farms, delaying t   ad
prevent them from   act
the troops at Cro tte
When the crusader hav
began to push for the t
volleys from the wood
unlimbered and opened

When the first soun
in the streets of Cas
galloped back along
Line drawn up on the
he cried, so that all the
sacks and charge with
the regiment swept like
and flowed headlong do
foam the gilded youth
rout with the peasants

Castelfidardo, the first files of Pimodan's column were seen emerging from the woodlands below Loreto, and making for the banks of the Musone by way of Arenici.

The North Italian army was taken by surprise. Various Austrian battalions, another small body of Irish, and the Franco-Belgian Zouaves splashed through the river and fell with all the fury of religious zeal upon two companies of Bersaglieri, who had been stationed as outposts in two farms near the river, known as the Lower and Upper House. Some more lukewarm Swiss and native troops followed up across the ford. The Bersaglieri held out in the farms, delaying the advance of the enemy long enough to prevent them from reaching the top of the Monte d'Oro before the troops at Crocette had been brought up to its crest. When the crusaders, having at length stormed the two farms, began to push for the top of the hill, they were met by rifle volleys from the wood above, while a battery of artillery unlimbered and opened fire on them down the slope.

When the first sounds of the distant battle were heard in the streets of Castelfidardo, Cialdini mounted and galloped back along the ridge. He found the Tenth Line drawn up on the top of the Monte d'Oro. ' Colonel,' he cried, so that all the ranks could hear him, ' pile knapsacks and charge with the bayonet.' In another minute the regiment swept like a wave over the edge of the hill and flowed headlong down the side, bearing before it like foam the gilded youth of Royalist salons, mingled in the rout with the peasants of Bavaria and of Tyrol.

For the next half-hour the plain between the Upper House and the ford of the Musone swarmed with confused masses of Italians, French, Germans, and Irish, trampling hither and thither, bayoneting each other in the frenzy of rage and firing wildly in every direction. Lamoricière himself rode into the *mêlée*, now far beyond the control

contained a smaller proportion of good troops.* They were first brought to a stand because their own artillery became entangled in the lane along which they were all advancing, and when the round shot came crashing in among them or flying over their heads, when the wounded and the fugitives from the north bank of the river began to stream back past them in terrified crowds, a panic seized the regiments of the rearguard. Before midday the Pope's army, half of which had never fired a shot, was running for dear life to the shelter of the wooded hills, whence they had so recently emerged. Cialdini let loose his lancers upon them. Four hundred were captured in the valley, and the rest climbed back to S. Mary of Loreto, whose magnificent dome had been in sight of the combatants during all that disastrous morning.

Lamoricière, when he saw the army break up under his eyes, rode off with the staff to find his way into Ancona, taking the coast track by which he had hoped to lead 6000

and began to fire into
into the sea. The infa
Lamoricière and forty
Ancona, and entered it
evening T⸺⸺on,
they had been waiting
joy, and the Governor,
come him. 'Here I a
army.' There was no
in Ancona.*

Meanwhile, Cialdini h
and accepted the surren
the shrine of Loreto.
away their arms and dis
natives who now attemp
side, changing their clot
acter of Italian peasant
few days the ⸺⸺

men.   He was accompanied for two miles by a few hundred German-speaking infantry whose officers had had
the presence of mind in the rout to make for the coast
instead of retreating by the way they had come.   This
remnant would have reached Ancona, had not Cialdini
seen them from the heights of Crocette and sent off the
Ninth Line at a double, to go round by the Concio hill and
cut them near Umana.   As the Germans were struggling
along ankle-deep in the sand beside the blue Adriatic,
the Italians appeared over the rocks at a few paces distance
and began to fire into their flank, literally driving them
into the sea.   The infantry had no choice but to surrender.
Lamoricière and forty-five horsemen alone escaped to
Ancona, and entered its gates between five and six in the
evening.   The garrison, recognising the General for whom
they had been waiting all day, broke out into shouts of
joy, and the Governor, Quatrebarbes, came down to welcome him.   'Here I am,' he said, 'but I have lost the
army.'   There was no more cheering heard that night
in Ancona.*

Meanwhile, Cialdini had crossed the valley of the Musone
and accepted the surrender of some 3000 crusaders around
the shrine of Loreto.   Two or three thousand more flung
away their arms and dispersed.   Most of these latter were
natives who now attempted to pass through the country-
side, changing their clothes and resuming their real character of Italian peasants.   But in the course of the next
few days the greater part of them were captured by Cialdini's flying columns.   Except the garrison of Ancona,
and a few small bodies nearer Rome, the crusaders had
been wiped off Italian soil.

---

* Part of the garrison had marched out earlier in the day to co-operate
with Lamoricière, but being carefully watched by some of Cialdini's battalions, had returned to Ancona.

8 a

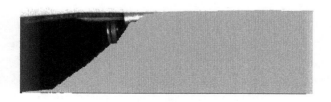

as a serious blow. It would be easy and it was tempting for Austria by use of her fleet to preserve the city from capture, as a preliminary to more active interference. Such, at least, were the fears entertained at Turin. Napoleon's ' *Faites vite* ' must still be the motto of the campaign.

The siege was pushed with energy on the land side; batteries were placed scientifically in position and the bombardment began. At the storming of various outer works both sides showed great courage, and Quatrebarbes, the Governor of Ancona, was amazed by the zeal of a small body of Irish under his command.* But his most vulnerable side was towards the sea. After a week's delay, which the event seemed to prove unnecessary, Persano on September 28 ordered his fleet to steam in close to the fortifications of the harbour and blow them to pieces. The order was gallantly executed, and after a severe duel ending with the explosion of a powder-magazine in the fortifications of the lighthouse, the defence of

of Abruzzi, contiguous
already risen and estab
in the name of 'Italy,
Dictator.' The leaders
both spirit and sense.
in the form of anarchy
Victor Emmanuel towar
the Tronto and annex
more delay. Similar ad
habitants of Naples. T
indignation because the
his Dictatorship, and e
stupid and incorrigible
wished the annexation to
yet ceased to hope that
turno would so far change
march on Rome. But
tained the idea of resisti

Ancona collapsed. On September 29 the formal surrender took place of Lamoricière, Quatrebarbes, and the whole garrison of four to six thousand men. The Pope's Generals and soldiers were treated with scrupulous courtesy by their captors, who knew that all over the world jealous eyes were watching for a chance to censure the conduct of the new Italian State.

Nothing now stood in the way of the entry of the North Italian army into the Neapolitan Kingdom. The Province of Abruzzi, contiguous to Umbria and the Marches, had already risen and established a Provisional Government in the name of 'Italy, Victor Emmanuel, and Garibaldi Dictator.' The leaders of this provincial rising showed both spirit and sense. Fearing a reactionary movement in the form of anarchy and brigandage, they petitioned Victor Emmanuel towards the end of September to cross the Tronto and annex the Neapolitan Kingdom without more delay. Similar addresses reached him from the inhabitants of Naples. These petitions aroused Garibaldi's indignation because they contained sharp criticism of his Dictatorship, and even spoke of his friends as 'a stupid and incorrigible faction.' And besides, he still wished the annexation to be postponed, because he had not yet ceased to hope that the military situation on the Volturno would so far change for the better as to enable him to march on Rome. But he never for one moment entertained the idea of resisting the advance of the North Italian army, even if it were to come sooner than he wished. His horror of civil war between the patriotic parties was one of those simple, fixed ideas that guided his sometimes too impulsive conduct throughout the whole course of his life.

Garibaldi's loyalty was soon put to the proof. On September 23, Tripoti, who commanded the Garibaldian

On September 27, two days before the fall of Ancona, and four days before the battle of the Volturno, Garibaldi issued the following proclamation, characteristically inaccurate, and characteristically loyal and generous :—

'Our brothers of the Italian army commanded by the brave General Cialdini are fighting the enemies of Italy and conquering. The army of Lamoricière has been defeated by these brave men. All † the provinces subject to the Pope are free. Ancona is ours.‡ Our brave soldiers of the Northern army have passed the frontier and are on Neapolitan territory.§ We shall soon have the good fortune to press these victorious hands.'

But the North Italian army had still to traverse some 200 miles of road before it could reach Capua. Nearly another month was to pass before they arrived on the scene, and during that month Francis II. had still the time, if he had the strength, to cut his way back to Naples over the ruins of Garibaldi's army. If he had succeeded, the moral effect of such a reversal on the public mind in Italy, Austria, and France would have rendered it impossible for Victor Emmanuel to turn him out once more, and European interference would have supervened in one form or another on behalf of a King who had won his way back to the allegiance of his subjects. The fate of Italy still hung on the issue of Garibaldi's defence of his lines before Capua.

CHAPTER XII

THE EVE OF THE VOLTURNO

'. . . Tifata, onde, aquila in agguato
spia presso e lungi tutto il fiume e il piano
di vastissima pugna incendiato.'
MARRADI. *Rapsodia Garibaldina.*

'. . . Tifata's summit, whence, an eagle in ambush, he watches near
and far all the river and the plain far around ablaze with the fires of war.'

THE military position on the Volturno was in itself an
additional inducement to Garibaldi to acquiesce in the
coming of Victor Emmanuel. By the middle of September
his observations from the summit of Monte Tifata had
shown him not only the uselessness for the time being
of any attempt on his part to attack Capua, but the grave
danger in which his own army would stand if General
Ritucci ventured on a counter-attack. In order to distract the enemy's attention from any such design, he sent
a few hundred men under the Hungarian Csufady to the
north bank of the Volturno, with a roving commission to
join hands with Liberal insurgents anywhere between
Cajazzo and Rome. Some bands around Alife and Piedi-
monte had been in arms for three weeks past.* With
their help Csufady was to threaten the line of Ritucci's
communications behind Capua, and so prevent him from
making a forward move. But Garibaldi had no intention

* For this chapter, see Maps IV. and V., at end of book.

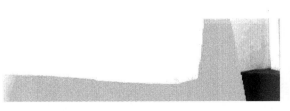

of attempting to hold Cajazzo or any other post nor
the river, still less of attacking the walls of Capua.

Such was the state of affairs when he was called ;
on September 16 to pay a political visit to Palermo.
pressing demand of the Sicilians, headed by his own
Dictator, Depretis, for immediate annexation to Piedn
required his presence. Türr, whom he left in comm
on the Volturno, ought not to have taken any impor
new step in his absence, but Türr's fault as a soldier
rashness, as he had shown the year before at Trepc
Finding himself in command for three days, he formed
ambitious scheme of occupying and holding Cajazzo
hill-town north of the Volturno—a far more serious unc
taking than the irresponsible gyrations of Csufady's fly
column. In order to distract Ritucci's attention fr.
Cajazzo, Türr made a reconnaissance in force agai:
Capua on September 19, the day after the battle of Cast
fidardo.

The reconnaissance procured, indeed, the unoppos
occupation of Cajazzo, but was itself ill-conducted a
disastrous. At dawn Rüstow's Milanese drove the enemy
advance-guard into Capua, but then, instead of retirin
from before the walls, remained for two hours round tl
railway station and on the open parade ground exposed t
the fire of the cannon on the bastions. They retreate
after severe losses, and the Bourbon troops sallied ou
after them from the gate, led on by old General Rossarol
who, though on the retired list, rode to the sound of th
firing and headed the advance in gallant style, until he wa
carried off wounded. Rüstow's men made a stand at th
cemetery and Cappuccini Convent and drove the Royalist:
back to Capua. But the events of September 19 had a
least all the appearance of a repulse for the Garibaldini
who had fired at the walls as if they intended to take Capu:

by a *coup de main*. Ir   some of the officers who served
that day under Rüsto   I believe that he was inspired
by a secret hope that   gates would be opened to him
by treachery, though   ever confessed as much. The
day cost the Garibaldin   ) in killed and wounded.

Meanwhile, the Dic   or had settled affairs in Sicily.
The love the people buie to him overcame their strong
desire for annexation and their indifference to his pro-
jects on Rome. He had another magnificent popular reception in Palermo on September 17. He replaced the
pro-Dictator Depretis by Mordini who had hitherto been
more opposed to Cavour. But Mordini was a man capable
of learning by experience, and although Crispi tried to
poison his mind with false rumours of treachery on the
part of Cavour,* the new ruler of Sicily had by the middle
of October discovered the absolute necessity for the immediate annexation of the island to Piedmont.

Garibaldi returned to the banks of the Volturno on
the afternoon of September 19, too late for the fighting
under the walls of Capua, but in time to join Türr in a
duel, which he was carrying on with the enemy's forces
on the other side of the river, across the ferry of Formicola. There is no reliable evidence as to what he said
to Türr that day, but he afterwards wrote in severe con-
demnation of his lieutenant for the attack on the walls
of Capua and for the occupation of Cajazzo.

The events of September 19, especially the sally of
the Bourbon troops under old General Rossaroll, gave
self-confidence to those forces, and suggested to them the

* On September 28 Crispi wrote to Mordini : ' The cession of the
islands of Sardinia and Elba is agreed on in favour of France. Sicily is said
to be promised to a Prince of the House of Bourbon. Victor Emmanuel will
have the mainland. As we cannot unseat Cavour we must organise our
party to resist these acts of violence.' There was not a word of truth in these
stories.

memoirs declares that the enemy would in this way have
succeeded in reaching Naples if his own force had meanwhile been held in check by false attacks. But the plan
was rejected as too dangerous by its author Ritucci, who
opposed as still more rash the frontal attack on Santa Maria
and Sant' Angelo, recommended by the Royal counsellors
at Gaeta.

All that Ritucci would as yet consent to do was to
recover Cajazzo. The Dictator made his one military
mistake of this year in not withdrawing from Cajazzo the
300 Bolognese under Cattabeni whom Türr had without
his consent placed in that isolated position across the
river. Matters were only made worse by the despatch
of another 600 men under Vacchieri; there were now
900 men collected in the hill-town to hold it against any
force that might come along the high-road from Capua.
On September 21 the best regiments in Ritucci's army—
the native *cacciatori* with a battery of guns, and a reserve
of three fine Swiss and German regiments—some 7000
in all came to retake Cajazzo. After a gallant defence of

the Swiss, who took no part i   he sack, observed with
compassion that many of the   nded were mere boys.
Two-thirds of the defenders unⁿⁿⁿ Vacchieri escaped with
difficulty by fording the flooded ferry of Limatola.

After the storming of Cajazzo, the Bourbon troops
were prepared for any adventure ; the spell that had so
long bound them was wellnigh broken, for they had proved
that they could defeat the red devils, at least where the
magician himself was not present. The King's counsellors
in Gaeta, who had learnt the disastrous news of Castelfidardo, perceived that unless they could at once cut their
way back to Naples their position on the Volturno, however
impregnable in front, would be taken in rear by the victorious armies of Piedmont. They therefore overruled Ritucci's
objections, and compelled him against his will to lead his
eager troops to the general attack on the enemy's lines.
It was the one chance left for the house of Bourbon on
this earth, and if the attack had been made within two
or three days after the victory of Cajazzo, before Garibaldi
had erected his batteries at Santa Maria and Sant' Angelo,
and if Ritucci's whole striking force had been directed in
one solid mass against those two villages, it is difficult to
see how it could have failed to succeed.

But again there was the delay of a week, and again
there was the division of forces. For both these errors
the counsellors at Gaeta were responsible. For although
they had done well in compelling Ritucci to fight, they
spoilt all by dictating to him a plan of battle of which
he rightly disapproved. They were unnecessarily alarmed
for the safety of the rear and flank of Ritucci's position,
conceiving it to be threatened by the really negligible
activities of Csufady and the Liberal bands round Piedi-
monte and Roccaromana. The council at Gaeta therefore
compelled the commander-in-chief to send great forces

they were planning rather to make victory complete than to make it secure. Misled by the golden hope of surrounding the enemy's headquarters at Caserta from east and west at once, they took the unnecessary risk of operating on an outer semicircle of which the two ends were not in effective communication. They thus gave to Garibaldi with his smaller force the advantage of acting on the inner ring, or rather along the straight diameter, while their communications ran round the circumference of the semicircle.* This advantage he used to the utmost on the day of battle, with the help of the railway-line running from Maddaloni through Caserta to Santa Maria.

The effect of this plan was to divide the Bourbon army into two separate forces, one under Ritucci at Capua, and the other under Von Mechel operating round Ducenta. Von Mechel, the brave Swiss whose stupidity in May had been one of the chief causes of Garibaldi's capture of Palermo, was nominally under the orders of Ritucci, but he chose to act as if he had an independent command and left the

Cajazzo in search of the missin,
discovered that he had on the :
from Amorosi through Ducenta
at Cantinella, and thence had ser
Bixio's force covering Maddalor
Valley. Von Mechel had there
as Amorosi on September 27. I1 ∼∽ ııau ∪
a determined assault on Maddaloni while K
sallied out in force from Capua against Sai
would have had a good chance of meeting ɛ
evening. But owing to their entire want c
tion, the great effort was postponed until th⌐
tober. 'This delay,' wrote Ritucci to Von ⅃
at last he was able to renew correspondenɔ
lieutenant, 'may well be fatal to our cause.'*

Ritucci was sulky but prepared to carry out ıı
the orders which he disliked.† His men were
the prospect of battle, and confident that they wo
in Caserta the first night and in Naples the next.
prospects were indeed bright, but they would haı
still brighter if the attack had not been deferred ı
beginning of October. On September 27 Garibald,

* Garibaldi in his *Memorie* writes: 'Our line of battle was defeɪ
because too far extended—from Maddaloni to Santa Maria.' But if he
not occupied both Maddaloni and Santa Maria he must have been taker
rear from one direction or the other : and if he had not held Sant' Ang
and M. Tifata, he could not have held Santa Maria, which stands on the plɛ
commanded by the Tifata range. No one of his critics has ever yet pointe
out which of his positions was superfluous, in view of the double attac.
from Capua and from Amorosi-Ducenta.

† Ritucci to the Minister of War. Capua, September 29 : 'Then the
attack will take place the day after to-morrow (October 1) at dawn. I free
myself from all responsibility as to the wisdom of this action, because it is
not due to my conviction but to the King's command and disposition; nor
am I responsible for what disappointments may occur owing to Von Mechel
not acting in unison with me, since he has been detached from my base of
operation with a strong column on his own account.'

only half a dozen field-guns and no ￼
in his lines against Capua, but in the la￼
month he and his men laboured day an￼
cannon that arrived from Naples, and th￼
in their front. In this they received skil￼
Dowling, a British ex-sergeant of artille￼
service before Sebastopol, two ex-capt￼
artillery, and twenty gunners of the Pie￼
army, sent up from Naples on the night of￼
request of Garibaldi, to Villamarina, and￼
next day by forty more of their number.

One of the new batteries was on the￼
Sant' Angelo and Capua ; another was in￼
the scattered village of Sant' Angelo itself￼
tended to fire at the enemy's batteries ac￼
was erected on the top of the precipitous￼
Jorio, whither the guns were dragged with￼
and considerable engineering skill. Finallj￼
was placed at the entrance of Santa Maria￼
ancient Roman archway which spans the r￼
from Old to New Capua. There were other m￼
of artillery on the road between Sant' Angelo￼
Maria.*

For the last time in his life Garibaldi had all￼
lieutenants with him : Avezzana, the former War 1￼

* Captain Deane, R.N., who served on board H.M.S. Aga￼
1860, tells me that he and some middies on leave from that shi￼
near the Bourbon lines at Capua, were fired at, and ran for she￼
nearest of the Garibaldian earth-works. They were pulled up ￼
of the battery by a rope flung over by friendly hands. When￼
safely landed inside the battery a moment of embarrassment foll￼
the faces of the Garibaldian gunners who had just helped them￼
exceedingly familiar and indeed curiously similar to those of som￼
who had recently been missing from H.M.S. Agamemnon. It wa￼
for the old proverb, ' The least said the soonest mended.' Captai￼
tells me that the enthusiasm for Garibaldi was perfectly univers￼
ranks from Admiral Mundy downwards.

the full advantage of being on the inside of the circle—of acting on the diameter while the enemy moved round by the circumference.

In spite of these preparations, which greatly strength-ened his position in the last three days of September, his army was still in evil case. ' Twenty thousand men, the greater part of them ill-armed and worse drilled,' many scarcely knowing how to use their rifles, had to stand the shock of twenty-eight or thirty thousand regular troops, coming on in the full confidence of victory. Exhausted with starvation, exposure, and overwork, many of the best men were physically prostrated, while the cowards were slinking back to Naples or preparing to fly at the first onset. There was none of that certain assurance of victory which had carried them through Sicily and Calabria. In the coming battle Garibaldi had to depend upon his own military genius, which was seldom

voice that seeme al
' Courage ! coura
Do you think I c ld
day we fought th .att

shoulder and simply said, with that low, strange, smothered voice that seemed almost like a spirit speaking inside me, '*Courage! courage! We are going to fight for our country.*' Do you think I could ever turn back after that? The next day we fought the battle of the Volturno."'

: Garibaldi obtained
ide of the circle—of
ly moved round by

:h greatly strength-
lays of September,
Twenty thousand men,
d and worse drilled,'
se their rifles, had to
thirty thousand regular
dence of victory. Ex-
and overwork, many
prostrated, while the
ples or preparing to
none of that certain
arried them through
battle Garibaldi had
ius, which was seldom
...perate day, and

A single blade against a circling horde,
And aye for Freedom and the trampled few.

'The cry of Liberty from dungeon cell
From exile, was his God's command to smite,
As for a swim in sea he joined the fight
With radiant face, full sure that he did well.

'Behold a warrior dealing mortal strokes,
Whose nature was a child's : amid his foes
A wary trickster ; at the battle's close,
No gentler friend this leopard dashed with fox.

'Down the long roll of History will run
The story of these deeds, and speed his race
Beneath defeat more hotly to embrace
The noble cause and trust to another sun.'
GEORGE MEREDITH. *The Centenary of Garibaldi.*

ON the last day of September, by way of prelude to their
coming attack, the Royalists kept up a heavy cannonade,
and their infantry skirmished along the line of outposts

to-night.' Next mor
to Caserta to arrange
Türr. 'He laughed—
left upon the terrace
their attack.'

After midnight a
plain, and wrapped
as they issued one by
In the Volturno regio
to a certain level abo
canic tufa, soft and
is hard, white limeston
on the lower slopes of t
of the two strata, and
stone ; while Santa M
are built, like Naples
which the soil i

ago out of the ruins of Roman villa
the centre of Medici's position, filled th
ing soldiers and on the morrow with th
dead. On the embanked terrace in fi
stood Garibaldi, with his back to the d
and his eyes fixed on the distant lights of
far away in the middle of the enemy's .
flame leapt up and flared on the night s.
it for some time in silence, and then turn
laugh. 'Sirs,' he said, 'we must not sl
to-night.' Next moment he was on his ho
to Caserta to arrange the last details with
Türr. 'He laughed—the old lion,' said on
left upon the terrace; 'that flame must be
their attack.'

After midnight a heavy fog crept over
plain, and wrapped itself round the Bourb(
as they issued one by one from the gate of
In the Volturno region all the ground that d
to a certain level above the sea is composed o1
canic tufa, soft and easy to cut. All above
is hard, white limestone rock. The village of Sa1
on the lower slopes of the mountain, stands on the .
of the two strata, and is built half of tufa and hal
stone; while Santa Maria and all the villages of
are built, like Naples itself, of the black, spungy
which the soil is composed—architecturally a sord
of discouraging and criminal appearance. The
cultivated plain between Capua and Monte Tifata
versed by the peasants and their flocks by mean:
network of lanes, sunk ten feet deep in the soft tufa
therefore invisible at more than a few yards' dist
The road that leads from Santa Maria to Sant' A:
crosses by bridges over four or five of these hidden l

up some of which Bourbon
dawn on October 1, and thus obt
inside Garibaldi's line at its w
undefended space between Sant' Angelo

Further to the south the fog serve
proach of other columns under Tabacchi,
routed the defenders of the cemetery and
Many of these first runaways fled by t
Naples, and arrived there before noon, s
like the first-comers from Waterloo in the 1
D'Ayala, who commanded the National
out the whole force and patrolled Naples and t
ing villages to prevent a reactionary movemen
the impressionable character of the Neapolita
sent out premature and exaggerated reports o1
counteract the tales of the runaways.

Meanwhile, Tabacchi's men seized the rai
bankment and a large group of buildings cal
Agostino, whence they enfiladed the trenches
of Santa Maria with cannon and rifle fire. Fort
since Garibaldi had come out by an early train from
and was already at Milbitz' side, Santa Maria itse
vigorously defended. Under the Roman archway
entrance two cannon, destined to be worked that da
many successive relays of professional and volunteer gun
began their ten hours' duel with the enemy's batteries
riflemen posted at Sant' Agostino. The Sicilians held
amphitheatre of ancient Capua, a fine defensive positi
in the plain just outside the town; while fifty Frenchme
who still named their company after De Flotte, their leade
slain on Aspromonte in August, held an isolated farm in
front of the amphitheatre with splendid courage all day
long. At Garibaldi's order Türr began thriftily to feed
Milbitz with portions of his reserve, which he sent up from

carelli bridge. At Garibaldi's side sat a young officer of the Piedmontese regular artillery, going to serve his guns at Sant' Angelo. He was Emilio Savio, one of a noble pair of brothers who with their mother, the poetess, were soon to be made famous by Mrs. Browning in every household of Europe and America where English poetry was read. Emilio as he sat by Garibaldi's side did not yet know that, three days before, his brother Alfredo had been ' shot by the sea in the east ' in the trenches beneath Ancona, any more than that he himself was in a few weeks' time, beneath the walls of Gaeta, to be ' shot in the west by the sea.' *

As the carriages drew near the Ciccarelli bridge, the Bourbon infantry in the lane beneath came scrambling up as if out of the bowels of the earth, and emptied their rifles at the Dictator twenty yards away. The horses

Medici's infantry from Sant' Angelo, who were fortunately not far off, came running up, and, led by the Dictator, they charged and repulsed the enemy.

After this incident, which had so nearly secured the restoration of the Bourbon dynasty to Naples, Garibaldi made his way on foot to Sant' Angelo, and spent the whole of the morning and the early part of the afternoon in heading charge after charge on the slopes of Monte Tifata and in the streets of the village. The enemy, in greatly superior force, had stormed the advanced battery on the road to Capua, where Dunne fell wounded at the head of his Sicilians, and had poured into the lower part of Sant' Angelo. At the top of the village Garibaldi's cannon were planted on the terrace in front of the church, and here the struggle raged hottest. Other Bourbon troops crossed from the north bank of the Volturno by the ferries and began to ascend Monte Tifata through the forest of S. Vito.

Garibaldi was here, there, and everywhere, now on horseback, now on foot, now at the church, now on the summit of Monte Tifata, whither he led the Genoese Carabineers of the Thousand. His criticism of the Bourbon method of attack was that though they advanced bravely, they advanced firing instead of charging with the cold steel. The chief feature of his own method of defence was a series of bayonet charges, each of which drove back the Royalists and relieved the pressure for awhile. Wherever one of these rushes was being made in defence of Medici's position, whether on the rocky mountain-side or on the plain below, there was Garibaldi organising and leading the charge. His presence put courage into the most faint-hearted of Medici's 4000 men and made heroes of the bravest. Soon after noon-day he began to cry 'victory' wherever he went, and to send off messages to all parts of the field reporting ' victory all along the line.' The phrase kept up the spirits of his outnumbered force, though the veterans muttered under their breath, ' Victory ! What victory ? '

In the attack on Sant' Angelo the Bourbon General, Afan de Rivera, who was in command, incurred censure for not appearing near the front. But in the attack on Santa Maria General Tabacchi did his duty, and the commander-in-chief, Ritucci, exposed himself all day in a manner more suitable to the part of a divisional commander. The knowledge that King Francis was in the field, with his brothers, the Counts Trani and Caserta, and his uncle of Trapani, greatly encouraged the assailants. Both sides, an observer noted, fought in silence, with the intensity of an Italian vendetta. The Bourbon cavalry made several charges on the plain to the north of the amphitheatre, and the infantry penetrated as far as San Prisco. Their guard regiments alone lost 460 killed and wounded, but the grenadiers of the guard sulked and refused to advance a second time against Santa Maria at a moment regarded by Ritucci as the crisis of the battle.

The attack directed from Capua on Santa Maria and Sant' Angelo was not the only part of the Bourbon operations on October 1. It has already been explained how Von Mechel with 8000 men, acting from the base of Amorosi, had orders to capture Maddaloni and thence advance on Caserta, where it was hoped that they would in the afternoon join hands with the victors of Santa Maria coming from the opposite direction. This wide division of the Royalist forces was a mistake in strategy dictated to Ritucci by the Council at Gaeta. Von Mechel now proceeded to make on his own account a further mistake of the same character in the manipulation of his 8000 men. Instead of attacking Bixio's position before Maddaloni with his whole force, he led only the 3000 German-speaking troops down the valley road from Ducenta, and detached the 5000 native troops under Ruiz to make a long circle through the mountains by Limatola, Castel Morrone, and Old Caserta. Von Mechel declares that he intended Ruiz and his 5000 to come over the top of Monte Caro and fall from above on to the left flank of Bixio's position near the Villa Gualtieri, at the moment when his own frontal attack was engaging the full attention of the Garibaldini at the Arches of the Valley. But it was an error to employ 5000 men for a flank attack which required speed and mobility rather than numbers, and to keep only 3000 for the main operation. Perhaps his Swiss pride inspired him to send away all the Neapolitans and to fight a pan-German battle in the valley. Whether from pride or sheer stupidity, he pushed on his own attack with such haste that Ruiz would barely have had time to make his way round over the rocky and trackless mountains, even if he had met with no resistance from bands of Garibaldini at Castel Morrone or elsewhere.

But Von Mechel's worst mistake was that he never gave Ruiz clear orders to cross Monte Caro and appear on the scene of conflict. He merely instructed him to occupy Old Caserta and there to await developments. ' You must keep up communications,' so Von Mechel wrote, ' between the column attacking Sant' Angelo and my column attacking the Arches of the Valley.' This cannot be read as constituting an order to assist in the battle of the Arches of the Valley, and yet Von Mechel conducted his whole operations there on October 1 on the assumption that Ruiz would hasten to his assistance, and after the event blamed him for ' adhering too literally to his instructions,' instead of marching to the sound of the guns. It may be pleaded in favour of Ruiz that he heard guns firing on both

sides of him, at Sant' Angelo and at the Arches of the
and that the instructions given him by Von Mech
to 'keep up communications' between these two
eight miles apart. No doubt a Clive or a Blucher
have marched off to decide one or other of th
battles, or else would have seized the opportunity to
the enemy's headquarters at New Caserta, but Ruiz v
ordinary Neapolitan officer, and was content to can
his actual instructions a few hours behind time.

Von Mechel, therefore, at six in the morning of Octol
with only 3000 infantry and six mountain guns, attem
to dislodge Bixio from a strong position which he
with an equal number of guns and 5600 volunteers.
was the only part of the battle of the Volturno in w.
the Royalists were inferior, not in quality, but in numl
The first of Von Mechel's three battalions of foreign tr
was composed of Austrians and Bavarians, brave but
disciplined, and inclined to be mutinous on questions
food and forced marches. The second battalion consis
chiefly, and the third entirely, of Swiss, many of whom l
been in the Bourbon service for years in the old privileg
Swiss regiments disbanded in 1859. They had been acc
tomed, when in garrison at Maddaloni, to field days in the
mountains, and knew every yard of the ground near tl
aqueduct. Better troops could not have been found in a
Europe for the purpose Von Mechel had in hand.

Bixio had chosen to defend Maddaloni at the poin
where the valley connecting it with Ducenta narrows t
a gorge, spanned by 'the Arches of the Valley'—Van
vitelli's colossal aqueduct that carries the water to Caserta
Palace. Along the top of the water-pipe runs a narrow
viaduct, some 200 feet above the valley bottom, and by
this aerial footpath Bixio was able to establish rapid
communication between his left wing on the slopes of

Monte Caro and his right wing on the slopes of Monte Longano. His reserve was behind the left wing, on Monte San Michele and at Villa Gualtieri.

The Swiss veterans of the third battalion, dragging up with them a mountain battery, ascended the wooded slopes of Monte Longano and stormed the Mills at the eastern end of the aqueduct, driving in flight Bixio's right wing, the 'brigade' Eberhardt. Von Mechel's son was killed at the head of the mountaineers of Uri and Unterwald. The attack at the bottom of the valley, directed against the base of the great arches, was successful in consequence of the victory on the hill-side above. Several Garibaldian officers at the aqueduct, apparently of Eberhardt's Genoese 'brigade,' led the flight to Maddaloni. A few days later, at Bixio's request, they were degraded in sight of the whole army, at a review held in front of Caserta Palace, with the advice from Garibaldi's own lips to beg for muskets and get themselves killed in the next action.

But the left wing under Dezza and Menotti Garibaldi and the reserves under Fabrizi behaved so well that even Bixio praised their conduct, especially that of the Sicilians.* Bixio, after his right wing had disappeared, still held the western mountain wall of the valley, the lower slopes of Monte Caro and the pass crowned by the Villa Gualtieri, over which Von Mechel now attempted to cut his way to Caserta in the plain beyond. The Austrians and Bavarians tried to ascend Monte Caro through the wood from the north, while the victorious Swiss began to climb out of the valley-bottom up the precipitous slopes to Villa Gualtieri, and to

* This praise is the more to be believed, because Bixio had been especially contemptuous of the conduct of the *squadre* in Sicily. On September 19 some of the Sicilians (the *Cacciatori d'Etna*) had behaved badly. But on October 1 the Sicilians behaved well, not only here under Bixio, but also at Sant' Angelo under Dunne, and at Santa Maria under the Sicilian officers, Corrao and La Porta. See Türr's and Avezzana's reports.

DEFENCE OF CASTEL MORRONE

pour across from Monte Longano along the top of the Arches
of the Valley. But the artillery got encumbered in endeavouring to cross the narrow viaduct, and as the infantry
struggled up-hill through the sparse vineyards and the
limestone rocks, they were met by vigorous bayonet charges
and hurled back again into the valley-bottom.

Now was the time that Ruiz should have appeared over
the top of Monte Caro, but he was not in sight, and the
messengers sent to find him had failed in their mission.
At midday, therefore, after six hours' fighting, Von Mech-
gave orders to retreat to Ducenta. He acknowledged a l...
of ninety men and one gun captured, and over 100 ...
killed and wounded. Bixio lost no prisoners, but ack...
ledged a loss of over 200 killed and wounded.

Meanwhile, Ruiz and his 5000 were wandering ab...
useless between the two battles, either of which co...
have been decided by their presence. Their only ord...
were to occupy Old Caserta. Arriving at Limatola ...
dawn, they drove out a few hundred Garibaldian irreg...
lars, and followed the road southwards through the hi...
on to the cultivated tufa plain that lies in the lap of tl...
group of mountains. On the plain stand half a dozen villag...
around the foot of a conical mountain crowned by the feud...
ruin of Castel Morrone. In the castle were stationed Pila...
Bronzetti and 280 men of Cosenz' brigade, and Ruiz turne...
aside to storm their position. Bronzetti had expected th...
villages of Sant' Andrea and l'Annunziata in the plain to t...
defended for awhile by the bands who had retired thith...
from Limatola, and by 150 of Sacchi's men who had com...
over from San Leucio. But these all decamped withou...
waiting for the enemy, refusing even to retire up the hi...
so as to join Bronzetti in the defence of the ruined castle...

* Later on, another small body of Sacchi's troops came on the sce...
further to the west and skirmished with Ruiz' men in the villages of Grotto...

9

Bronzetti and his 280 men were therefore left alone in Castel Morrone against Ruiz and his 5000. The attack was delivered, first from the north only, and finally from all sides at once. The Bourbon General himself has recorded that his handful of Garibaldini held out for ' four hours of fierce fighting.' Castel Morrone was a well-chosen position for a determined body of men to resist more than ten times their number. The lonely mediæval keep, raised high above the modern life of the plain below, has been inhabited for hundreds of years past only by yellow hawks, darting in and out of the upper windows, whence the robber Normans once watched the traffic along the banks of the Volturno. The keep itself is surrounded by a ruined parapet a few yards out, which Bronzetti had caused his men to repair. From the foot of this outer wall the mountain falls away on every side in a smooth glacis for several hundred yards, and on the south side the straight, bare slope continues for half a mile as far as the villages of the plain. Only on the west is there a neighbouring hill-top within long rifle range of the castle.

Firing from behind the parapet the Garibaldini again and again repulsed the enemy advancing up the glacis of the mountain-side. At length their ammunition ran out, but still they resisted, using the bayonet and hurling the heavy blocks of limestone which lay everywhere to their hands. When the Royalists at length burst over the wall and into the chambers of the castle they found Pilade Bronzetti sitting wounded on the ground, and stabbed him to death while he was attempting to negotiate the surrender of his men. He left a name as memorable in

and Casali. But Sacchi himself and most of his 1800 men remained far away at San Leucio, in accordance with Garibaldi's orders, which were to guard the communications of Caserta with Sant' Angelo.

Garibaldian story as that of his brother, Narciso, who had been killed the year before at the foot of the Alps. His men were all captured, but not before at least a third of them had been killed or wounded.

In the latter stages of this four hours' siege, Ruiz with a part of his force had been skirmishing at Casali against a few of Sacchi's men, and had then begun to push on towards Old Caserta. After the fall of Castel Morrone his whole force proceeded southwards, ascended the Lupara range over the western shoulder of Monte Viro, and reached Old Caserta in the middle of the afternoon, three and a half hours after Von Mechel had retreated from before Bixio at the Arches of the Valley.*

The appearance of Ruiz' blue-coats on the ridge overlooking the great plain, and the sight of the Bourbon flag floating from the Castle of Old Caserta, were greeted with the ringing of joy bells in the reactionary villages of Casolla, Santa Barbara, and Tuoro at the foot of the mountain, and struck terror into the Liberal inhabitants of New Caserta. The headquarters at the Palace were now practically destitute of troops, for Türr, though with some misgivings, had obeyed Garibaldi's orders and started for Santa Maria about an hour before with the last of the reserves. Ruiz, however, having no orders to proceed farther than Old Caserta, remained on the top of the mountain all the rest of the day, looking down on the unprotected heart of the enemy's

---

* Bronzetti's brave lieutenant, Giuseppe Mirri, thought that his commanding officer should have fallen back from Castel Morrone and resisted on the range of mountains running out of Monte Viro. Mirri, before he died, persuaded his friend, the fine old Garibaldian Senator Cadolini, of the justice of this criticism of Bronzetti's wisdom. Senator Cadolini has spoken to me about it, but I still venture to think that Bronzetti was right, for although the position he took up ensured the ultimate capture of all his small force, it also ensured a long delay to Ruiz, which was the all-important military object. Except on the top of a smooth, conical hill 280 men could not have held out for four hours against more than ten times their number.

position, but never striking the blow that might so well have proved fatal if delivered in time.

The four hours' delay purchased by the heroism of Bronzetti and his handful of men at Castel Morrone, very probably saved Garibaldi from destruction. For if Ruiz had arrived at Old Caserta before noon, he would either have been in time to help Von Mechel to a victory over Bixio ; or else he would, by threatening New Caserta in the plain, have prevented the departure thence of Türr's reserves for Santa Maria. In the latter case Santa Maria and Sant' Angelo would have been taken before nightfall.

At three in the afternoon, the last reserves from Caserta —the Hungarians,* Rüstow's Milanese and Eber's North Italians,—all picked troops, were brought up by Türr himself to Santa Maria. Almost at the same hour Garibaldi returned thither from Sant' Angelo. He had been forced to ride round by a long and dangerous circuit through Casapulla, for the whole plain, as far as San Prisco, was occupied by regiments of Royalist foot and horse. He found Santa Maria still holding out, but more like a besieged town than a point in the line of battle. The Frenchmen still held their farm-house, the Sicilians the amphitheatre, and men and guns were still lodged on part of the railway embankment. But every one else in that part of the field was packed into the streets of Santa Maria, which presented for hours together a scene of confused resistance and continual slaughter. All through the day fresh men were

---

* The foreigners fighting for Garibaldi on October 1–2 were about 200 Hungarian cavalry ; 200 Hungarian infantry ; about 50 French of De Flotte's company ; and 100 of Wolf's foreigners, deserters from the Neapolitan army. The British Legion had not yet arrived, but a few score English were fighting in various capacities. The foreigners in the Bourbon army on October 1–2 were six times as many, for besides Von Mechel's 3000 at the Arches of the Valley, a few companies of Swiss were fighting against Santa Maria.

found ready to die beside the two cannon under the old Roman archway. The town band of Santa Maria, whose 20,000 inhabitants were devoted partisans of the new order, stood playing in the middle of the crowded street to hearten their defenders.

Arrived in the middle of this welter, which would have confused a less able soldier, Garibaldi took in the situation on the whole battlefield, and saw that the opportunity of the day had come. He at once determined to lead out northwards the last reserves whom Türr had just brought into the town. In this way alone could he relieve the pressure on Santa Maria and at the same time clear the enemy off the line of communications with Sant' Angelo. While he was giving his last orders in the street before riding out to try the final issue of his own and his country's fortune, his old friend, Jessie White, Mario's English wife, came up to him with a glass of water and some figs. He had tasted nothing all day, and he gladly took food and drink from her hands. As he did so, he observed that she was being followed about by a group of British sailors on the spree, with no officer among them, on leave from H.M.S. *Hannibal*.* Being unskilled in Italian, they had fastened on their country-woman and were imploring her to have them supplied with muskets. ' What, Jessie ! you are helping these sailors to desert their Queen ? ' said Garibaldi, good-naturedly, as he sat on his horse eating the figs she had brought him. ' They have only come to amuse themselves,' she said. They were not supplied with arms, but stood by to bear a hand in some way more befitting their country's attitude of benevolent neutrality.†

* Not to be confused with the *deserters* from the *Agamemnon*, who were helping to fight the guns at Sant' Angelo.

† After the charge of Hungarian horse that followed a few minutes later, the Royalist battery on the road near Sant' Agostino was seen lying dismounted and derelict. A handful of Garibaldini rushed out from under the

The decisive movement now began. Garibaldi, followed by the Hungarians, by Eber's men and by the Milanese, issued from Santa Maria along the northern road and cleared the enemy off the communications with Sant' Angelo. Eber, continuing up the road towards the Ciccarelli lane and bridge where Garibaldi had fallen into the ambush in the morning, relieved the pressure on Medici. But the Dictator himself, followed by the Hungarians and Milanese, wheeled to the left not far outside Santa Maria, and swept the field in the direction of Capua. The onslaught with fixed bayonets of fresh and vigorous troops under such a leader could not be resisted by the masses of the enemy, who had been firing for hours past without making further headway. The 200 Hungarian cavaliers, Garibaldi's only mounted force, were at length let loose. They went right over the batteries and on through regiment after regiment. Too few to rout the whole army, they were too brave, and too skilled with horse and sword, to be stopped anywhere on this side the walls of Capua. Singly and in small groups, as evening fell, the survivors rode back, well satisfied that they had honoured the Magyar name before the eyes of Europe.

Behind the 200 horsemen followed the ranks of levelled bayonets with Garibaldi in the midst of them. Two hundred Hungarian infantry and 600 Milanese, deploying to north and south of Parisi farm-house, with their faces towards Capua station, drove the enemy's tired regiments before them. The Royalists, as they retreated, turned round to fire, and still here and there rallied for a stand

Roman arch to drag off the enemy's guns, but they had not the skill to remount them. Then the sailors from H.M.S. *Hannibal*, seeing that their time had come, ran up to help, and the spectacle seen a few minutes later of sailors in British uniform dragging two captured guns into Santa Maria was reported far and wide, scandalised Royalist Europe, and became the subject of diplomatic correspondence.

under a covering charge of cavalry. But Garibaldi still came on, and in the rear and on the left of the men whom he was leading, came the defenders pouring out from Santa Maria, men of Sicily, of Calabria, of Tuscany, and of all the other provinces of United Italy. Sant' Agostino had been deserted by the enemy, and now the cemetery and the Cappuccini Convent were stormed, and De Angelis farm to the north of the road. Medici, too, relieved by Eber's advance, sallied out from Sant' Angelo and recaptured the battery where Dunne had been wounded in the morning. All the advanced positions which had been lost at dawn when the Bourbon army came out of Capua in the fog, were reoccupied before sunset. The masses of the beaten Royalists, converging from north and south upon the parade ground before Capua, retreated sullenly through the gate whence they had issued with such high hopes twelve hours before. While Garibaldi rode back to Sant' Angelo through the dusk, his men lay down exhausted and hungry on the ground, each man where he stood, knowing that they had saved Italy.

An epilogue to the decisive battle of the first of October took place on the following day. Ruiz and his five thousand on the hill-top of Old Caserta had spent the afternoon and night in complete ignorance of the result of the fighting before Capua or at the Arches of the Valley. Early on the morning of October 2 news reached them of the double defeat of Ritucci and of Von Mechel. Ruiz thereupon held a Council of War at which he decided to retreat at once to the north bank of the Volturno, while the way was still open. Nearly three thousand of his men obeyed the order to retreat and escaped through Limatola, but more than two thousand, seized by a sudden impulse for battle and plunder, refused to obey their General, and descended off the mountain, officers and men together, to attack Caserta in the plain below.　**Part** of them advanced through the park and by way of the cascade, driving a company of Sacchi's men before them down the wooded hill-side. Others made straight into Caserta town through Casolla and Altifreda. A panic seized the few troops defending Caserta, and the Royalists entered in triumph and commenced sacking the houses.

But all this while Garibaldi was throwing his net round them with equal energy and skill. He had already caused orders to be conveyed to Bixio bidding him come over Monte Viro and cut them off from the north-east. He himself with such of the troops from Sant' Angelo as were not completely prostrated by their efforts of the day before crossed the tracks over Monte Tifata and arrived at San Leucio, a little after nine in the morning. Here he effected a junction with Sacchi and with some troops just arrived by train from Naples, who had taken no part in the battle of October 1, namely, Stocco's Calabrians and a few companies of Piedmontese Bersaglieri and other regulars. Led on by Garibaldi himself, the picked troops of Victor Emmanuel's army in their round hats with the cock's feathers, climbed through the steep park in the direction of Old Caserta, side by side with the red-shirts and the gaitered Calabrians in their brigand costume.

Before he himself began to mount the hill from San Leucio, the Dictator had detached thence a few score of Genoese Carabineers of the Thousand by the lower road, to save the Palace and to clear the enemy out of Caserta in the plain. The Genoese charged into the main street of Caserta, singing Mameli's hymn of '48, and after a sharp struggle in which a dozen fell on each side, drove the horde of plunderers back out of the town and up the hills towards Old Caserta. Meanwhile, the larger force under the Dictator was shepherding the other flocks of

Bourbon infantry out of the park, and up towards the same point on the hills above. Before long the whole two thousand, emerging from brush-wood and the olive groves below, were to be seen flying for their lives along the stony flanks of the mountain towards Old Caserta. At this moment Bixio's force appeared over the top of Monte Viro, barring their flight northwards. The net closed in upon them, and after another hour spent in hunting detachments of various sizes over the great bare plateau, 2012 men and 77 officers were secured as prisoners of war.

Taking all parts of the battle of the Volturno together, the Garibaldini officially acknowledged a loss on the two days of 306 killed, 1328 wounded, and 389 missing. Of these losses scarcely fifty can be attributed to the fighting on the second day ; at Castel Morrone there were under 300 lost, most of them prisoners ; and at the Arches of the Valley rather more than 200 killed and wounded. It follows that some 1400 must have been killed or wounded in the main battle of October 1, in defence of the line of Santa Maria and Sant' Angelo over against Capua. The Bourbon Generals officially acknowledged a loss in that part of the field of 1065 men—260 killed, 731 wounded, and 74 prisoners ; besides 200 more lost at the Arches of the Valley on October the first, and 2089 prisoners taken near Old Caserta on October the second.

Garibaldi had now nearly 1500 wounded on his hands, besides large numbers of sick, disabled by constant exposure and under-feeding at the outposts. As the autumn drew on, long grey overcoats were served out, which gave the army a more uniform appearance, besides some chance of warmth at night. But the conditions of service before Capua continued to be very severe.

9 a

The Neapolitans did little or nothing to make life more comfortable for their deliverers. Those of the wounded who were sent back to the Capital fared worse than those left at the front, for the usual peculation and carelessness of the hospital officials and the consequent dirt and absence of necessaries were not remedied on behalf of the Garibaldini, except to some degree by British help in the form of materials and money from England and personal service by some of our country-women in Naples. The field hospitals at Caserta and Santa Maria, though far from perfect, were better, being under the control of the medical staff of Türr's division, and under the eye of Jessie White Mario herself. The English women in the hospitals of Naples were deeply affected by the patience and gentleness of the North Italian wounded, and by their complete unselfishness. Indeed their only anxiety seemed to be not to give trouble, by any complaints, however reasonable, to Garibaldi or to those who had volunteered to nurse them. In spite of the pain and squalor of their lot, the wounded were not unhappy, for there were days in October on which Garibaldi was in the Capital, when he never failed to visit them, stopping to speak to each one and make the dying envied by some special mark of his gratitude and love.

' All the men,' writes an English lady, ' when they heard him coming, began to sit up in their beds and clap their hands and shout, *Papà nostro, papà nostro!* They long to be allowed coffee in the morning instead of grease and water, so my sister said to one of them, " Now ask the General to order that you have coffee." The young man answered, " O lady, how could I trouble him with that, when he has so much to see to, and when his very presence gives us new life." '

The battle of the Volturno, the last of Garibaldi's great

feats of war, differs from Como, Calatafimi, Palermo, Milazzo, and the Crossing of the Straits, firstly, because it shows him acting on the defensive, and secondly, because it shows him handling some 20,000 men, a larger number than the handful of guerillas which according to his critics was all he could command with success. His defensive strategy on this occasion is excellent, and proves that he had learnt much about the conditions of European warfare since his defence of Rome in 1849, on his return from the South American pampas. While the Bourbon generals on October 1 went out of their way to divide their army and attack him from east, north, and west at once, Garibaldi made full use of the central position in which they thus placed him. Communications between the various parts of the assailing force were therefore lost, with the result that Ruiz' division was of no practical use to Ritucci on the great day and was destroyed in detail on October 2. Garibaldi, on the other hand, took advantage of his central position, and of his short line of communication, strung together by the Maddaloni-Caserta-Santa Maria railway, to keep his reserve under Türr at the central point between the various battlefields until the very last moment. He could thus postpone the vital decision as to whether the reserve should be sent from Caserta to Santa Maria, or from Caserta to Maddaloni, until events showed where they were most needed. The arrival of this body of fresh troops at Santa Maria, half-way through the afternoon, and the vigorous use which he made of them to attack the enemy's tired regiments, decided the even balance of the day. The success of the National army in holding its own against greatly superior numbers is therefore to be attributed, apart from the valour of the volunteers, to three qualities shown on this occasion by Garibaldi : the personal inspiration of his presence at so many of the important points, the combined caution and vigour of his offensive-defensive tactics, and last, but not least, a sound strategy governing the disposition of his men over the whole region of conflict from the Arches of the Valley to the gate of Capua.

CHAPTER XIV

THE MEETING OF GARIBALDI AND VICTOR EMMANUEL

'To watch the new Kingdom of Italy rising as it were by magic is a marvellous sight. When time has veiled the events of the period and wiped away all that is perfidious and adventurous, Cavour, Victor Emmanuel, and Garibaldi will stand forth as heroes of this epoch. While I am writing of the struggles and sufferings of Rome in the Middle Ages, the observation of the present, which is realising the work of which centuries have despaired, is an experience of inestimable value to the historian.'—*Gregorovius' Diary.* Rome, November 7, 1860.

THE battle of the Volturno saved Naples from the Bourbons, but it did not deliver Capua to Garibaldi. It redressed the balance of war which had begun to incline against him, but it did not weigh down the scales on his side. A condition of military stalemate continued for more than three weeks of October, until Victor Emmanuel's army arrived upon the scene.

During this period of waiting, the only military event of interest was the expedition to Isernia.* That town, like most others in the Molise and in the neighbouring province of Abruzzi, had been seized by the citizens in the name of Garibaldi and Victor Emmanuel. But on the day before the battle of the Volturno it was invaded by peasants from the hills, authorised to act for the good cause by their Bishop and by the authorities at Gaeta, and led on by Royal gens-d'armes. During the following

---

* See Map VI., at the end of book.

week pillage, massacre, torture, and mutilation were the lot of the inhabitants of Isernia and of other centres of Nationalism in the neighbourhood. This system of 'reaction' or 'brigandage,' accompanied by all the bestial cruelty of which the half-savage peasants of the South were still capable, afforded a last weapon for the expiring system of Church and State. Francis II., when finally driven from Gaeta by Victor Emmanuel's army, took refuge in Rome in 1861, and thence, under the protection of the Pope, continued to foster this kind of 'brigandage' in his lost dominions in the Abruzzi for nearly seven years to come. No such horrors were committed on the other side by the Garibaldian peasantry of Calabria, Basilicata, Abruzzi or any other province of the mainland, and the difference may fairly be attributed to the higher ethical standard of the local Nationalist leaders—men like Stocco and Pace, touched by the idealism of the *risorgimento* movement—as compared with the reactionary clergy and the Bourbon officials, who had been brought up in an evil school on frankly mediæval ideas of religion and government.

Early in October, Nationalist refugees from the neighbourhood of Isernia arrived at Caserta, told the tale of horror to Garibaldi, and assured him that if he would send some of his officers into the Molise they would there find 3000 peasants ready to place themselves under their orders and suppress the reaction. The Dictator accordingly sent Nullo, Mario, and Zasio in command of a few hundred Sicilians and irregulars from the Alife district, and a few dozen North Italians. But when they arrived in the Molise, there was no sign of the 3000 friendly natives who were to have joined them. The reactionary peasants, backed by several battalions of Bourbon regulars, fell upon them near Isernia on October 17, and drove them out of the Molise with heavy loss. In the Abruzzi the Liberals held their own, but eagerly awaited the crossing of the Tronto by Victor Emmanuel.

On October 15 the British Legion, otherwise called the 'Garibaldi Excursionists,'* landed in Naples, over 600 strong. They looked a fine body of men as they marched up the Toledo in their red tunics with green facings, the muzzles of their Enfield rifles stuffed with flowers by the admiring populace. Four days later they gave a good account of themselves in a skirmish in front of Sant' Angelo, conducted up to the walls of Capua, where they lost two killed and eight wounded. But the warning that Dunne had uttered when Garibaldi consulted him at Milazzo as to the advisability of allowing such a Legion to be recruited, was unfortunately borne out by events. One part of the Excursionists consisted of roughs principally from Glasgow and London, who considered that they were out for a holiday at other people's expense, and though they did not object to the fighting, expected a maximum of food and good quarters and a minimum of discipline. The other half, old soldiers, 'volunteers,' and generous enthusiasts of all classes from a Duke's son downwards, could not, by their own better conduct, save the Legion from acquiring a name for disorder similar to that which the Pope's Irish had acquired in Rome. ' You see,' said the Italians indulgently, ' these men are not accustomed to a country where wine is cheap.' Peard, whom the Dictator set over them as Colonel, was not so well qualified for this

* A thin pretence that such was their innocent character had been kept up in England to save diplomatic appearances. The advertisement that enlisted most of them ran as follows : ' *Excursion to Sicily and Naples.* All persons (particularly Members of Volunteer Rifle Corps) desirous of visiting Southern Italy and of *aiding* by their presence and influence the *Cause of Garibaldi* and *Italy*, may learn how to proceed by applying to the Garibaldi Committee at the offices, No. 8 Salisbury Street, Strand, London.'

difficult command as for the individual knight-errantry which had made him a well-beloved figure in the Garibaldian field armies for eighteen months past. If the campaign had been prolonged and carried to the walls of Rome, as the Committee in London had expected when it raised the Legionaries, there is little doubt that they would have done us credit. As things were, although the Legion came too late, the fame of our country had been upheld throughout the campaign, and yeomen's service rendered to the Italian cause by the English free lances, by Dunne and Wyndham, by Peard and Dowling, by Dolmage and Patterson.

Garibaldi estimated accurately the limits of the degree to which he had improved his position by the recent victory on the Volturno. One day soon after the battle he came to Mario with a letter from Mazzini in his hand. ' Read this,' he said. ' Mazzini urges me on to attack Rome. You know that I have long been thinking of it. On the first of October we defeated the enemy so that they cannot meet us again in the open field. But I cannot advance on Rome leaving behind me 60,000 men intrenched in Capua and Gaeta, who can march into Naples the moment my back is turned.' He fully accepted the political consequences of the military situation. He abandoned all idea of advancing on Rome, and prepared to welcome the immediate advent of Victor Emmanuel.

Cavour, gravely anxious that Italy should present a united front to the Monarchs of Austria, Prussia, and Russia, who were about to hold an ominous conference at Warsaw, desired above all else that the Dictator should go out to welcome the King in the face of Italy and Europe, and was much concerned lest he should sail home to Caprera in dudgeon before Victor Emmanuel's arrival. This, rather than any fears of actual civil war, appears to have been the limit of Cavour's anxiety with regard to Garibaldi, from the first days of October onwards.* The Minister wisely sought counsel with Garibaldi's oldest and best friend, Augusto Vecchi, who had worn the red shirt beside his chief in South America, who had fought shoulder to shoulder with him in the midnight *mêlée* when the French troops burst through the defences of the Janiculum, and from whose house at Quarto, Garibaldi had sailed with the Thousand for Sicily. On October 1 Vecchi wrote to Garibaldi to implore him to hasten the plebiscite for the annexation of Naples, and to send a message inviting Victor Emmanuel to march without delay into his new dominions. Three days later Vecchi wrote again : ' Invite the King personally by a telegram to come quickly to Naples. And go to meet him. I ask this of you in the name of Italy, our mother, for whose greatness we two swore many years ago to make every kind of sacrifice.'

On the very day when Vecchi was writing in this strain, Garibaldi had already yielded the point and was inditing his famous letter to Victor Emmanuel, which, besides many expressions of goodwill and desire for unity, contained the following words :—

* On September 24 he had feared a collision with Garibaldi (*Chiala*, iv. 15), but this fear had been removed by Garibaldi's manifesto of welcome to the Royal troops a few days later. On October 4, Augusto Vecchi writes to Garibaldi : ' Cavour sent me word to call on him. I will tell you about our two hours' conversation. I laid bare to him all your noble heart. He regretted that you had not answered a letter of his. At the end of our interview, he told me to accompany you to meet the King. And he ended by saying that Venice would be ours six months sooner, if you did not separate yourself from Victor Emmanuel,—to put it more clearly, if you did not obstinately retire to Caprera ' [*viz.* before welcoming Victor Emmanuel to Naples]. If Cavour had still thought there was any chance of civil war, he would have been only too glad that Garibaldi should 'retire obstinately to Caprera.'

'CASERTA, *October* 4, 1860.

' SIRE,

' I congratulate Your Majesty on the brilliant victories won by your brave General Cialdini and on their happy results. . . . Since Your Majesty is at Ancona, you must make the journey to Naples by land or by sea. If by land, as would be best, Your Majesty ought to march with at least one division. If I were informed in time, I would move forward my right wing to meet you, and would come in person to present my homage and to receive your orders as to the final operations. . . .'

Cavour, therefore, as early as October 4 had gained his point that Garibaldi should invite the King and go out to meet him. But for another ten days there was trouble on the further question of the plebiscite, a controversy which became the storm-centre of the last political crisis of the Dictatorship. The question at issue was the proper method of obtaining the consent of the inhabitants of the Neapolitan Kingdom to their absorption in the Monarchy of Victor Emmanuel. Should they be consulted directly by plebiscite, by a simple referendum on the question of annexation, to which each elector could answer by his vote, ' yes ' or ' no ' ? Or should they place their fate in the hands of an assembly of elected representatives, who might then propose conditions on which the South would come into the National union ? Such were the two alternatives, and the choice between them was a question of more than mere form.

If Italy had had no armed enemies to fear either within or without the barrier of her guardian Alps, if she had been in safe possession of her own house, then indeed she ought to have gone about the difficult business of setting it in order with long and careful deliberation. the union of North and South Italy, like the union of Nor

and South Britain in 1707, had been proposed in a year
when the two Kingdoms were immune from invasion and
revolution, then indeed a Parliament at Naples and a
Parliament at Palermo might reasonably have sat for many
months bargaining with the Parliament at Turin. In such
a case some of the evils that have actually resulted from
a too close union might possibly have been avoided. Those
who know South Italy of to-day deplore the rigid and
mechanical application of the Piedmontese laws and administrative system to a state of society very different from
that of the sub-Alpine populations; and they deplore no
less the immense powers of self-government which under
the constitution of 1860 have been committed to the back-
ward communes of the South. But this was the necessary
price that Italy paid for her existence. In the crisis of that
autumn, with war and revolution still in the bowels of the
land, with an Austrian army eagerly awaiting the word to
cross the Mincio and rush on Milan, with the French Minister
already withdrawn from Turin, and every great European
Power except England hostile to the unification of Italy,
it would have been the height of unwisdom to waste two
months in electing and calling together Neapolitan and
Sicilian assemblies, and half a year more in bargainings and
intrigues of every kind, public and personal, into which
Southern Parliamentarians would instinctively plunge and
revel, if they found that they had their country in their
gift and Cavour on his knees to them to hand it over. If
Italian unity were to be accomplished at all—and all were
agreed that there was no other port of safety in sight—
then it must be done at once by direct acceptance of Piedmontese law and custom for the whole Peninsula, not
because that was best for all, but because that alone could
be established everywhere without delay. A plebiscite for
unconditional annexation could be held in a fortnight,

but an assembly might sit until it was dispersed by Austrian bayonets.

The men who in the second week of October besieged Garibaldi with petitions for an assembly instead of the plebiscite, were not, with the exception of the 'federalist' Cattaneo, primarily interested in obtaining a separate system of administration for the South. Their opposition to the plebiscite was essentially factious. Crispi and his friends desired an assembly where they might hope to dominate, and they objected to a plebiscite because it would in a fortnight's time bring to an end the Garibaldian Dictatorship which, so long as it lasted, left the executive power in their hands and kept out the hated Cavour. They played on the Dictator's distrust of the Minister. They cunningly reminded him that the plebiscite had been the device by which Napoleon III. had filched Nice and Savoy. There had arisen one of those complicated situations through which Garibaldi was least able to see his way in the light of the few simple rules by which he guided his conduct. His mind was darkened and he sat stupefied at the head of the council-board while the rival parties of plebiscite and assembly defied each other shrilly across the room.

Between October 11 and 13 a series of such councils were held at Caserta and in Naples. Old Giorgio Palla vicino, ' the martyr of the Spielberg,' the Austrian dungeon where he had sat for fourteen years in the early days of the *risorgimento* movement, was now Garibaldi's Pro Dictator of the Neapolitan mainland. He it was who stood in the breach against Crispi and Cattaneo, on behalf of immediate Italian unity. On October 11, at Caserta, Garibaldi decided for Crispi and an assembly. Pallavicino once gave in his resignation, and the city of Naples rose in great demonstration of protest in his favour. On all door windows, carriages, coats, and hats appeared cards inscribed *sì* (' yes '),—the vote that all desired to be allowed to give in plebiscite. Garibaldi returned to the Capital to find the streets in an uproar. He heard Pallavicino's name coupled with his own for *vivas*, while *morte* was cried out against Mazzini, Crispi, and the others who had persuaded him to summon an assembly. All along the Toledo it 'snowed *sìs*' into the carriage. Garibaldi was much perturbed by this clear manifestation of the popular will, for obedience to the people was one of the formulæ of his creed, in accordance with which he had long ago abandoned his republicanism in order to be in touch with his fellow-citizens.

On the thirteenth another council was held in his rooms at the Palazzo d'Angri. Pallavicino refused to take back his resignation unless the plan for an assembly were cancelled. In the middle of an angry dispute between the Pro-Dictator and Crispi, Türr produced a petition signed by thousands of hands in favour of the plebiscite. Garibaldi bowed his head over it in melancholy silence, and for some minutes his face was hidden. When he looked up the clouds had cleared away, and he wore the ' serene gaiety ' of his happiest and gentlest mood. ' If this is the desire of the Neapolitan people,' he said, ' it must be satisfied.' ' *Caro Giorgio*,' he said to Pallavicino, ' we need you here still.' The same evening Crispi resigned the secretariate, and his part in the history of Italy came to an end for that year.

The plebiscite was held on October 21. The elector-ate had no choice but to vote *yes* or *no* to the following proposition : ' The people wishes for Italy one and indi-visible with Victor Emmanuel as Constitutional King, and his legitimate descendants after him.' The result was shortly afterwards declared as follows :—

Neapolitan mainland 1,302,064 yes ; 10,312 no.
Sicily . . . . . 432,053 yes ; 667 no.*

The voting was open, and every one who voted ' no ' did
so in the face of a disapproving world.   No doubt, therefore,
the real minority was a very much larger proportion of the
citizens.   But if the plebiscite exaggerated, it did not belie
the opinion of the people.   Whether the majority of the
inhabitants of South Italy wished for Italian unity on its
own merits is fairly open to question, but they had shown
in more ways than one their earnest desire for immediate
and unconditional annexation as the only security against
the return of the House of Bourbon and the dreadful past
from which Garibaldi had delivered them.

Meanwhile, Victor Emmanuel was coming to take
possession of his new dominions.   On the afternoon of
September 29 he left Turin on his triumphal progress
that was yet a most perilous adventure, hoping that when
he wanted to return he would not find his northern capital
occupied by Austrians or by French.   Passing through
Bologna to the Ravennese coast he embarked on October
for Ancona.†   A storm arose, the frigate was in great
danger, and the seamen declared that the safest course was
to run across the Adriatic towards Pola in Austrian territory
But Victor Emmanuel, refusing to be put into the hand
of his enemies at such a crisis of Italian affairs, came o
deck to encourage the sailors, and remained there througho
the storm, while his staff officers were prostrated belo
Towards evening the sea went down, and before midnig

* In the Papal dominions the vote, held a few days later, went
follows :—

Marches 133,072 yes ; 1,212 no.
Umbria 99,628 yes ; 380 no.

† See Map VI., at end of book, for the King's route from Rave
southwards.

they entered the harbour of Ancona, where the King was welcomed ashore by Fanti, Cialdini, Della Rocca, and their victorious troops.

Some delay occurred in starting from Ancona, but on October 9 the great march began, the whole army moving, with the King in the midst, along the road to Naples. He passed near the battle-field of Castelfidardo, through Macerata and Loreto and thence along the Adriatic coast. He reached Grottammare, the last town in Papal territory, on October 11, and remained there four days inactive, probably from some cautionary reasons of diplomacy or politics. These were the days during which the political crisis on the question of the plebiscite was taking place in Naples. Only on October 15, after Pallavicino had triumphed over Crispi, did the King cross the Tronto and enter the Neapolitan Kingdom.

After following the coast-road as far as the fortress of Pescara, which had already come in to the national cause, they turned inland by way of Chieti and Popoli to Sulmona. Thus far, in Papal and in Neapolitan territory alike, the enthusiasm of the liberated people for their new King had been abundantly shown. All classes, including very many of the clergy, joined in the demonstrations, and triumphal arches and addresses of welcome impeded the rate of military progress. It was felt that no offence must be given to the King's new subjects, and he showed as much rough graciousness as his impatient nature contained. Other causes of delay were the neglected state of the high-road, and the absence of bridges over the innumerable dry torrent beds through which the siege-guns and commissariat waggons had to pass. For this was not a Garibaldian army; it moved slowly, but it was bringing with it the means to take Capua and Gaeta.

After they had passed Sulmona, the political sym-

pathies of the inhabitants were less unanimous. There
was still an enthusiastic ' Italian ' party to welcome them,
but at every turn of the road they saw fresh evidence of
civil war and massacre. The ' good Italians ' came in
with stories, usually only too true, of massacre and mutilation which their relations and friends had suffered. Rough
justice was administered on the roadside by Piedmontese
court-martials assisted by firing parties, and a proclamation
was issued that all peasants found with arms in their hands
would be shot. Even in this district some of the parish
priests showed themselves on the national side.

Cialdini with the vanguard was now two days' march
in front of the King. On October 20, near Isernia, where
a handful of Garibaldini had been repulsed only three
days before, he fell in with 5000 Bourbon troops under
General Scotti. Scotti neglected to send out scouts or
advance-guard, and marched his men in column right up
to Cialdini's hidden batteries. The Bersaglieri and line
regiments were let loose upon the enemy's surprised and
disordered mass, and the lancers of Novara charged through
the whole length of their column. In a few minutes Scotti
with nearly a thousand of his men had been captured,
and the rest dispersed over the country-side in hopeless
disbandment.

On October 25 Garibaldi crossed the Volturno by a
crazy bridge of planks a yard wide, supported on boats,
which had been flung across at the ferry of Formicola
The Italians had failed to make any bridge at all with the
scant materials to hand, but the task had been accom
plished by the British Legion with the expert assistance o
some ' handy men ' who appeared to be their fellow
countrymen and showed a suspicious readiness for an
service connected with ropes and water. The making c

the bridge had been conducted under fire, but the Bourbon troops, who had already abandoned Cajazzo, withdrew towards Capua and did not attempt to dispute the passage of the river after the bridge had been completed.

Leaving Medici to protect the lines at Sant' Angelo, Garibaldi with a few regiments of Italians and the British Legion advanced northwards through Bellona and Calvi to meet Victor Emmanuel. They bivouacked on the night of October 25 to 26 in the broad valley between the hills of Cajanello and Vajrano, where the high-road then, as the railway now, debouches from the gates of the wooded mountains into the flatter country that soon broadens out into the great plains of Capua. Most of the troops slept by the roadside below, but some were stationed on the heights of Vajrano, whence their watch-fires could be seen afar by three armies : for below them lay the camp of their fellow-Garibaldini ; close at hand to the south were Bourbon regiments ; and a few miles to the north lay Victor Emmanuel's army, the corps of Della Rocca and of Cialdini side by side on two converging roads, with the King's quarters between them.

On the morning of October 26 an Englishman among the Garibaldian outposts, who was sleeping in a dry ditch, was awakened by shouts of *Viva il Re!* Accustomed to hear 'Long live the King' as the Bourbon war-cry, he sprang up half-awake, thinking the enemy were upon them. Next moment he saw his mistake. Victor Emmanuel, King of Italy, was riding by.

About the same hour the Garibaldini on the hills of Vajrano awoke to see the whole Italian army, in all the panoply of war, move swiftly along the valley below towards the camp of the red-shirts on the edge of the great plain.

Garibaldi had overnight sent on Missori and Zasio to the Royal camp to announce his presence and offer his homage. At dawn he himself rode out with his staff to find the King, and stationed himself in front of the Toll-bar Tavern (*Taverna la catena*)—' a rustic cottage with a few poplars near it '—at the point of junction of the two roads along which the Royal army was coming.*

The Dictator and his staff, including Canzio and Mario, with Missori and Zasio who had now rejoined them, dismounted in front of the tavern and took their stand a little off the road along which the Northern regiments filed past. Battalion after battalion went by, gazing on Garibaldi, some with unmingled enthusiasm, gratitude, and love, others with a greater or less admixture of professional jealousy and political distrust. Generals Della Rocca and Cialdini both greeted him warmly that morning and were warmly welcomed in return, for neither of them was touched with that jealousy of the volunteers which embittered Fanti and many others among the regular officers. The victor of Castelfidardo and the Liberator of Sicily and Naples were divided by no cloud of petty rivalry, and if Cialdini instead of Fanti had been commander-in-chief of the Italian army, Cavour's instructions to show gratitude to the Garibaldini would have been heartily obeyed, much might have been forgotten and forgiven on both sides in the enthusiasm of the meeting, and the Serbonian bog of mutual reprisals and recrimination might have been shunned.

So the early morning wore on, while regiment after regiment of the Royal army marched past the Liberator It was a damp autumn air, and Garibaldi was not onl wearing his *poncho*, but had in homely fashion bound coloured handkerchief over his head. His staff, in the war-stained red shirts, presented a curious contrast to th brilliant uniforms that were filing by them hour by hou

* The modern railway-station of Cajanello-Vajrano is built within a f yards of the historic cross-roads.

Suddenly the strains of the Royal march were heard, and the cry arose, 'The King! The King is coming!' Garibaldi and his staff mounted their horses and rode forward to the edge of the road. Victor Emmanuel, on a prancing Arab, dashed up to meet them. The Dictator, sweeping his hat off his kerchiefed head, cried aloud—'*Saluto il primo Re d' Italia*'—'I hail the first King of Italy.' * The King stretched out his hand and the two men clasped and held hands for more than a minute.

'*Come state, caro Garibaldi ?*'

'*Bene, Maestà, e Lei ?*'

'*Benone.*'†

Then they rode on together, and the two staffs behind them, red shirts side by side with resplendent uniforms, crosses, and cordons of honour. It was an epitome of the union of conservative and revolutionary forces that had crushed the obscurantists and expelled the foreigners. The constrained conversation between the two groups betrayed the heart-burnings on either side, and the grudging sacrifices that each was making to the other. But although there was cold politeness where there should have been enthusiasm, none the less that ride together was the making of Italy, and seen down history's lengthening vista, remains evermore a goodly sight.

After a while Garibaldi and his men turned off the road to the left and made their way back by country lanes to Calvi, while the King held on to Teano. 'Garibaldi's countenance,' writes Mario, ' was full of melancholy sweetness. Never did I feel drawn to him with such

* Missori was always very particular to say that the words he heard uttered by Garibaldi were '*primo* re,' not merely 're.' Missori told me that Garibaldi's idea was to make a kind of implied 'investiture' or at least ' ceremony.'

† ' How are you, dear Garibaldi ? ' ' Well, your Majesty; and you ? ' ' First rate.'

tenderness.' He said little that evening to his friends. Next morning they met Jessie Mario, who had crossed the Volturno to provide hospital arrangements north of the river. 'My wounded,' said Garibaldi to her somewhat sternly, ' are all on the south of the Volturno.'   And then, relapsing into his gentlest mood, he added, ' Jessie, they have sent us to the rear ' (' *ci hanno messi alla coda* '). During their ride together Victor Emmanuel had told him in soft words the hard decree that the Royal army would take over all the operations of war and that the Garibaldini were no longer required.

CHAPTER XV

THE RETURN TO CAPRERA

'Semplice in atti e semplice in parole,
Chi della Patria cavalier si cinse
Dona tutto alla Patria, e nulla vuole.'
                    MARRADI. *Rapsodie Garibaldine.*

'Simple in act and word, his country's knight,
He gives his country all and nothing takes.'

THAT part of the enemy's force which had been in the
neighbourhood of the two national armies at the moment
of their junction on October 26, retired in the afternoon
towards Gaeta and effaced themselves behind the line of
Garigliano. On the morning of the 27th Victor Emmanuel
rode from Teano to Calvi in search of Garibaldi. Finding
that he had returned to the south bank of the Volturno, the
King pushed on alone with his staff in the same direction,
crossed the rickety little bridge, and entered the Garibaldian
lines at Sant' Angelo. The volunteers came swarming out
to welcome the unexpected visitor, with cries of devotion
and enthusiasm which showed how far a very little attention
from the official world would have gone to win the hearts
of the main body of Garibaldini. Unfortunately this
surprise visit was the last effort which His Majesty was
permitted to make by way of showing personal gratitude
to the rank and file of the volunteers.

Since Garibaldi was absent, not knowing of the King's
visit, Medici did the honours of the occasion, helped by

286 GARIBALDI AND THE MAKING OF ITALY

Nino Bixio's lieutenants. Bixio himself was in hospital at Naples. At the crossing of the Volturno two days before, whence he was to have accompanied the Dictator to meet the King, Nino had headed a hue and cry after a priest suspected of acting as spy, and riding furiously after the man to arrest him had let his horse slip in a narrow lane, and fractured his leg against a wall. He lay, however, quite happy in the hospital at Naples, for his wife came out from Genoa to nurse him, and since the volunteer's part in the fighting was over he was able to turn his mind to the docile family affections which shared dominion in his heart with the rage for his country's service.

Victor Emmanuel, after having fraternised with Medici's men, and ridden close up to the walls of Capua at the greatest risk of being cut off by the enemy's outposts, recrossed the Volturno and returned to Teano. His army was there divided into two, one part going on towards the line of the Garigliano and Gaeta, and the other under General Della Rocca coming south to besiege Capua. Della Rocca had to negotiate a delicate situation with Garibaldi. Although the red-shirts were no longer to be allowed to take part in the serious operations of the campaign, yet on October 2 their services were still required for yet a few days longer to help guard the lines for the royal siege batteries. Garibaldi fearing that his men might be annoyed at receiving orders from Della Rocca if they considered that a slight was being put upon themselves or their chief, not only placed the whole of his army at the absolute disposal of the Piedmontese general, but was at pains to devise a plan where by Della Rocca's orders were conveyed to the red-shirts through Sirtori, as though they still came from Garibaldi himself. He strictly enjoined on his staff to prevent the men from knowing that the orders did not in reality ema nate from him. Shaking his supplanter warmly by the hand, he wished him luck, and rode off to Caserta.

Two days later Della Rocca, who had been deeply touched by Garibaldi's generous conduct, hearing that he was ill at Caserta, went there to pay him a visit. He found him in a little room over the guard-house of the Palace, exactly above a large store of gunpowder.

'I begged him,' writes Della Rocca, ' to move immediately, and smiling he promised to do so. Propped up with pillows, he was wrapped in a military cloak, a little cap on his head, and a silk handkerchief knotted round his neck. As I entered, he held out his hand, and seemed quite touched when I told him I had only come to ask how he was. He was still more pleased when I told him how well I got on with his generals, Cosenz and Sirtori, notable personages and most excellent men, and how I regretted the enforced absence of Bixio. . . . Mine were no idle compliments. I meant what I said, and I saw that Garibaldi was pleased that I appreciated his friends.'

Meanwhile, Della Rocca's batteries were being scientifically erected by the engineers of the regular army, in front of the Garibaldian lines. On November 1, at four in the afternoon, all was ready, and a red flag run up on the summit of Monte Tifata gave the signal for the bombardment. The enemy replied and the duel lasted on through the night. Some of the houses in the town were set on fire, and the Capuans, many of whom secretly hated the falling dynasty, protested to the General of the garrison the necessity for instant surrender. At dawn of November 2 the officers on the terrace of Sant' Angelo Church eagerly turned their telescopes towards Capua, and saw the white flag hoisted on its walls. The garrison of 10,000 men became prisoners of war, and the fortress that had set a limit to Garibaldi's career at length surrendered to the Italian army.

While Della Rocca was taking Capua, Fanti and Cial·

dini were drawing the net round Gaeta. On October 29 a reconnaissance against the enemy's strong position on the hills behind the mouth of the Garigliano was pushed too far, partly by the carelessness of the generals, partly by the unwillingness of the Bersaglieri to obey the orders to retreat. The action cost the Italian army over fifty men and showed that their opponents could still fight. But a day or two later, when the Italian fleet opened fire on their flank and rear, the Bourbon forces abandoned the position on the Garigliano and fell back towards the great fortress. On November 2, the day of the fall of Capua, a successful action at Mola di Gaeta on the coast placed the Italian army in a situation to besiege Gaeta in form.

During the first ten days of November some 17,000 Neapolitan soldiers, closely pursued by Victor Emmanuel's troops, escaped over the frontier into Papal territory at Terracina, and were disarmed and interned among the Alban hills by the Papal authorities and the French garrison of Rome. The remainder of the Bourbon army that had not already disbanded or surrendered, was now shut up in the citadel of Messina, in one or two small forts in Sicily and the Abruzzi, or with the ex-King and Queen in Gaeta.

The siege of Gaeta was protracted all the winter, because Napoleon III. kept the French fleet in those waters with orders to prevent the Italian fleet from bombarding the fortress. The siege operations had therefore to be conducted entirely from the land side, and were not brought to a successful issue until February, 1861. The long siege enabled Maria Sophia, Francis II.'s young Bavarian Queen, to display to Europe from the battlements of the bombarded fortress a heroine's courage, which illuminated with sunset glow the last vision of that inglorious dynasty which had known no rays at noontide.

Napoleon's action in stopping the war at sea while allowing it to be carried to its conclusion on land, had no permanent effect save to irritate Italians and to efface from their minds all claims of gratitude for his recent complaisance with regard to Umbria and the Marches. It is difficult, at first sight, to assign a reason for an interference at once so feeble and so exasperating. The Emperor's biographer, La Gorce, unable as ever to understand his sympathy with Italian freedom, supposes that he wished to ' clear his personal honour ' by this tangible protest against Victor Emmanuel's piratical attack on the Kingdom of Naples. Such may be the feelings of a French Clerical in face of the Liberation of Italy, but it is difficult to suppose that they were those of Napoleon III., only two months after he had given his consent to Cavour's invasion of the Papal Marches. The secret agreement which he had made at Chambéry was that the North Italian army should invade and traverse the Papal territory, so as to arrive at Naples in time to stop Garibaldi and ' absorb the revolution.' In making this arrangement Napoleon did not imagine that Victor Emmanuel had undertaken to put down Garibaldi merely in order to restore Francis II. to the throne. The Emperor did not like the annexation of South Italy by Piedmont, but he had agreed to it as the least of many possible evils. Therefore his motive in sending the French fleet to Gaeta was probably not so much genuine indignation at the conduct of the King of Italy, as the perception that he must appear to be angry for the sake of the French Clericals, whose loyalty, so essential to his throne, he had strained almost to breaking-point.

On the 8th of October, Cavour had written to Farini, the Minister in attendance on Victor Emmanuel :—

10

'If Garibaldi's army acclaims the King, it must be treated well. We have to contend against the requirements and pedantries of the regular army. Do not give in. Reasons of State of the first importance demand firmness. Woe to us if we show ourselves ungrateful to those who have shed their blood for Italy! Europe would condemn us. In the country there would be a great reaction in favour of the Garibaldini. I have had a warm argument with Fanti on this point. He spoke of military requirements. I replied that this was not Spain, and that here the army had to obey.'

It was a great misfortune that Cavour was unable to secure the fulfilment, in spirit as well as in letter, of hi wise and benevolent intentions. Victor Emmanuel, wh had hitherto been more enthusiastic for Garibaldi tha Cavour himself, fell at this critical moment under th influence of Fanti and the military pedants. Garibal and his troops had welcomed the King and his arm and had taken the place assigned them in the rear, in manner which no one had been able to criticise, and whi had elicited the gratitude and praise of Della Rocca, t General most concerned. There was therefore not t smallest provocation for the official insult to which whole body of Garibaldini were subjected on November On that day they had been instructed that the King wo come to review them at Caserta. The Dictator was present his Generals and his favourite officers to t Sovereign, and the red-shirts were to march past. S a day might well have been a turning-point in the of the new-born nation. Old feuds, instead of taking fresh and more virulent forms, would have been soo or healed. The Garibaldini assembled at Caserta feelings of loyalty and pride. They were drawn u front of the Bourbon Palace in their picturesque regin —good, bad, and indifferent, Sicilian and Calabrian, N

erner and Tuscan. They waited till after the appointed
hour and then learnt that the King had determined not
to come.

No apology or explanation was sent, or has ever since
been offered. Further to point the moral, Victor Emmanuel did not even write an order-of-the-day thanking the
men who had won for him the crown of the Two Sicilies.
Still less would Fanti, the commander-in-chief, put his
name to such a document. It was signed by Della Rocca.

The man who suffered most from the consequences of
this ungracious conduct was the man who had vainly striven
to avert the folly. It was against Cavour that Garibaldi
turned his wrath; his personal devotion to Victor Emmanuel
stood the shock. He persuaded himself that these acts of
petty meanness had been specially ordered by the Minister
at Turin, though in fact they had been suggested either
directly by Fanti or indirectly by the atmosphere of jealousy
natural to a regular army in the presence of volunteers.
This jealousy, common to every professional service in the
world, and aggravated at Naples by the fact that these
volunteers had really won their laurels, Cavour was unable
to control from his cabinet in Turin. Next spring, in the
first session of the first Parliament of United Italy, Garibaldi's pent-up wrath boiled over in a misdirected and
malicious attack on the statesman who had been his guardian-
angel throughout the year of wonders.

Garibaldi was sometimes unjust, but he seldom missed
an occasion to be generous. And on the very afternoon
of the thwarted review he had a magnificent opportunity.
General Cialdini arrived at Caserta, commissioned to
obtain his promise to enter Naples on the following day
in the same carriage with the King. It was very desirable that the Dictator should appear at Victor Emmanuel's side, for if it became known that he had absented

himself with a grievance, it was doubtful wl
reception the Royal party would obtain. Tl
indeed have been a fair case for him to refus
Naples with the King who had failed his appoi
the review. But he liked Cialdini well, and a
demur, and a good deal of strong language aga
and Cavour, he finally consented to go.

On November 7 the first King of Italy en
southern capital, with Garibaldi sitting beside hi
carriage. They were both out of temper, and
in torrents. But the Neapolitans were again in
of frantic enthusiasm, which the rain could no
although it ruined the triumphal arches and cai
rows of paste-board allegorical figures to double
they had been shot.

If the King had been permitted to use common c
to the Garibaldian army in the matter of the revi
had shown more imaginative sympathy with me
haps over-sensitive, little complaint could justly
been made of the treatment accorded to their m
interests. In this matter Victor Emmanuel wa:
to see the right thing done, saying, ' I cannot sho
generosity than Garibaldi.'

It had been Cavour's original intention to divic
Garibaldini into three sections : the first and fa
largest to be disbanded at once with a gratuity for
man ; the second to constitute a separate volu
division of the army under the title of *Cacciatori*
Alpi ; the third to consist of a small number of of
to be given commissions in the regular army. But
plan was not carried out. It was decided not to
stitute a permanent force of volunteers attached to
army, partly for fear of professional quarrels and polii
complications that might arise out of the existence of s

a force, and partly because nearly all the genuine volunteers who had done the fighting were anxious to return at once to their families and their work in life. The privates, therefore, were sent back each to his home with a gratuity. The Hungarians alone, who had no homes to which they could return, were taken into the Royal service, and were engaged for many years in the inglorious but dangerous task of tracking down the reactionary brigands of Molise and Abruzzi.

There remained the question of the officers. Since Cavour's scheme of a permanent volunteer force had been abandoned, it was felt to be only just that a very large number of Garibaldi's officers should be given posts in the regular army. A military commission, on which Sirtori, Medici, and Cosenz had seats, chose out the officers most fit to be admitted into the King's service. It was a difficult task, for there were six or seven thousand so-called ' officers ' of all sorts, drawing Garibaldi's pay in Sicily and on the mainland in the first days of November, about one ' officer ' to every seven privates. Half or more of these must have been absolutely unworthy of permanent commissions. In the course of the next two years 1,584 of the best men were picked out and admitted as officers to the regular army. Medici, Bixio, Cosenz, and nine others were made Generals. These arrangements were regarded with intense indignation by Garibaldi and his intimates at Caprera, who had expected that the volunteers would be kept in being as a permanent force, to form a nucleus for the national *levée en masse* in the coming war for Venice and Rome. But the settlement cannot, in a fair review of all the circumstances, be called either impolitic or unjust, although there were many individual cases of harsh treatment of men who had deserved well of their country.

Although Victor Emmanuel was now in full possession of Naples, the half-formed Kingdom of Italy was still in grave danger. On October 22 Cavour had felt 'the certainty that Austria will attack us.' Every day that passed in safety added to the chances of peace and to the meagre possibilities of resistance in case of war. But the Emperors of Austria and Russia and the King of Prussia had met in conference at Warsaw, an ill-omened gathering of the murderers on the tomb of their victim, and Europe looked on to see whether they would decide to slay Italy as they had slain Poland. At this crisis the Italian position was strengthened by the pronouncement of the British Foreign Minister in favour of the right of the Italians to settle their own affairs. Lord John's famous despatch was his own spontaneous act, a personal proclamation of the principles of Charles James Fox, the gospel by which Russell's life had been inspired and guided. England, who had often supported these principles and often opposed them, was in one of her generous moods, and applauded to the echo her champion's defiance of despotic Europe. The first sentence plunges *in medias res*: 'It appears that the late proceedings of the King of Sardinia [Piedmont] have been strongly disapproved by several of the principal Courts of Europe.' After telling some home-truths about the character of the Papal and Neapolitan Governments, Lord John announces that—

'Her Majesty's Government must admit that the Italians are the best judges of their own interests.' 'It is difficult,' he proceeds, 'to believe, after the astonishing events that we have seen, that the Pope and the King of the Two Sicilies possessed the love of their people.' Therefore 'Her Majesty's Government can see no sufficient ground for the severe censure with which Austria, France, Prussia, and Russia have visited the acts of the King of Sardinia. Her Majesty's Government will turn their eyes rather to the gratifying prospect of a people

building up the edifice of their liberties, and co.
work of their independence.'

This despatch, written on October 27 and
in the early days of November, was greeted v
of joy by the Italian people. Cavour, who l
been somewhat annoyed by Lord John's insist
that Italy must not go to war to liberate Veni
that he had now more than made amends.* :
despatch has sometimes been depreciated as a m
of trumpets over the *fait accompli* of United l
such was not the view of the men who best ι
Italy's needs. Hudson wrote to Russell that wh
first read it, ' he shouted, rubbed his hands, ju
sat down again, then began to think, and when
up tears were standing in his eyes. Behind your
he saw the Italy of his dreams, the Italy of his h
Italy of his policy.' Cavour himself wrote to thanι
in the strongest language for ' the immense servicι
rendered Italy,' and his trusted agent Villamarι
the despatch was worth an army of 100,000 men.

The feeling of Cavour's countrymen for Lorι
Russell, as one of the chief instruments in their
tion, was shown in many different ways during
mainder of his life. Once, in 1869, when he and his
were staying in a villa at San Remo, they found the
of the principal room frescoed with portraits of four na
heroes. The four turned out to be Mazzini, Gari
Cavour, and, to their surprise and delight, Lord

* Lord John feared in 1860 that a war for Venice, under the eι
conditions of Europe, would mean a renewal of Italian dependence on F
more Napoleonic aggrandisement, and a general European war. H
not lukewarm in his desire to see Austria quit Venetian territory, for
that happy event took place in 1866 he went with his family to see and rι
over the official act of the liberation of Venice, and the entry of V
Emmanuel up the Grand Canal.

himself ! Neither had the house been specially prepared for their reception.

It has of recent years been somewhat the fashion to blame Lord John Russell for his failures, but never to praise him for his triumphs. Fashions in history come and go, more often the reflex of tendencies in the present than the result of new knowledge of the past. It is probable that very few British statesmen in the course of their lives did as much to reinvigorate and secure the institutions of our country as was done by Russell in 1830-32, or won for her as much well-deserved gratitude and such enduring friendship abroad as was secured by his action in 1859-60. On the Italian question England secured peace with true honour, and has never since, either in point of interest or of conscience, had reason to repent of her work.

On the day of their entrance into Naples and on the following day, Victor Emmanuel and Garibaldi held private colloquies. The out-going Dictator asked to be continued in power for another year as the King's Lieutenant, and to have the grade of all his officers recognised. Such requests showed how utterly incapable Garibaldi was of understanding the difficulties of administrative and military reorganisation that confronted the new State.

On November 8 the throne-room in the Palace was the scene of an imposing ceremony, the official presentation of the result of the plebiscite, and the investiture of Victor Emmanuel with the Kingship of Sicily and Naples. The new Monarch was seated on his throne. Garibaldi and his friends stood in one group, the courtiers and army officers in another, and small cordiality was shown between them. But the act of annexation was duly signed by all parties, and Garibaldi, formally resigning the Dictatorship,

left the room a private citizen once mor(
in that capacity was to publish a letter callir.
to rally round Victor Emmanuel, and to
follow him next spring, a million strong, a€
Venice. ' By the side of the *Re galantuo1*
' every quarrel should disappear, every ran
pated.' Garibaldi's public utterances durin
of strained relations were as loyal as if eve:
made had been conceded by the King.

Before nightfall he sent Missori to tell
Admiral that he would leave for Caprera ea.
morning, November 9, and would come aboard t
to pay a farewell visit before he quitted th(
spent the night in the Hotel d'Angleterre (or
anniche) in the Chiaja, talking with Missori, Ma.
Zasio, and others of his intimate friends. As
these last days, he was in a melancholy and ger
moving his followers to tears when he spoke of th(
on the morrow. In spite of the brave words of
lamation in which he thanked his soldiers, and ,
them to be ready against the next spring, all felt
hearts the presentiment that their day of glory w
end. And so these men, who had seized occasion
forelock and had performed at the appointed 1
the miracle never to be repeated, sat up all night
hotel and talked sadly of what they had done a:
undone.

Next morning, before dawn, they went down to,
to the port. The city was still asleep, and there w
one to witness the departure, which had been kept :
from every one except the British Admiral. They
a boat, rowed over to the *Hannibal*, and came up
side of the great three-decker, between the darkness
the first twilight. Admiral Mundy, still in his cot,

10 *a*

told that Garibaldi was in the cabin, and turned out with all haste to receive the strange man whom he had learnt to admire and love, while still keeping the open eye of common sense on his single-minded fanaticism. During a long talk in the cabin, Garibaldi invited Mundy to be his guest in his cottage at Caprera, ' and spoke much of the beautiful harbour between the island and the main, where Nelson had once anchored for the protection of his fleet.' As they passed up from the cabin to the quarter-deck, Garibaldi saw the Admiral's visiting-book lying on the small table upon which, six months before, at Palermo, he and the Bourbon Generals had signed the armistice, the source of such mighty consequences. He sat down and wrote in the book in French :—

' G. Garibaldi owes to Admiral Mundy the most lively gratitude, which will last all his life, on account of sincere proofs of friendship with which he has been loaded in all kinds of circumstances.'

As he went down the ship's side many of the officers and crew of the *Hannibal* were deeply moved, and the expressions which some of them afterwards used about ' the look of intense love ' upon his face testify to the unique effect of his presence upon men trained in no sentimental school of thought or character.

From the *Hannibal* he rowed to the *Washington*, the steamer that was to take him home. On her deck he parted from Canzio, Missori, Mario, and his other friends, who returned to the quay. His last words to them were ' To meet again at Rome.' Only his son Menotti and one or two persons of less importance sailed with him to the island. He returned thither as poor a man as he had left it in the spring. In the last two days Victor Emmanuel had offered him an estate for Menotti, the title of King's

aide-de-camp for his younger son, a dowry for his
a royal castle and a steamer for himself. Bu
refused them all. His secretary, Basso, had
a few hundred francs of paper-money from a f
necessary expenses. He himself had stowed on l
Washington a bag of seed-corn for his farm. W
spoils the steamer, almost unobserved, left port
of day.

He was soon back at his old daily occupations ₁
primitive struggle with nature, at which, but for
of a great epoch and a great cause, he would so
have spent his whole life. Again the dawn and ₁
light on the Straits of Bonifacio saw him at work
the granite boulders, industriously putting seed i₁
scrapings of earth which he called his fields; sh₁
a few sad vines from the sweeping winds of the ₣
calling up his cows by name from their pasturage
the wild, odorous brushwood; and seeking the ₰
goats on the precipice-top. Under these conditio₁
melancholy of his last days on the mainland soc
him. When, a few weeks later, a visitor came on b₁
from Genoa, he found Garibaldi 'robust in health
radiant with a calm and serene joy.' For when on
had been left alone again with his mother Earth, be
rock and sea and sky, no disappointment could pr
him from feeling in his heart the truth, that he had
a mighty labour, and taken his share in a task whicl
years would soon complete and the long generations ₁
—the Making of Italy.

EPILOGUE

I HAVE now told the story of Garibaldi for the two years 1849 and 1860 that give him his title to enduring fame. It is not my intention to carry any further the chronicle of his life; partly because the documents which alone could unfold the inner history of the affairs of Aspromonte and Mentana are not available; still more because Garibaldi's actions after 1860 are no longer the hinge on which the fortunes of Italy revolve, but are merely important episodes in the movement to liberate Venice and Rome, which was brought to fruition by very different forces. But I feel the need to add here a few pages of summary, unnecessary to the student, but perhaps useful to the reader unfamiliar with the bare outlines of Garibaldi's subsequent career.

In 1861 the spell of Italy's amazing good fortune was broken by the irreparable calamity of the death of Cavour. If he had died two years before, it is not improbable that Italy might still at this day be divided and enslaved; if he had lived ten years longer the young country would have escaped many falls in learning to walk.* Cavour was succeeded by smaller men, who made it their custom to court popularity one day by flattering Garibaldi's designs on Rome, and on the next to arrest his movement in panic,

* There is now an adequate biography of this great man available for the Anglo-Saxon public in Mr. W. R. Thayer's *Life and Times of Cavour* (1911).

/ any further the chronic[le]
le documents which also
· of the affairs of Aspr[o]
available; still more becaus[e]
o are no longer the hinge o[n]
revolve, but are merely in[-]
ement to liberate Venice and
o fruition by very differen[t]
to add here a few pages of
e student, but perhaps use-
ith the bare outlines of Gari[-]

s amazing good fortune was
nity of the death of Cavour,
re, it is not improbable that
be divided and enslaved; if
. . . would

'Italian bullet.' He was carried down, a prisoner and in great pain, from the mountain where two years before he had triumphed over the Bourbon armies.

He had not fully recovered from the wound of Aspromonte when in 1864 he paid his famous visit to England. Never has any foreigner, hardly ever any native hero, been received as Garibaldi was received by our fathers. The quiet square in front of Stafford House,* near St. James's Palace, is one of the rare places in modern London which is still 'a haunt of ancient peace,' and few of those who hurry across it on their daily avocations would guess what scenes it witnessed when Garibaldi was lodged there. When the Duke of Sutherland's four-horse carriage, containing the son of the skipper of Nice in his red shirt and grey blanket, struggled in the course of six hours through five miles of London streets, amid half a million of our people who had turned out to greet him, the wild procession carriage, in which he had come, literally fell to pieces in the stable, strained to breaking-point by the weight of thousands of strong arms that had snatched at and clung to its sides as it passed through a London gone mad with joy.

After the long interval following the Chartist collapse, the tide of British Democracy was just beginning to stir again with that peaceful but irresistible ground-swell that resulted three years later, after the quietest of great crises, in the enfranchisement of the working men. The successful emancipation of Italy and the visit of Garibaldi had their part in stimulating this movement in England. To the common people it was an unexampled privilege to carry one of themselves in triumph through London streets, as if he had been Wellington or Cæsar. But he won, no less, the hearts of the English upper classes, at that time heartily antagonistic to continental clericalism and despotism. The Duchess of Sutherland drove him into School-yard at Eton, followed by boys and masters shouting after him as if he had just won them the match against Harrow.

While he was staying under Mr. Seely's roof in the Isle of Wight, he went to visit his brother poet, always an enthusiast for Italian freedom. They smoked and repeated Italian poetry to each other with great fervour. 'What a noble human being!' wrote Tennyson when he had parted from his guest. 'I expected to see a hero and I was not disappointed. One cannot exactly say of him what Chaucer says of the ideal Knight, "As meke he was of port as is a maid." He is more majestic than meek, and his manners have a certain divine simplicity in them, such as I have never witnessed in a native of these islands, among men at least, and they are gentler than those of most young maidens whom I know.' In

worldly matters, Tennyson noted \
stupidity of a hero.' *

During the same month he sa
stone, his ' precursor,' as he called
of Naples. Mr. Gladstone, though $
ated belief,' thus spoke of his visit
who then saw Garibaldi for the firs
us never forget the marvellous effec
minds by the simple nobility of his
manners and his acts. . . . Besides hi
and his wide and universal sympathies,
tive simplicity of manner which never c
and that inborn and native grace which
all his actions, I would almost select
quality this, which was in apparent contrast
in Garibaldi—the union of the most profi
humanity with his fiery valour.'†

In 1866 the quarrel of the two German
Italy to acquire her present North-Eastern \
that barter of her independence to Franc
John Russell had always feared would be the \
While the Prussians defeated the main Aus
the plains of Bohemia, their Italian allies \
attacked the Venetian quadrilateral. The \

---

* It was on this visit that Garibaldi planted the tree \
long afterwards celebrated as—

> ' . . . the waving pine which here
> The warrior of Caprera set,
> A name that earth will not forget
> Till earth has roll'd her latest year.'

† ' The General's gestures,' wrote Bruzzesi, one of Garibalc
cerning followers, ' are marvellous, and much more perfect than \
In his language he sometimes repeats himself, in his gestures
language is not invariably good ; but his gestures are alway
perfect. They are never comic, always dramatic. I believe if l
Garibaldi, he would be the greatest tragic actor known.'

under La Marmora and Della Rocca was repulsed by the Austrians at Custozza, owing to bad generalship, which failed to bring the great mass of the troops into action. The naval disaster at Lissa, under Persano, was much worse. The only glimmer of partial success shone on the arms of Garibaldi and his volunteers in the Trentine Alps, though Garibaldi scored no remarkable victories such as he had won over the Austrians in his Alpine campaign of 1859. His vigour was not what it had once been. The regular army was preparing to renew the attack on Venetia when the war came suddenly to an end. The complete Prussian victory at Königgrätz had led to the surrender by Austria of her Venetian territory. All Italy was now free, except the Trentino and Rome, with the small province in which it stood.

In the autumn of 1867 Garibaldi, now turned sixty, headed another rush on Rome, with an ill-selected mob of followers, very different from the thousand youthful veterans who had been so carefully picked out to follow him to Sicily seven years before. At Mentana the intervention of the French troops on behalf of the Papalists turned the day against the Garibaldini, part of whom stood their ground and were mowed down by the *chassepots*, while part ran, as Garibaldi said, like ' cowardly rabbits.' Hedged by French bayonets, Rome remained to the priests for three years more. Aspromonte and Mentana had at least kept the country's passion fixed steadily on Rome, and prevented the Government from acquiescing in a state of things that appeared only too likely to become permanent, though it could never have given peace.

But the end came at last. The result of the first battles in the Franco-Prussian war caused the withdrawal of the French garrison from Rome, and on September 20, 1870, less than three weeks after Sedan, Victor Emmanuel's

id. The complete Prussian
:o the surrender by Austria
Italy was now free, except
the small province in which

;aribaldi, now turned sixty,
le, with an ill-selected mob
rom the thousand youthful
refully picked out to follow
ore. At Mentana the inter-
on behalf of the Papalists
ibaldini, part of whom stood
d down by the *chassepots*,
id, like ' cowardly rabbits.'
ome remained to the priests
onte and Mentana had at
\.\.\.\. .\.\.\.\.\.dily on Rome,

gimento epoch came to an end. Two years later Mazzini died.

In the winter of 1870, after the withdrawal of the French
from Rome, the deposition of Napoleon III., and the proclamation of the Republic in Paris, Garibaldi's sympathies
went round to the side of France, whom he regarded in the
later stages of the struggle as a free country once more,
despoiled and oppressed by a power representing the military
and despotic principles of Eastern Europe. The old man
summoned his followers and went off to defend the French
Republic against the Prussians. Much controversy has
raged as to the part played by the gallant Italians in that
winter campaign. But whether it is true or false that
Garibaldi's powers were atrophied by advancing years, at
least he had not grown old in generosity to a sister nation
or in his will to succour the oppressed.*

After his return from France he lived on another dozen
\.\.\.\. .\. .\.\. .\.\. .\.\.\.\.\.\. five. He was nearly always

Rome. It is entirely to the credit of his countrymen that they continued to regard him as a demi-god when his star had paled for the rest of Europe, and when it was only too apparent that this demi-god was no more exempt than Tithonus from the ravages of age, and from other weaknesses of mortal men.

The end came in his white house at Caprera, on a June evening in 1882. The old sailor, farmer, and fighter was propped up on the pillows to watch for the last time the sunlight gilding the waves and the granite rocks. While his life was slowly ebbing out, two little birds whom he had taught not to fear him fluttered in from the moor, and sat chirping on the window-sill. The attendants were about to drive them away lest they should disturb him, when that voice was heard once more by men, bidding them let the little birds come in, and always feed them after he was gone. And having given these orders, he went upon his last expedition.

Garibaldi is not to be judged as a professional soldier leading modern armies, but as the greatest master that the world has seen of that department of human activity known as revolutionary war. In that special kind of warfare, the political and moral atmosphere in which the campaign is conducted is more than half the battle ; and in the creation of this atmosphere Garibaldi excelled all men of whom history has left record. His military plans, absurd by any ordinary rules of war, succeeded because of the terror his name struck into his foes, because of the enthusiasm his presence aroused among his own army and in the civil population, who are often the decisive third factor in a revolutionary campaign. And in the purely military side of his methods he had genius of the first order as a leader of voluntary armies of moderate size. He

could never have commanded a regular force of 10(
men, but he managed to defeat one.

But Garibaldi's claim on the memory of men rest
more than his actual achievements. It rests on
which was one part of his professional equipment
soldier of revolution, but which surpasses and transc
it—his appeal to the imagination. He was a poet, i
save literary power. He was guided in political
somewhat even in military situations by a poet's inst
and motives. He is perhaps the only case, except B
for a few weeks in Greece, of the poet as man of ac
For most poets, if they ever take part in action, cea:
be poetical. While he was alive this quality was botl
strength and his weakness—Samson's locks and Ach
heel. But now that he is dead, the poetry in his chari
and career is all gain in his race for immortal laurels.
history of events is ephemeral and for the scholar;
poetry of events is eternal and for the multitude.
the acted poem that lives in the hearts of millions to w
the written words of history and the written word
poetry are alike an unopened book. So Garibaldi bec(
the symbol of Italia to her children in all ages to (
and on either side of the Atlantic. As the centuries sli]
carrying into oblivion almost all that once was nobl
renowned, Mazzini's soul and Cavour's wisdom wil
forgotten by the Italian who tends the vine or sweats b
the furnace sooner than the old grey cloak and the red
and that face of simple faith and love. And to us of (
lands, and most of all to us Englishmen, Garibaldi wil
as the incarnate symbol of two passions not likely
to die out of the world—the love of country and the
of freedom, kept pure by the one thing that can tam(
yet not weaken them, the tenderest humanity for all
kind.

APPENDIX

By the great kindness of Mr. Rollo Russell, to whom, as to his sister, Lady Agatha Russell, I am much indebted for materials for the history of 1859–60, I have been allowed to see the private correspondence with Italy of Lord John Russell while Secretary for Foreign Affairs. I have spoken at the end of Chapter I. above of the very great importance of these private letters, more particularly those of Henry Elliot, the British Minister at Naples, and Sir James Hudson, the British Minister at Turin. We see in them the process by which British statesmen were induced during the course of Garibaldi's expedition of 1860 to accept the idea of Italian Unity contrary to their previous views and intentions. Russell, Palmerston, and Gladstone had long been friends of Italian liberty, but they did not see that unity was the condition of liberty until they were convinced by events and by the letters of Hudson and Elliot, who were themselves converted to the doctrine of Unity only by Garibaldi's success in Sicily. The following extracts and analyses will interest, I think, the general reader.

1860, May 1. *Hudson to Russell.* From Turin. [Garibaldi still at Quarto, preparing to sail for Sicily.]

'I feel convinced that both France and Austria mean mischief, France will not tolerate the substantial aggrandisement of this country [Piedmont] and its institutions, and Austria yet dreams of reconquest. If you abstain in Sicily and at Naples, Italy, in my opinion, has not much chance of being left to the Italians.'

May 4. *Hudson to Russell.* [Two days before Garibaldi sailed.] Hudson encloses a letter of Mr. Fenton's from Flor-

much indebted for mai...
ve been allowed to see the
of Lord John Russell while
. have spoken at the end of
at importance of these private
of Henry Elliot, the British
s Hudson, the British Minister
rocess by which British states-
urse of Garibaldi's expedition
alian Unity contrary to their
Russell, Palmerston, and Glad-
Italian liberty, but they did
tion of liberty until they were
letters of Hudson and Elliot,
to the doctrine of Unity only
The following extracts and
e general reader.
ell. From Turin. [Garibaldi
.. Sicily.]

Italy, because— 1. Naples cannot be ruled from Turin or
Florence with the Papal States intervening.' [This objection
of Hudson's was removed in September when the Piedmontese
overran and annexed the Papal Marches and Umbria.]

2. ' The Neapolitans are too corrupt and the entire civil
and military administration is so abominable that their junction
with North Italy, where honesty is the rule in public affairs,
would merely produce a social decomposition and then a political putrefaction.' We must therefore, argues Hudson, find
a *mezzo-termine* in order to arrive at the end Russell desires,
viz. to check the Murat party and the French designs on
South Italy. The *mezzo-termine* recommended by Hudson is
a Prince of the House of Savoy on the throne of Naples and
Sicily, guaranteed by France and England. This is to be got
by ' amicable representation ' at Naples by France and England,
which would result in either the grant of a constitution, or an
abdication. Either would do, but the latter would be best, for
then a Prince of the House of Savoy might be put into the
vacant throne. ' I believe Cavour heartily desires an Anglo-
French intervention at Naples. I cannot go and speak to him

'I received your telegram this morning instructing me to ask Cavour to stop any more expeditions from Genoa and Tuscany. He told me some days ago he would not permit any repetition of the Garibaldi expedition, and I believe him.' [If so, Hudson was unusually credulous, for Cavour was at that moment helping his friends to fit out the expedition of Medici.]

May 31. *Hudson to Russell.* [First day of the armistice at Palermo.]

Hudson discusses whether there is truth in the rumours that Italy will make ' further concessions ' of territory to France, in return for Venice or the South. Cavour denies it, and Hudson believes him. ' For my part my belief is based not upon Cavour but upon Cavour's necessities. . . . You speak of Cavour as though he were Dictator. But he depends on public opinion.' The deputies supported him in the cession of Savoy, because they knew they must pay France for Central Italy, and because the greater part of Nice is French in population, and Savoy ' is as reactionary as Ireland or the Vatican.' But he could not command fifty votes to give away Sardinia or Genoa. ' The King told me that he had made the sacrifice of Savoy and Nice with a heavy heart, but there was no means of avoiding it. He added that he had paid his shot to France and he would hang the first Minister who proposed to make another cession. Supposing the King's word is worth no more than Cavour's, why should Venice be worth Genoa ? In my opinion Genoa is the real *tête de pont* of the King of Sardinia's Dominions. To give Genoa means to give Spezia, in which case there is no Italy at all, and the Italians have no intention of changing an Austrian master for a French one.'

' Cavour and Farini were here with me for an hour last night. They went over the whole question of Italy and her independence. They came here with a telegram announcing the fall of Palermo. I did not detect a word which smacked of further concessions to France. But I perceive very clearly that the more you hang back, the more easy do you make the propagation of French notions in Italy. Upon whom can the constitutional party in Italy lean save upon us ? And if we refuse to allow them to lean upon us, you force them to lean upon France. Consequently if you abstain from interference in some shape or other in these Sicilian movements you leave a free field to France.'

June 2. *Elliot to Russell.* From Naples. [During armistice at Palermo.]

' It is extremely fortunate that the protest of the Admiral [Mundy] against the bombardment' [of Palermo; see *Garibaldi and the Thousand*, Chapter XVII.] 'was not listened to, for if it had been abandoned on that account the success of the insurgents would indubitably have been put on our shoulders, but nevertheless, as it was not listened to, I am delighted that the protest should have been made. . . . I do not feel much fear that the bombardment will be renewed, but it was charming to see how its defence was taken up by the Nuncio, who gesticulated in favour of shells and shrapnel till his purple stockings got almost scarlet with excitement.'

July 10. *Elliot to Russell.* [More than a month after fall of Palermo.]

Elliot says he is favourable to complete annexation by Piedmont, either by means of Garibaldi continuing his career of victory, as he will do if the Sicilian settlement is delayed till he has crossed the Straits : or else, as Elliot would prefer, by Piedmont declaring open war on the House of Bourbon. If Piedmont ' would come forward openly and say that she intends to take up arms for her Sicilian brothers, I think it would simplify matters much, for the whole concern would probably tumble down without much further trouble, and it would moreover be an infinitely more manly and creditable course.'

The treaty ceding Sardinia and Genoa to France is apocryphal, and comes from Vienna. But false rumours, adds Elliot, have often preceded such objectionable pretentions of France.

July 16. *Hudson to Russell.* From Turin. [Four days prior to the battle of Milazzo.]

' The Unionists of North and Central Italy hold that policy because they see in it their principal means of escape from all foreign influence, and for my part I cordially and entirely agree with them for the very same reason that heretofore I advocated the annexation of Tuscany. Because now that the notion of a Prince of the House of Savoy ' [see his letter of May 18 above] ' has been set aside by the force of circumstances, I do see very great danger to the Balance of Power in the Mediterranean if France should in the midst of the Neapolitan confusion find means to place a creature of her own on that throne or on both of the Sicilies. As to further compensation to France in the event of annexation of one or both of the Sicilies,' . . . Cavour ' exclaimed vehemently only last night— *" I will guarantee that nothing of the sort shall happen. I want Italy for the Italians, not for the French."* I replied, that you were of opinion that if he only *ran straight* all would yet be well, and to this he solemnly declared that he would *run straight.*'

July 22. *Farini to Russell.* From Turin.

Farini, Cavour's principal colleague, writes solemnly denying rumours circulating in Europe that Italy and France are negotiating for a cession of Sardinia and the Ligurian coast to France.

July 31. *Russell to Farini.* From Chesham Place. (Reply to last.)

' Sir,

' I beg to assure you that I entirely believe your denial of the sinister rumours which have been spread. But we know that Count Cavour thought himself compelled to yield, contrary to his declarations on the subject at Savoy and Nice. So that many say what happened once may happen again. For the present I entirely disbelieve in any secret treaty.'

July 25. *Ricasoli to Russell.* From Florence.

Ricasoli writes to thank Lord John for his support of the Italian cause. 'La régénération italienne repose uniquement sur son unité. Veuillez bien en être persuadé, My Lord. Il n'y a de salut pour l'Europe que dans l'Italie-Nation, et il n'y a pas de Nation que dans l'unité.'

July 27. *Hudson to Russell.* [Garibaldi's army, victorious at Milazzo on the 20th, is arriving at Messina on the Straits.]

' To state what are the plans of Cavour would be to do that which he himself would not dare to attempt, for my belief is that he has no plan. He is a waiter upon Providence and the chapter of accidents.' . . . ' The general aspect of affairs is a complete imbroglio for which there would, as a choice of evils, appear to be no other remedy than annexation. If, therefore, I am an advocate of that principle, it is rather because it appears to me to be less prejudicial to *British interests* (of which you remind me) than the anarchy of Sicily and Naples, and the discontent of North Italy.'

July 28. *Elliot to Russell.* [Three or four days after Lacaita's visit to Russell's house, see Chapter V. above.]

' De Martino [Neapolitan Minister for Foreign Affairs] is evidently much vexed that you will not join in preventing Garibaldi from crossing the Straits, though I scarcely think he can have really expected that you would, as I have over and over again told him not to reckon on any such help.'

July 31. *Hudson to Russell.* [Garibaldi still at Messina.]

A long reasoned letter to prove that the Unity of Italy is in accordance with British interests.

' To constitute Italy under Duality is not easy with public opinion opposed. I was then a Dualist. I continued to be so till the capture of Palermo. I then proposed a Prince of the House of Savoy. [See letter of May 18, above.] You received the notion coldly and did nothing to promote it. The tidal wave of unity which the victory of Palermo set in motion carried that idea to the frozen sea of diplomatic nostrums.'

The Neapolitans are turning to Victor Emmanuel as to the only man to save them from ' anarchy and civil war, plunder and massacre, a licentious foreign soldiery, and a degraded mob.'

After stating many suggested solutions and the objection to each, he writes, ' It is not then my *sympathies* with Italy but my sympathy with British interests which leads me in the face of existing circumstances to advocate the least prejudicial of these various issues, the Unity of Italy.'

' The interests of Italy turn, naturally, rather towards

Germany than France, provided Germany will allow her. There is no reason why Austria should not give a real, efficient protection to Italy ; they have great interests in common, and they have a common danger, France. But then this protection should be a moral one—not such an interest as Rudolf of Hapsburg tried to create in Italy by a corrupt bargain with Rome. It should be a protection shared by England and Prussia, with no other guarantee, no other pact than that which springs from natural necessities shared in common and felt by all. . . . If Austria would consent to cede Venice she would find security, compensation, and safety. She would re-establish her finances and gain a barrier on her Western frontier which would be impregnable so long as England is mistress of the sea.'

Such a league of Austria, Prussia, Italy, and England, argues Hudson, would put an end to all our fears of French hegemony.

[In view of the arguments used by Hudson in this letter in favour of Italian Unity, compare the letter of Lord Palmerston on January 10, 1861 (*Queen's Letters*, vol. iii.). ' Upon the subject of Italy your Majesty reminds Viscount Palmerston that he stated last summer that it would be better for the interests of England that Southern Italy should be a separate Monarchy, rather than that it should form part of a United Italy. Viscount Palmerston still retains that opinion, because a separate Kingdom of the Two Sicilies would be more likely, in the event of war between England and France, to side, at least by its neutrality, with the strongest naval Power, and it is to be hoped that such Power would be England. But then it would be necessary that the Two Sicilies as an independent and separate State should be well governed, and should have an enlightened Sovereign. This unfortunately has become hopeless and impossible under the Bourbon Dynasty, and no Englishman could wish to see a Murat or a Prince Napoleon on the Throne of Naples. The course of events since last summer (1860) seems to have finally decided the fate of Sicily and Naples, and there can be no doubt that for the interest of the people of Italy, and with a view to the general balance of

Power in Europe, a United Italy is the best arrangement. The Italian Kingdom will never side with France from partiality to France, and the stronger that Kingdom becomes the better able it will be to resist political coercion from France. The chief hold that France will have upon the policy of the Kingdom of Italy consists in the retention of Venetia by Austria.']

August 11. *Elliot to Russell.* [Garibaldi still on Sicilian side of Straits of Messina.]

' Villamarina told me this morning, but again swore me to secrecy, that Victor Emmanuel has just received a letter from Prince Napoleon saying that *the time has come for securing the independence of Italy : courage on your part is all that is now required.'* But Elliot adds that the Piedmontese Government, frightened of the men around Garibaldi, have instructed Villamarina ' to do all he can to prevent Garibaldi from coming over,' but without letting it appear as if Piedmont was doing so. The object in this is to get a revolution in Naples for annexation without a Garibaldian dictatorship. But Elliot prophesies [correctly] that the Neapolitans have so little pluck that the attempt to anticipate Garibaldi will fail.

August 20. *Elliot to Russell.* [Garibaldi just crossing the Straits.]

' The only tolerable solution which I see remaining is that there should be war between Naples and Sardinia. The former dare not quarrel, and I am afraid the latter may continue to think it more profitable to go on working underground. But open war would be infinitely more creditable, and it would avoid the dangers both of Mazzinism and reaction through which we shall otherwise have to pass. If this were to be done, Naples would be settled, but we should then have the affairs of Rome and Venetia which must arise out of the annexation of Naples. If the Neapolitans shook off their King for themselves it is perhaps possible that they might be induced to be satisfied with the second son of Victor Emmanuel ; but there is little chance of their doing their work for themselves, and those who do it will impose the new arrangement on them,' viz. annexation.

August 24. *Hudson to Russell.*

' The expeditions of Garibaldi have ceased, *bonâ fide*, and, as the fine weather has set in, the country people are thinking more of their harvest than of politics. Turin is deserted. The King is in the mountains shooting chamois, and nearly all the diplomats gone too.' [And Cavour was meanwhile making his final arrangements for the invasion of the Papal States. I wonder whether Hudson really knew this.]

September 1. *Elliot to Russell.* From Naples. [Six days before Garibaldi entered Naples.]

Narrates discovery of what is called Count Trapani's reactionary plot, which has led to the resignation of the constitutional Ministers. But their resignation is not yet accepted. The National Guards almost insist on the Ministry remaining in, and say that if it does so the tranquillity of the town will be guaranteed by them. But the Ministers, or rather De Martino, insist on going, and say that if the King becomes privy to plots for their arrest, which was part of the programme of Trapani's plot, they cannot remain in to please the National Guard, or to become the Government not of the King but of the people. In a few hours it must be settled one way or other.

' I cannot yet give any true details of this plot, but the French connection of the leaders both of it and of Count Aquila's [plot of August 11] is a remarkable feature. The most prominent man in the present one is Prince Castropiano, and Prince Ischitella is also said to be in it, and both of these men I pointed out to you as devoted to French interests. It was also a Frenchman in whose rooms the compromising papers were found, and I believe Brenier has called for his liberation. In fact on all sides there is an atmosphere of intrigue that bewilders me.'

September 7. *Hudson to Russell.* [Day of Garibaldi's entry into Naples; a few days prior to Cavour's invasion of Papal States.]

' Cavour must choose between one of the horns of his dilemma—either intervention with Victor Emmanuel, or anarchy with Garibaldi. Of course he chooses for the former, but we see now what the Garibaldi expedition has produced. Cavour told me this morning that he would willingly have avoided all this, but being determined not to let Garibaldi and the Mazzinians get the whip-hand, he is forced to resort to extreme measures in order to avoid the Venetia difficulty. When I read your despatch to him this morning he said : *Believe me, Garibaldi shall not attack Venice ;—if Venice is ever attacked it will be by an Italian army. I have no intention of attacking Venice, and this Lord John may rely on.* This appears to mean he will attack Venice when he is strong enough to do so, but that day appears to me to be distant.'

October 16. *Elliot to Russell.* [A fortnight after the battle of the Volturno.]

' General Türr, who is Garibaldi's right hand, says that the town of Naples furnished eighty fighting men ' [to Garibaldi's army of 20,000 Italian volunteers at the front, protecting Naples].

October 30. *Elliot to Russell.* [Last days of Garibaldi's Dictatorship.]

' No change of any kind has taken place here since I last wrote, except that the necessity of having a Government becomes daily more and more apparent, and each day adds immensely to the difficulty that will be experienced in setting matters a little straight, after the universal and wholesale plunder and confusion, which is by degrees becoming a system.'

October 19. *Hudson to Russell.* [Victor Emmanuel advancing from Ancona to Naples.]

' The King has sent me through General Solaroli a message to the following effect. That considering the jealousy with which his constitutional system of government is regarded by most sovereigns, and especially by Austria, Russia, and France, and the lukewarm support of Prussia, he has no one to rely on for moral support save England, and he would esteem it as a favour if on his arrival at Naples he could be supported by a British representative.'

[The ' moral support ' was forthcoming in Lord John Russell's famous despatch of October 27 (No. 195 in the *F. O.* MSS.=No. 136, p. 125, in the *Br. Parl. Papers*, vii.). It contained the sentiment—' It appears that the late proceedings of the King of Sardinia have been strongly disapproved by several of the principal Courts of Europe.' But ' Her

Majesty's Government must admit that the Italians themselves are the best judges of their own interests.' The publication of this despatch produced in Italy the effect recorded in the following letters.]

November 2. *Hudson to Russell.*

' Cavour begs me to make to you his warmest acknowledgments for your despatch No. 195. . . . Yesterday it would have done your heart good could you have seen him read your No. 195. He shouted, rubbed his hands, jumped up, sat down again, then he began to think, and when he looked up tears were standing in his eyes. Behind your despatch he saw the Italy of his dreams, the Italy of his hopes, the Italy of his policy.'

November 12. *Elliot to Russell.*

' For the last week Naples, and I believe Italy, have been more occupied about your despatch to Hudson than about anything else, and though you must have been in great measure prepared for it, you can hardly quite have expected the immense sensation it has made. Villamarina's first exclamation was that it was worth more than 100,000 men, and King Victor Emmanuel appears to have spoken to Admiral Mundy in terms almost as strong.'

November 16. *Cavour to Russell.* Thanking him for the despatch.

' L'appui moral que vous nous prêtez dans cette circonstance suprême, nous permettra, j'espère, d'établir sur des bases larges et solides l'édifice de la nation Italienne. . . . Ma vive reconnaissance pour le service immense que vous venez de rendre à l'Italie.'

The following letter has already been printed in Spencer Walpole's *Russell*, ii., pp. 328–329.

' MR. ODO RUSSELL TO LORD JOHN RUSSELL.

' MY DEAR UNCLE,   ' ROME, *December 1st*, 1860.

' Ever since your famous despatch of the 27th you are blessed night and morning by twenty millions of Italians. I could not read it myself without deep emotion, and the moment it was published in Italian, thousands of people copied it from each other to carry it to their homes and weep over it for joy and gratitude in the bosom of their families, away from brutal mercenaries and greasy priests. Difficult as the task is the Italians have now before them, I cannot but think that they will accomplish it better than we any of us hope, for every day convinces me more and more that I am living in the midst of a *great* and *real* national movement, which will at last be crowned with perfect success, notwithstanding the legion of enemies Italy still counts in Europe.

' Your affectionate nephew,

' ODO RUSSELL.'

While this book was being printed (1911) an important document came to hand, through the kindness of Mr. William Warren Vernon,* who had just found in his diary under the date February 22, 1870, the following contemporary entry :—

' Reached the Hotel Vittoria at San Remo at 5.30. We dined with Lord and Lady Russell, who live close by. Lord Russell is looking very well. Lacaita, he, and Lady Russell discussed how in July, 1860, when Persigny was trying to induce Lord John to stop Garibaldi's landing in Italy from Messina, he (Lacaita) being very ill at the time, managed to see Lady John, who was ill in bed. She, however, received him and sent for Lord John, who was mightily surprised to find Lacaita there, who immediately attacked him on the treaty he was supposed to be arranging with Persigny, to have an Anglo-French fleet in the Straits of Messina to prevent Garibaldi from crossing to Italy.

' After a long discussion which nearly exhausted Tino [Lacaita], who was very ill, Lord John said to him " go to bed, and don't be so sure that I am going to sign the treaty yet." Tino went home to bed ; and two hours later, George Elliot, then Lord John's secretary, came to him to tell him from Lord John to be of good cheer. Tino took the hint, sent for

---

* It may be explained that Sir James Lacaita and Mr. Warren Vernon were intimate friends, and in 1870 were travelling together to Tuscany by the Riviera. Mr. Vernon was married to a first cousin of Lady Russell.

D'Azeglio and dictated a telegram to Cavour, implying that the intended treaty was at an end. Garibaldi was accordingly undisturbed. How few people knew that this was owing to Lacaita. I myself heard Lord Russell confirm this story.'

This passage from Mr. Vernon's diary puts the story of Lacaita's visit to the Russells, told pp. 112–117 above, beyond all possible doubt, by proving that Lord and Lady Russell bore out Lacaita's account of it.

THE END.

PRINTED IN GREAT BRITAIN AT
THE PRESS OF THE PUBLISHERS.

MAP II.

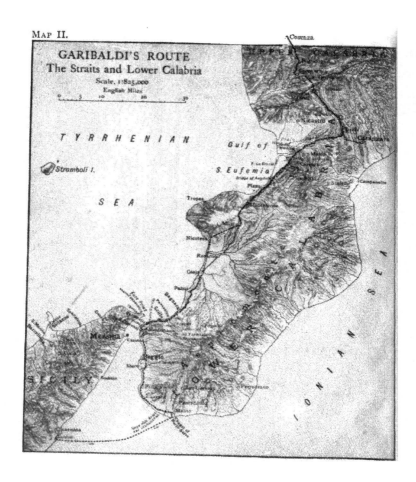

GARIBALDI'S ROUTE
The Straits and Lower Calabria
Scale, 1:825,000
English Miles

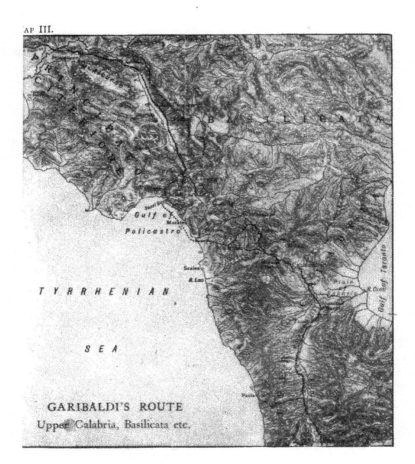

GARIBALDI'S ROUTE
Upper Calabria, Basilicata etc.

MAP IV.

MAP V.

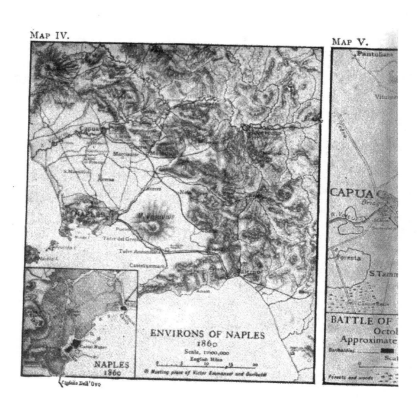

ENVIRONS OF NAPLES
1860
Scale, 1:500,000
English Miles

NAPLES
1860

Castello Dell'Ovo

CAPUA

BATTLE OF
Octol
Approximate

THE VOLTURNO
er 1, 1860
positions at noon

Bourbon troops
1:105,000
3 Miles
Olives

MAP VI.

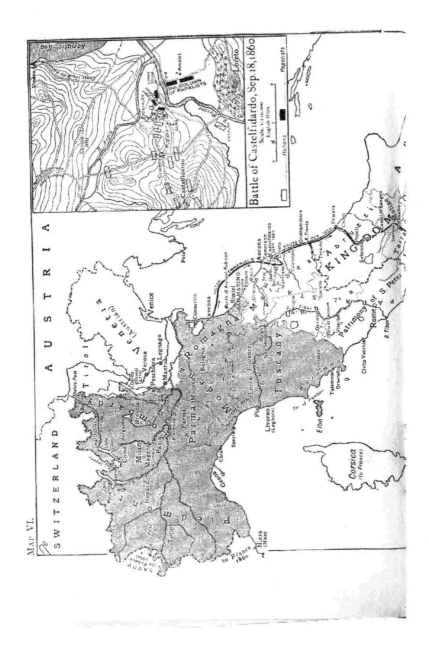

Battle of Castelfidardo, Sep. 18, 1860

Scale, 1:250,000

4 English Miles

Italians   Papalists

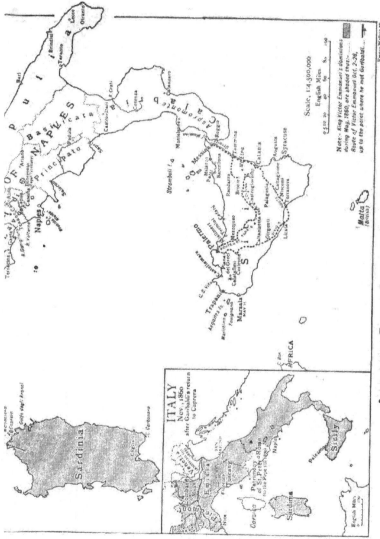

ITALY AT THE TIME OF GARIBALDI'S CAMPAIGN, 1860.

Lightning Source UK Ltd.
Milton Keynes UK
UKHW022140100521
383500UK00003B/192